PROGRESS IN BEHAVIOR MODIFICATION

Volume 25

CONTRIBUTORS TO THIS VOLUME

Barbara Fleming

Dorothy Ginsberg

Robert G. Hall

Sharon M. Hall

Thomas Koepke

Jamie K. Lilie

John E. Lochman

Mark E. Oakley

Christine A. Padesky

James L. Pretzer

Arthur L. Robin

Russell P. Rosenberg

PROGRESS IN BEHAVIOR MODIFICATION

EDITED BY

Michel Hersen

University of Pittsburgh School of Medicine
Pittsburgh, Pennsylvania

Richard M. Eisler

Department of Psychology
Virginia Polytechnic Institute and State University
Blacksburg, Virginia

Peter M. Miller

Hilton Head Health Institute
Hilton Head Island, South Carolina

Volume 25

1990

For information address:

 SAGE Publications, Inc.
2111 West Hillcrest Drive
Newbury Park, California 91320

SAGE Publications Ltd.
28 Banner Street
London EC1Y 8QE
England

SAGE Publications India Pvt. Ltd.
M-32 Market
Greater Kailash I
New Delhi 110 048 India

Printed in the United States of America

Library of Congress: 75-646720

ISBN 0-8039-3701-6

FIRST PRINTING, 1990

CONTENTS

Pharmacological and Behavioral Treatment
for Cigarette Smoking

Sharon M. Hall, Robert G. Hall, and Dorothy Ginsberg

Cognitive-Behavioral Approaches to Personality Disorders

Barbara Fleming and James L. Pretzer

Behavioral Treatment of Insomnia

Jamie K. Lilie and Russell P. Rosenberg

Behavioral Assessment and Treatment of Parent-Adolescent Conflict

Arthur L. Robin and Thomas Koepke

CONTRIBUTORS

BARBARA FLEMING, Department of Psychiatry, Case Western University Reserve School of Medicine and Cleveland Center for Cognitive Therapy, has clinical and research interests that include cognitive-behavioral therapy, personality disorders, and anxiety disorders.

DOROTHY GINSBERG is Assistant Research Psychologist at the University of California at San Francisco. She is interested in the treatment of addictive behaviors and in the role of social support in promoting health behaviors.

ROBERT G. HALL holds appointment at the VA Medical Center in Palo Alto and at Stanford University. He provides clinical service, training to psychology interns and medical interns/residents, and pursues his interest in smoking cessation treatment and research.

SHARON M. HALL, Department of Psychiatry, University of California, San Francisco, and San Francisco Veterans Administration Medical Center, has research interests in the treatment of drug dependence, including nicotine dependence, in commonalities across drugs of abuse, and in relapse.

THOMAS KOEPKE, Children's Hospital of Michigan and the Department of Pediatrics at Wayne State University School of Medicine, Detroit, Michigan, has clinical and research interests that include therapeutic interventions with parents and adolescents, assessment of parent-adolescent conflict, and behavioral and learning disorders in children.

JAMIE K. LILIE, Department of Psychiatry, University of Illinois at Chicago, has research interests that include behavioral treatment of sleep disorders, objective personality assessment, and measurement of alcohol and drug effects on sleep and waking function.

JOHN E. LOCHMAN, Department of Psychiatry, Duke University Medical Center, Durham, North Carolina, has research interests that include social-cognitive deficiencies in aggressive children and the effectiveness of cognitive-behavioral therapy with aggressive children.

MARK E. OAKLEY, Ph.D., is Assistant Clinical Professor, UCLA School of Medicine, Department of Psychiatry and Biobehavioral Sciences, Los Angeles, California, and Director, Center for Cognitive Therapy, Beverly Hills, California. He has clinical and research interests in cognitive-behavioral applications to behavioral medicine, anxiety, and depression.

CHRISTINE A. PADESKY, Ph.D., is Director, Center for Cognitive Therapy, Newport Beach, California. She is a psychotherapist who has conducted cognitive therapy training programs for professionals, groups, and hospitals in the United States and Europe. She has published articles on depression, stress, personality disorders, and women's issues, usually emphasizing a cognitive therapy perspective.

JAMES L. PRETZER, Department of Family Medicine, Case Western Reserve University School of Medicine, Cleveland, Ohio, and Cleveland Center for Cognitive Therapy, has clinical and research interests that include cognitive-behavioral treatment of personality disorders and of marital dysfunction.

ARTHUR L. ROBIN, Department of Pediatrics, Wayne State University School of Medicine and Children's Hospital of Michigan, has research/ service interests that include parent-adolescent conflict, adolescent eating disorders, and attention-deficit hyperactivity disorders. He is the Chief of Psychology in a large metropolitan children's hospital.

RUSSELL P. ROSENBERG, St. Mary's Medical Center and University of Tennessee, has research interests that include behavioral treatment of insomnia, compliance with medical and psychological treatment, and health psychology.

COGNITIVE THERAPY FOR ANXIETY DISORDERS

MARK E. OAKLEY
Center for Cognitive Therapy
Beverly Hills, California

CHRISTINE A. PADESKY
Center for Cognitive Therapy
Newport Beach, California

I. INTRODUCTION

While traditional exposure-based behavior therapies are well-established treatments for certain anxiety disorders (e.g., agoraphobia and simple phobias), cognitive therapies have become increasingly popular approaches for the treatment of anxiety. This chapter will be devoted to a discussion of several concerns that are encountered when attempting to answer two broad questions: (1) What constitutes cognitive therapy for anxiety disorders? (2) What is the empirical evidence regarding cognitive therapy's efficacy with anxiety disorders?

The first section will be devoted to a brief description of several varieties of cognitive therapy that have been empirically evaluated with anxiety disorders. The second section will present a cognitive theory of anxiety and review results from empirical tests of four predictions derived from this theory. Because it appears that Beck has presented the most systematic and elaborated cognitive approach to anxiety to date, the third section will provide a detailed description of procedures that constitute the therapeutic process of Beck's cognitive therapy for anxiety. The fourth section will review empirical evaluations of cognitive therapies to date. This discussion will focus on methodological pitfalls that preclude definitive conclusions regarding the relative efficacy of behavior therapy versus cognitive therapy for anxiety disorders. The final section will provide a summary of the critical review and also highlight some suggestions for future research.

II. COGNITIVE THERAPY:
ONE TREATMENT OR MANY?

The cognitive therapies differ from behavior therapy in that they place an emphasis on thinking rather than motor behavior. A cognitive therapist would maintain that the individual's thoughts and perspective will be an important determinant of anxiety and avoidant behavior patterns.

For example, the treatment of an agoraphobic who avoids grocery stores may be conceptualized by a behavior therapist as an example of conditioning and then treated with systematic desensitization. A cognitive therapist might also see this as a learned response but would consider the internal cognitions as the central focus of change in therapy (e.g., "I have had a panic attack here before. I know I will have another panic attack. If I have a panic attack I'll die."). Cognitive therapies also include exposure techniques and, therefore, are sometimes appropriately termed cognitive-behavior therapies.

While the basic tenet that thoughts influence emotion and behavior is central to all cognitive therapies, there are actually many varieties of cognitive therapy that differ in conceptualization, techniques, and the processes by which change is attempted. These various approaches often differ to a significant degree. The four most influential cognitive therapies are Ellis's (1962) rational emotive therapy (RET), Meichenbaum's (1977) self-instructional training (SIT), Bandura's (1977) approaches to enhance self-efficacy and Beck's (1976; Beck, Emery, & Greenburg, 1985; Beck, Rush, Shaw, & Emery, 1979) cognitive therapy (CT).

A. Ellis's Rational Emotive Therapy

Rational emotive therapy is based on the theoretical premise that, when an emotional consequence (C) follows a significant activating event (A), A may be perceived to, but actually does not, cause C. On the contrary, Ellis argues that the ostensible emotional consequences of situations are determined by an intervening variable (D), the interpretation of A. Ellis notes that when an undesirable emotion is experienced, such as severe anxiety, the emotion can usually be traced to irrational beliefs, and when these beliefs are "effectively" disputed (at point D) by challenging them rationally, the disturbed emotional consequence disappears and eventually ceases to recur.

RET maintains that virtually all maladaptive emotions are caused by irrational, empirically untenable thoughts. The purpose of RET is to vigorously dispute irrational thinking by logical-empirical thinking to eliminate or minimize irrational beliefs and their emotional by-products. Ellis identified 12 irrational beliefs that he believed were particularly important in the genesis of emotional problems (see Table 1).

Ellis (1979) has stated that, despite his designation as a cognitive therapist, he does not focus the majority of his therapeutic efforts on combating irrational beliefs. Ellis describes RET as "an exceptionally multifaceted or multimodel form of therapy" that includes a wide range of techniques such as "emotive-evocative-expressive" methods (i.e., role-playing, unconditional acceptance of the client, self-disclosure, and shame-attacking exercises) and a sizable number of behavioral methods (i.e., operant conditioning, desensitization, aversive penalties, and skill training).

Most cognitive therapies include methods that are not strictly cognitive. Some cognitive therapies are broader than Ellis's model (see Beck, 1986) and recognize that it is not always thoughts that lead to emotion. However, all cognitive theories state that, when anxious, a person has anxiety-producing thoughts and/or images that, if modified, can serve to reduce anxiety.

Cognitive therapies also differ in terms of what is believed to be the most "effective" way to change maladaptive beliefs. For example, Ellis (1984) does not believe that a warm relationship between the therapist and client is a necessary or sufficient condition for change. Ellis states that it is

Table 1   Ellis's Irrational Beliefs

1. The idea that it is a dire necessity for an adult to be loved by everyone for every-thing he does.
2. The idea that certain acts are awful or wicked, and that people who perform such acts should be severely punished.
3. The idea that it is horrible when things are not the way one would like them to be.
4. The idea that human misery is externally caused and is forced on one by outside people and events.
5. The idea that if something is or may be dangerous or fearsome one should be terri-bly upset about it.
6. The idea that it is easier to avoid rather than to face life difficulties and self-responsibilities.
7. The idea that one needs something other or stronger or greater than oneself on which to rely.
8. The idea that one should be thoroughly competent, intelligent, and achieving in all respects.
9. The idea that because something once strongly affected one's life, it should indefi-nitely affect it.
10. The idea that one must have certain and perfect control over things.
11. The idea that human happiness can be achieved by inertia and action.
12. The idea that one has virtually no control over one's emotions and that one cannot help feeling certain things.

important for RET therapists to accept their clients but also to criticize and point out the deficiencies of the clients' beliefs and behavior. They may use a variety of techniques including didactic discussion. Further-more, to keep clients from becoming unduly dependent on the therapist, RET therapists often deliberately use "hardheaded methods of convinc-ing clients that they had damned well better resort to more self discipline" (Ellis, 1984). As will be seen below, Beck, Emery, and Greenburg (1985) differ from Ellis on this point.

B.   Bandura's Self-Efficacy

Self-efficacy is defined as a prediction generated by a particular indi-vidual of his or her perceived ability to competently manage a particular situation. Bandura's social learning theory states that the initiation and process of transactions with the environment are partly determined by judgments of self-efficacy (Bandura, 1977). This theory predicts that peo-ple tend to avoid or to feel anxious in situations that exceed their per-ceived coping abilities but initiate and perform assuredly activities they judge themselves capable of managing (Bandura, 1982).

Furthermore, when difficulties are encountered, a heightened sense of self-efficacy results in more vigorous and persistent efforts. In contrast, with low self-efficacy, efforts are abated or abandoned (Brown & Inouye,

1978; Schunk, 1981). These studies demonstrate that self-efficacy is generally a good predictor of how people are likely to behave and of how much emotional arousal they will experience during specific tasks. The hypothesis that anxiety results from a lack of self-efficacy within a particular situation implies that increasing self-efficacy would reduce anxiety in that specific situation (Bandura, Reese, & Adams, 1982). Bandura has also argued that the most effective way to increase self-efficacy is to provide occasions for successful behavioral performance via participant modeling (Bandura & Adams, 1977; Bandura, Adams, & Beyer, 1977; Bandura, Adams, Hardy, & Howells, 1980).

C. Meichenbaum's Self-Instructional Training

Self-instructional training (SIT) has its conceptual roots in the work of Luria (1961), who proposed a developmental sequence of verbal-symbolic control over behavior in which children develop internal speech at first controlled by instructions from others, then, by overt self-instructions, and, eventually, by covert self-instructions. Meichenbaum's (1977) therapeutic application of these principles to the process of SIT has been summarized by Wilson (1978, p. 15) as follows:

1.) Train the client to identify and become aware of maladaptive thoughts (self-statements).
2.) The therapist models appropriate behavior while verbalizing effective coping strategies which include an appraisal of task requirements, self-instructions that guide graded performance, self-statements that stress personal adequacy and counteract worry over failure, and covert self-reinforcement for successful performance.
3.) The client then performs the target behavior first while verbalizing aloud the appropriate self-instructions and then by covertly rehearsing them. Therapist feedback during this phase assists in ensuring that constructive problem solving self-talk replaces previously anxiety-inducing cognitions associated with that behavior.

Instead of being developed as a treatment for anxiety or other emotional problems, Meichenbaum's SIT was originally tested on kindergarten and first-grade children who were judged to be impulsive. Meichenbaum and Goodman (1971) found that SIT helped these children decrease their errors on a cognitive task. Later, Meichenbaum and his colleagues applied these ideas to test anxiety (Deffenbacher & Hahloser, 1981; Hussain & Lawrence, 1978; Meichenbaum, 1972), interpersonal and dating anxiety (Glass, Gottman, & Shmurak, 1976; Jaremko, 1983), public speaking anxiety (Fremouw & Zitter, 1978; Jaremko, 1980), performance anxiety (Sweeney &

Horan, 1982), flying phobias (Girodo & Roehl, 1978), and stress management for adults (Meichenbaum, 1985). Meichenbaum notes that many of these published studies describe demonstration projects and do not include careful controls or follow-up measures of effectiveness (1985, p. 26). More careful empirical evaluation of SIT is needed. In addition, Meichenbaum now incorporates Beck's cognitive therapy methods (Beck, Rush, Shaw, & Emery, 1979) into his SIT program (Meichenbaum, 1985, p. 58), so current SIT overlaps somewhat with Beck's cognitive therapy described below.

D. Beck's Cognitive Therapy

In contrast to Ellis, Beck, Emery, and Greenburg (1985, p. 173) state that "one of the principles of cognitive therapy is that a sound therapeutic relationship is a necessary condition for effective cognitive therapy." Beck notes that the anxious patient is so bombarded with frightening thoughts that he or she is often unable to view problems in other ways. He argues that creating a warm therapeutic relationship based on trust and acceptance is necessary to enable patients to talk openly about fears that they would typically avoid discussing. Without this, the techniques and procedures of cognitive therapy are unlikely to work. Furthermore, Beck (1985) reports that patients who have learned to manage anxiety often attribute a large part of their success to the therapeutic relationship.

Beck's cognitive therapy essentially consists of the following steps:

(1) Teach clients to see the connection between thoughts and feelings.
(2) Teach clients to critically appraise thoughts.
(3) Teach clients to change inaccurate beliefs and develop more accurate ones.
(4) Teach clients to do all of the above independent of the therapist.

Beck's cognitive theory and therapy for anxiety is arguably one of the most elaborately described models. Therefore, in the following sections, Beck's cognitive approach is described in detail along with an overview of other theoretical positions.

III. BECK'S COGNITIVE MODEL OF ANXIETY

Beck's cognitive therapy for anxiety is based on the same model of emotions previously proposed for depression and other disorders (Beck, 1967, 1976). Central to his model is the concept that it is not events per se but rather a person's interpretation of events that is instrumental in the experience of a negative emotion such as anxiety. This is not to say that all emotion is *caused* by thinking. In fact, Beck, Emery, and Greenburg,

(1985) have argued that disordered thinking is characteristic of strong emotional states whatever the original cause of the emotion (e.g., biological, cognitive). Because the domains of emotion, biology, behavior, and cognition are interactive, changes in thinking can produce changes in the other domains.

Beck has delineated cognitive themes that are specific to different emotional difficulties (Beck, 1976, 1986; Beck, Emery, & Greenburg, 1985; Beck, Rush, Shaw, & Emery, 1979). In anxiety, common themes involve perceived threat regarding personal loss, damage, sickness, or death. Beck (1976) claims that in pathological anxiety these perceptions of threat are unfounded in that they are overestimates of danger inherent in a given situation. These overestimates of danger are assumed to arise from one of the four cognitive errors listed below (Beck, 1976; Clark & Beck, in press):

(1) overestimating the probability of a feared event,
(2) overestimating the severity of the feared event,
(3) underestimating individual coping resources, and
(4) underestimating rescue factors (what other people can do to help).

Once an individual interprets a situation as threatening, a complex constellation of cognitive, emotional, physiological, and behavioral changes take place. These include the subjective feeling of anxiety or fear, marked changes in autonomic arousal (i.e., increased heart rate, sweating, dry mouth, increased muscle tension, and alterations in breathing), an inhibition of coping and/or an increase in maladaptive behavior (i.e., avoidance or escape), and a cognitive selective scanning of the environment for threat. Important to the cognitive model of anxiety is that cognitive resources are diverted from the processing of nonthreat data and selectively focused on the processing of threat-related information. This cognitive process leads to the selective enhancement of any danger-relevant stimuli as well as to the selective suppression of disconfirming evidence against such danger. Beck, Rush, Shaw, and Emery (1979) have called this process selective abstraction and we illustrate this concept schematically in Figure 1.

Anxiety often serves a useful function in situations where there is a realistic threat in that it can serve to motivate action toward an effective solution. However, pathological anxiety is characterized by maladaptive emotion and behavior that do not lead to productive solutions but instead cause a significant disruption in the quality of life. When threat is misperceived, anxiety does not initiate corrective action but can serve as a secondary source of threat leading to a vicious "upward spiraling" of anxiety that exacerbates the anxiety reaction. For example, a sudden increase in heart rate may be interpreted as evidence of an impending heart

SELECTIVE ABSTRACTION   ANXIETY

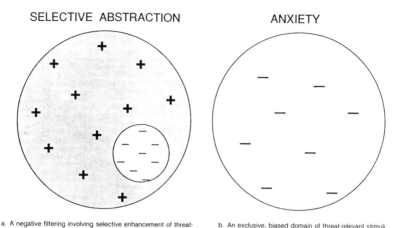

a. A negative filtering involving selective enhancement of threat-   b. An exclusive, biased domain of threat-relevant stimuli
relevant stimuli (−) and suppression of disconfirming evidence (+)   leading to anxiety and/or panic.
leading to b.

Figure 1. Selective abstraction and anxiety.

attack, shallow breathing as indication of fainting or a total cessation of breathing, a dry mouth as evidence predicting imminent social dysfunction and consequent embarrassment, and the disorientation sometimes produced by the above anxious thoughts as evidence of impending insanity. Because of this reciprocal and maintaining/exacerbating relationship between perceived threat and symptoms of anxiety, a central focus of cognitive therapy targets the secondary fears related to the behavioral, cognitive, and somatic symptoms of anxiety.

IV. RESEARCH EVALUATING THE COGNITIVE MODEL OF ANXIETY

At least four testable predictions can be derived from the cognitive theory of anxiety (Clark & Beck, in press):

(1) Cognitions of anxious patients will be characterized by thoughts concerned with the perception of danger.

(2) Within anxious individuals, anxiety ratings will correlate with the believability and frequency of thoughts concerned with the perception of danger.

(3) The temporal occurrence of thoughts concerned with danger will be such that they *could* logically contribute to the initiation or maintained activation of the anxiety reaction.

(4) Experimental manipulations of the frequency and believability of thoughts concerned with the perception of danger will have systematic effects on patients' levels of anxiety. Increasing the frequency and believability of danger-related interpretations should increase anxiety and decreasing the frequency of believability of danger-related interpretations of events should decrease anxiety.

An excellent analysis of current research evaluating the hypotheses generated by the cognitive model of anxiety is presented by Clark and Beck (in press). In summary, they cite research providing support for the first three hypotheses. Six studies have investigated the first prediction in clinical populations and all report that cognitions of anxious patients are indeed characterized by concern with perceived danger (Beck, Laude, & Bohert, 1974; Beidel, Turner, & Dancu, 1985; Butler & Mathews, 1983; Hibbert, 1984; Last & Blanchard, 1982; Rappee, 1985). The second prediction receives support from Last, O'Brien, and Barlow (1985), who report significant positive correlations between negative thoughts and anxiety ratings in five out of six agoraphobic cases. Furthermore, Sewitch and Kirsch (1984) have shown that this relationship between danger-related thoughts and anxiety is not simply due to demand effects. The third prediction, involving the temporal relation between perceptions of danger and anxiety, receives support from results consistent with the mediation hypotheses (Beck, Laude, & Bohert, 1974; Hibbert, 1984; Last & Blanchard, 1982). As Clark and Beck (in press) point out, this is an important finding because, if danger cognitions occurred only *after* the peak of an anxious episode, then these cognitions would clearly not play an important role in the production of anxiety. With the fourth prediction we find only partial support from studies reporting a reduction in "negative thoughts" and "irrational beliefs" concomitant with reductions in anxiety (Emmelkamp, Mersch, Vissia, & Van der Helm, 1985; Waddell, Barlow, & O'Brien, 1984). However, it was not reported whether or not these thoughts and beliefs were danger related. Furthermore, a causal link cannot be assumed because it remains equally plausible that reductions in anxiety from other effects lead to reductions in these thoughts and beliefs. A manipulation of the frequency and/or believability of danger-related thoughts in anxious patients will be necessary to adequately evaluate this fourth prediction.

Studies by Lazarus and his colleagues, in the 1960s, of cognitive appraisal and stress provided a model for this type of research and yielded results consistent with the fourth prediction. In one study (Lazarus, Opton, Nomikos, & Rankin, 1965) subjects viewed a gory workshop accident film in which one worker cuts off a finger and another is killed by a wooden plank. Subjects given information to change their cognitive appraisal of this film (e.g., either that the events were staged or that these real events would help increase worker safety) experienced lower

physiological arousal than those who watched the film without explanation. This was one of many studies where Lazarus and colleagues demonstrated that the interpretations of events influence stress reactions
(Koriat, Melkman, Averill, & Lazarus, 1972; Lazarus & Alfert, 1964;
Nomikos, Opton, Averill, & Lazarus, 1968; Speisman, Lazarus,
Mordkoff, & Davidson, 1964). Further studies should be conducted
where specific manipulation of danger-related thoughts are correlated
with anxiety.

V. COGNITIVE THEMES SPECIFIC TO
DIFFERENT ANXIETY DISORDERS

Although most anxiety disorders share in common the general "theme
of threat" including personal loss (i.e., embarrassment, deflated sense of
worth or self-esteem), injury, sickness, or death, there also appears to be a
subset of cognitions that are characteristic of each anxiety disorder. Beck
and his associates (Beck, 1986; Beck, Emery, & Greenburg, 1985) suggest
that sets of cognitions specific to each of the DSM-III anxiety disorders
can be delineated. To date, three anxiety disorders have received particular attention in the literature. In the following sections, cognitive themes
are delineated for three anxiety disorders that have received particular attention from cognitive-behavioral researchers: panic disorder, agoraphobia, and social phobia.

A. Panic Disorder

Characteristic cognitions with panic involve a theme of danger regarding an impending internal disaster and a sense of lost control over
physical and mental functions (e.g., heart attack, cessation of breathing,
fainting, loss of sanity). Many of the thoughts that precede, maintain, or
exacerbate panic appear to result from a catastrophic misinterpretation
of somatic sensations such as increased heart rate or a slight feeling of
breathlessness. This casts the patient in an "endless loop," where
catastrophizing leads to increased anxiety, leading to more pronounced
somatic symptoms—all of which are interpreted as further evidence of
impending personal disaster (Beck, Emery, & Greenburg, 1985; Clark,
1986).
    These conceptualizations have roots stemming from the "fear-of-fear"
hypothesis that has been described in a variety of ways (Evans, 1972;
Frankl, 1975; Goldstein & Chambless, 1978; Jacob & Rapport, 1984;
Malleson, 1959; Stampler, 1982; Weeks, 1977), which involves a fear of

the somatic concomitants of fear. While this theory has face validity it leaves unexplained the phenomenon of dramatic symptoms characteristic of panic attacks (heart palpitations and dyspnea) that often *precede* fear (Ley, 1987). Furthermore, as Ley (1987) points out, it also does not explain the termination of a panic attack. What accounts for the variability in length of panic attacks? Why do some people experience fear without panic attacks? A hyperventilation theory of panic disorder has been proposed, which assumes a primary role of hyperventilation in the initiation and maintenance of panic attacks (Clark, 1986; Ley, 1985a, 1985b, 1987). This theory proposes that the sudden, unexpected, and often unexplainable somatic consequences of hyperventilation (especially the misattribution of these somatic consequences) are the cause of the initial fear experienced in some panic attacks.

Specifically, it is proposed that overbreathing causes too much CO_2 to be blown off, which raises blood pH level, resulting in alkalosis and a decrease in arterial tension (pCO_2). These physiological changes produce symptoms that are the most frequently reported in panic attacks — palpitations (including tachycardia), dyspnea, dizziness, and trembling (Barlow et al., 1985). The hyperventilation theory also accounts for the termination of panic attacks by proposing that the drop in arterial pCO_2 causes a response in the respiratory reflex center of the medulla, which dampens respiration, allowing CO_2 to build back up and restore pH homeostasis. This process is experienced as dyspnea due to a reflexive weakening of intercostal and diaphragmatic muscles that causes respiration to be reduced dramatically.

It has been shown that patients experiencing panic attacks indeed do have resting pCO_2 levels lower than normal controls and that teaching controlled breathing produces a return to normal levels (Salkovskis, Jones, & Clark, 1986). These results were taken as evidence that study patients were chronically, mildly hyperventilating. It has also been argued that the process of adapting to a chronically lowered pCO_2 level could reduce the efficacy of the blood buffer systems and, therefore, potentiate the effects of even brief and subtle periods of acute hyperventilation (Lum, 1976) such as those produced by physiological stressors and exercise (Okel & Hurst, 1961). It has also been shown that the effects of overbreathing are most marked when resting levels of pCO_2 are the lowest (Damas-Mora, Davies, Taylor, & Jenner, 1980).

However, it has been proposed that hyperventilation may be a necessary but not sufficient condition to produce panic. It has been observed that there are considerable individual differences in the emotional response to hyperventilation ranging from pleasant to frightening (Clark & Hemsley, 1982). Thus it has been argued that hyperventilation only leads to panic if the sensations are interpreted in a catastrophic fashion (Clark, 1986).

B. Agoraphobia

Conceptualizations regarding the etiology of agoraphobia differ according to the relative contribution of individual differences, environmental factors, and their interactions. It is generally recognized, however, that a
pattern of stressful life events typically precedes the onset of an initial panic
attack by three to twelve months (Michelson, 1987). Subsequent to the initial panic attack, anticipatory anxiety leads to panic in similar situations followed by avoidance of those situations where panic is predicted to occur.

It has been hypothesized that life stressors, and possibly deficient coping skills, cause excessive autonomic reactivity, which, when interpreted
catastrophically, lead to hypervigilence and a general upward spiraling of
state anxiety. It has been reported that agoraphobics in fact do exhibit
higher autonomic arousal and overreactivity as well as delayed habituation processes relative to normals (Lader, 1967). These factors, therefore,
place the predisposed individual at increased risk for an initial panic attack in stimulating situations such as cars, crowds, shopping malls, and so
on. Panic attacks subsequently lead to further interoceptive and environmental phobic conditioning, which generalizes to a variety of previously
"safe" situations and thus perpetuates the vicious fear-of-fear cycle
(Goldstein & Chambless, 1978).

Characteristic cognitions of agoraphobics with panic overlap with
those typical of panic disorder (Chambless, Caputo, Bright, & Gallagher,
1984), with the added thought that panic attacks are more likely to occur
in certain situations. Hence these situations are avoided. In addition,
such patients typically carry a belief that they are safer if they have access
to a "lifeline." This may be a significant person in their lives or, in some
cases, proximity to a hospital or some source of help if they should en-
counter a personal disaster. In contrast to agoraphobia with panic, relatively little is known about the ideation of agoraphobia without panic.

Recently, more attention has been paid to the methodology of assessing and quantifying the agoraphobic's cognitions. Schwartz and
Garamoni (1984, 1986) have developed a structural model of positive
and negative states of mind that incorporates principles of information
processing, cybernetic self-regulation, interpersonal communication, and
the "golden section" hypothesis based on mathematical formulas of
Pythagoras. The "golden section" can be defined geometrically as the
point on the line that divides it into two segments such that the ratio of
the smaller to the larger segment is equal to the ratio of the larger segment
to the whole. Psychologically, the "golden section" can be defined as an
optimal balance between positive and negative cognitions that is characteristic of adaptive psychological functioning.

The golden section hypothesis, reviewed extensively by Schwartz and
Garamoni (1986), and summarized by Michelson (1987), proposes five

distinct states of mind (SOM) that generate variables depicting various ratios between positive and negative cognitions. Quantification of these cognitive ratios has been shown to reliably characterize the presence and severity of agoraphobia as well as sensitivity to treatment successes and failures (Schwartz & Garamoni, 1984, 1986; Schwartz & Michelson, 1987). Therefore, this model represents an important attempt at quantifying the cognitive structure that characterizes agoraphobics and their effective treatment.

C. Social Phobia

The characteristic cognitive themes for social phobia involve exaggerated fears of negative social evaluation with the resulting misinterpretation that negative evaluations from others provide evidence for deflated self-worth and negative self-labels (e.g., worthless, stupid, unworthy of love). The social phobic continually monitors his or her performance in social situations, fears that this performance will be viewed as evidence that he or she is inept, boring, or stupid, and expects rejection or failure that will have catastrophic implications (Clark & Beck, in press).

This fear of interpersonal evaluation has emerged in empirical studies as the predominant feature of social phobia and differentiates it from other anxiety disorders (Schlenker & Leary, 1982). For example, Nichols (1974) found that fearfulness of criticism or disapproval from others was a central feature of people with severe social anxiety. Leary (1983a) reports that people who worry about how others evaluate them experience more anxiety than those who are less concerned about evaluations made by others. In a study of dating skills training (Glass, Gottman, & Shmurak, 1976), socially anxious persons expected that their efforts would be unfavorably judged by others even when this was not the case. It is not clear whether subjects in these studies would have met DSM-III-R (American Psychiatric Association, 1987) criteria for social phobia. However, most studies of social anxiety describe a phenomenon that is similar to social phobia, even if it is in a milder form (Leary, 1983b, p. 19).

An alternative line of research to the cognitive view has been followed by those who argued that social anxiety and phobia involve social skills deficits (e.g., Bellack & Hersen, 1979). A number of studies have found that socially anxious people were judged by others to be less socially skilled than nonsocially anxious people (Bellack & Hersen, 1979; Curran, 1977; Farrell, Mariotto, Conger, Curran, & Wallander, 1979). However, Leary (1983b, p. 41) notes that attempts to identify specific "skill differences have come up empty-handed." He points out that low levels of social participation are not necessarily indicative of poor social skills. In one recent study (Turner, Beidel, Dancu, & Keys, 1986), patients meeting DSM-III criteria for social phobia were judged to have adequate social skills in a structured role-play and in an impromptu speech situation. The socially anxious may well be divided into two groups: those with social skill deficits and those who have adequate social skills yet are socially phobic (Emmelkamp, Mersch, Vissia, & Van der Helm, 1985; Heimberg, Becker, Goldfinger, & Varmilyea, 1985; Marks, 1985; Turner & Beidel, in press).

Leary (1983b) summarizes a study by Fischetti, Curran, and Wessberg (1977) that begins to effectively address the role of specific skill deficits in social anxiety by studying the timing and placement of social responses rather than their frequency or duration. They found "high skill-low anxiety and low skill-high anxiety men did not differ in the number of times they responded to a woman's remarks. . . . However, they differed in the timing and placement of their responses . . . the highly socially skilled men recognized . . . appropriate points [in the conversation] and confined most of their responses to them" (p. 42). A similar study with female subjects reports similar results (Peterson, Fischetti, Curran, & Arland, 1981).

It is not clear from these studies if people with high social anxiety lack social skill or if their anxiety interferes with otherwise normal skills. In any case, while skills deficits may be found in some people who are socially phobic, many with social phobias may have high levels of social skills. For example, it has been shown that, regardless of skill level, when people believe they will not be able to handle a social situation and/or when they judge themselves negatively, they are likely to experience social anxiety (Clark & Arkowitz, 1975; Meichenbaum, Gilmore, & Fedoravicius, 1971). Additionally, it has been documented that socially anxious people make many negative self-statements before and during interpersonal encounters (Cacioppo, Glass, & Merluzzi, 1979; Glass, Merluzzi, Biever, & Larsen, 1982). Cognitive theories assume that these cognitive factors exacerbate and maintain the anxiety and are, therefore, primary foci for treatment.

VI. DESCRIPTION OF COGNITIVE
THERAPY FOR ANXIETY

The goal of cognitive therapy is to teach patients to control anxiety by providing skills to identify, critically appraise, and modify inaccurate thoughts. In addition, patients are taught methods to control physiological arousal and to improve behavioral skills when appropriate (e.g., for social skills deficits). Beck's cognitive therapy for anxiety is arguably one of the most elaborately described models. Therefore, in this section, Beck's cognitive approach is described in detail. While a more complete description of cognitive therapy is available to the reader (Beck, Emery, & Greenburg, 1985; Clark & Beck, in press) a summary of the general "principles" of cognitive therapy are outlined below.

(1) The cognitive model is presented to the patient as the rationale for treatment, in general, and techniques, in specific. Examples from the client's presenting complaint are discussed in the context of the model (see Figure 2).

(2) Cognitive therapy is based on an educational and skill-building model: Clients are taught general skills in the course of working on specific problems so that they are equipped to deal with different problems with similar themes in the future.

(3) Cognitive therapy is goal oriented and time limited. Treatment of anxiety generally lasts from six to twenty sessions. This time frame is largely due to goals inherent in the second principle, which seeks to provide the client with self-sufficient coping skills.

(4) The therapeutic relationship is a collaborative one. The interaction of therapist and client is not presented as that of doctor-patient but of teacher-student, where the therapist serves to enable the client to view anxiety-provoking thoughts, assumptions, and beliefs as hypotheses to be tested for accuracy. Beck had termed this relationship collaborative empiricism. This has important implications for the course and process of therapy because, according to this principle, the client assumes an active role in setting each session's agenda, determining therapy goals, and selecting treatment alternatives (e.g., homework assignments).

(5) Cognitive therapists primarily use a Socratic approach. The therapist does not lecture the client or criticize the relative validity of thoughts but, instead, asks a series of questions that lead the client to experience a "test of the assumptions" that are inherent in anxiety. This serves to illustrate experientially the empirical approach to controlling anxiety that cognitive therapy attempts to teach clients.

(6) A sound therapeutic relationship is a necessary condition for effective cognitive therapy. This was discussed previously in elucidating fundamental differences between Beck's approach and that of Ellis.

(7) Cognitive therapy is directive and goal oriented. Each session begins with setting an agenda with the client, where problems are specified and goals are set that are periodically and systematically reviewed.

(8) Every session ends with a homework assignment that has the purpose of providing the practice necessary to building anxiety-management skills. The specifics of these assignments will be discussed subsequently.

The following techniques have the goal of helping clients to (1) identify the connection between thoughts and feelings, (2) critically appraise the validity of thoughts, and (3) arrive at more accurate thoughts. The reader should note that this should not be confused with positive thinking, which seeks to supplant negative thoughts with more adaptive self-statements. Beck's cognitive therapy places a great emphasis on procedures that *change* beliefs through the empirical-experiential process described below.

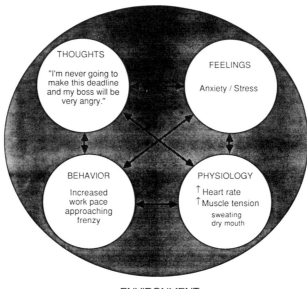

ENVIRONMENT

Figure 2. Example of discussing client's complaints in the context of an interactive model.

A. Discovering the Connection Between Thoughts and Feelings

Often the first opportunity a therapist has to demonstrate how thoughts influence feelings is when recent life events are discussed during the intake evaluation. At this point the therapist can elicit the cognitions associated with the initiation, exacerbation, and maintenance of anxiety by asking questions like "What was going through your mind then?" "What did that situation mean to you?" "What image or mental picture did you have just then?"

A vignette can also be very useful to illustrate how most events are inherently neutral until we interpret a situation and assign meaning to it. For example, consider the following hypothetical situation: There are four people having dinner together in a crowded restaurant and they observe a couple at a nearby table erupt in a loud argument that culminates with the woman exclaiming: "I've had it!" and then storming out of the restaurant. Each of the four observants experienced distinctly different emotions. How could this be, when it was exactly the same situation that all observed? The answer lies with how each person interpreted, or what they associated with, the identical situation.

One man who was recently separated from his wife responded with marked anxiety. This situation prompted an image of a recent fight with his wife and the resulting threat of abandonment. A young boy responded with anger because of his thought: "She reminds me of my sister who is always grouchy and overreacting, making everyone's life miserable." A young therapist felt a sense of joy as she thought: "I wish some of my patients could see this model of assertion!" Finally, a sage elderly person continued enjoying her dinner without feeling any disruptive emotion and she thought: "It's too bad they're not getting along, but I certainly can't do anything about it, so I might as well enjoy this delicious food."

Although vignettes are useful illustrations of the cognitive model, it is obviously important to demonstrate this with the personal material of the client. An opportunity is presented to the therapist when a shift in mood is observed from the client's body language. At this point the therapist can respond by saying: "I notice you seem to be upset by that; what is going through your mind right now?" This can provide for an emotional understanding of how thoughts influence feelings as opposed to an intellectual understanding provided by a hypothetical vignette.

The connection between thoughts and feelings can also be accomplished through a variety of homework assignments such as those described below:

Daily record of dysfunctional thoughts. One of the first homework assignments is designed to teach the client how to be more aware of thoughts that influence anxiety. Clients are instructed to self-monitor their anxiety and, when they notice a sudden increase (particularly during exposure assignments), to "tune in" and record any thoughts or images on a homework form. For various reasons clients often have difficulty identifying thoughts that are directly related to anxiety (see Clark & Beck, in press). A common misconception is that thoughts will be in complete sentences. On the contrary, they are often extremely brief (less than one second; Clark, 1986) and, with anxiety, are likely to be in the form of an image (Beck, 1970). Asking the client to write a brief description of the situation where anxiety was first noticed can help the therapist lead the client to discover the most provocative anxiety-producing thoughts or images.

Discovering "hot thoughts." Once the client is able to see a connection between thoughts and feelings, the next homework assignment involves the difficult task of identifying which thoughts are responsible for the increase in anxiety. This is complicated by the fact that several unrelated thoughts may be noted by the client. Furthermore, many of the thoughts may represent surface structure rather than deep structure meaning. For example, deep structure is composed of abstract units of meaning, which Lang (1977) referred to as propositions (i.e., "Others are responsible for my feelings") from which surface structure is produced ("He made me anxious"). (See Emery & Tracy, 1987, for a more detailed discussion.)

The deep structure meaning (analogous to Beck's terms: assumption, belief, or schema) that is connected to a particular emotion has been called a "hot thought" and can be identified by the "downward arrow" technique (Burns, 1980, p. 235). This technique enables clients to identify the belief behind the thought by repeatedly asking themselves: "What is upsetting about that?" or "What does that mean to me?" Clients are instructed that they will know when they have discovered the hot thought by determining that, if they asked 100 people if they truly believed that thought, most would also feel that particular emotion, at the same intensity. Beliefs and assumptions can also be identified by looking for recurrent themes in thoughts recorded on the thought records over time.

B. Critical Appraisal of Thoughts and Beliefs

Once beliefs related to anxiety are identified, the next step is to inculcate a spirit of critical inquiry. Clients are reminded that as students we were often told: "Don't believe everything you read"; now the corollary "Don't believe everything you think" is put into action. Teaching clients about common cognitive distortions can help them begin to critically appraise the accuracy of their beliefs. A summary of Beck, Rush, Shaw, and Emery's (1979) common cognitive distortions is provided by Burns (1980, pp. 40-41).

Clients are requested to become conversant with this list so that they will be more able to recognize an inaccuracy when they see it. It is important to realize that, because most clients are not accustomed to questioning their thoughts, they may not be able to see the inaccuracies in their thinking and may need training to do this. Some common cognitive distortions related to anxiety are as follows:

Jumping to conclusions. Anxiety-provoking interpretations are made that have no supporting evidence. Two special cases of this are (1) "*mind reading*," where a person believes that another person is thinking about them in a way that provokes anxiety, even though there is no such evidence; and (2) "*fortune telling*," where a person confuses negative predictions for hard facts.

Catastrophizing. The person jumps to the "worst possible" conclusion—this pertains to the confusing of low probabilities with high probabilities. The worst possible scenario is assigned an inordinately high probability.

Dichotomous thinking. Unnecessary anxiety can be caused by thinking in "all or none" terms (i.e., "If I don't do this perfectly it's worthless"). Failure to appreciate the continuous nature of most of life's elements creates anxiety by forcing an inordinate number of these elements into the unacceptable category.

Overgeneralization. One negative experience is viewed as a perpetual pattern of future negative experiences.

Personalization. This involves assuming an inordinate amount of responsibility when in fact other factors are involved. This is particularly important with anxiety related to guilt.

Emotional reasoning. Emotions are interpreted as evidence of fact ("I feel so anxious so therefore something disastrous must be about to happen").

Selective abstraction. This cognitive process involves the active enhancement of any danger-relevant stimuli as well as the selective suppression of disconfirming evidence against danger.

C. Modifying Inaccurate Thoughts

Once the client is able to recognize how a particular thought or belief is inaccurate, that belief may change spontaneously. However, merely identifying how a belief is inaccurate often does not lead to a change in the belief. Therefore, the following techniques can be helpful.

Behavioral experiments. Once the client recognizes the inaccuracies in his or her anxious thoughts, the therapist helps discover more accurate views that may be accompanied by lower anxiety. Cognitive restructuring is not always straightforward. If a client has had a particular belief for a long time, it may take some experience before an alternative view is credible. In these cases, the therapist can encourage the client to scrutinize both old and new beliefs by making and testing predictions. For example, an anxious client believed her husband would become angry if she expressed her opinions. She began expressing her opinions on small and then more important issues and each time predicted he would get angry. After about six experiences where he did not get angry, she began to change her predictions and her underlying belief: "My husband doesn't mind hearing my opinions."

In another case, a client with panic disorder assumed his tachycardia meant he was having a heart attack. As part of this belief, he thought his symptoms were uncontrollable and always dangerous. Several experiments could be conducted to test this belief. A typical behavioral in vivo exposure method would require him to experience the symptoms long and frequently enough to disarm his belief that the "uncontrollability" of these symptoms is equivalent to a heart attack.

However, other types of behavioral experiments are possible and are used more frequently by cognitive therapists. One such experiment would be to demonstrate control of symptoms in session by increasing the tachycardia through hyperventilation or imagery and decreasing the symptoms through controlled breathing or relaxation training. These experiments directly test the assumption that the symptoms are uncontrollable. Then the client would be asked to reinterpret the meaning of the tachycardia based on this data. The alternate beliefs generated (e.g., rapid heartbeat means arousal and can be due to anxiety or breathing changes) can be written on index cards for review during in vivo experiences of tachycardia.

Distraction. Clients are taught that one way of controlling anxiety symptoms is to distract themselves from thoughts of threat. Distraction basically involves a deliberate change in focus from inward preoccupation with bodily sensations or mental fears to an outwardly directed concentration on any number of things in which the client can become absorbed (e.g., conversation, counting objects, singing). This often has the effect of modifying catastrophic misinterpretations by restructuring those thoughts on more accurate beliefs. For example, the therapist can ask the patient: "What does this mean if you reverse your symptoms by simply taking your mind off them?" The patient is thus led to a restructured belief, such as "If I can reverse my symptoms by not thinking about them, perhaps they were not a signal that something was wrong but a result of my anxious thoughts."

VII. WHEN ACCURATE THINKING DOES NOT DECREASE ANXIETY

Even when the validity of a more "accurate" thought is acknowledged by a client, they may still experience continued anxiety. This may be due to several reasons.

A. Emotional Experience Versus Intellectual Understanding

A client may be able to appraise a belief as inaccurate outside of an anxiety-provoking situation but when exposed to the perceived threat the belief is now seen as accurate once again. This may be, in part, because intellectual understanding is often attained outside a state of emotional arousal. Furthermore, emotional reasoning during emotional states often makes thoughts that appear inaccurate while calm seem more real (e.g., "I feel like something is wrong so, therefore, something is"). For example, a client when calm may realize that he or she will not lose control of his or her behavior (i.e., scream or run) but when panicking will have the perception that behavior must be concordant with the emotion.

In these cases, behavioral tests are particularly appropriate to test the general notion that "because I *feel* like doing it, I must *do* it." An example of this process is illustrated by a client who, during a panic attack in the therapist's office, felt that he *couldn't* walk back to his car but would have to run, and therefore, draw a lot of attention to himself. Emotional reasoning was pointed out by the therapist and the client was instructed to test this belief (rated by the client as 100% accurate) by purposefully walking slowly in spite of *feeling* like running. In this way, the belief that panic equals loss of behavioral control was effectively disproven.

In summary, it is important that clients learn to test anxious beliefs while experiencing an anxious state. For example, someone may receive information and assurance from the doctor that he or she is in perfect physical health and that the symptoms he or she is experiencing are those of anxiety, not a heart attack. Subsequently, this person may recognize the catastrophic distortions in their thoughts and may even be able to see the role they play in the exacerbation and maintenance of symptoms, and hence state that he or she does not really fear a heart attack. However, when experiencing panic, this same person may say something to him or herself such as: "I know what my doctor said, but what if he 'missed' something and is wrong?" Or "What if I'm that one person in 100 who has a heart attack because of this intense heart rate?"

B. Disqualification of "More Accurate" Thought

In the above example the client has essentially disqualified the previous "more accurate" thought, which makes the original anxiety-provoking thought more believable. The therapist can next help the client identify and test the accuracy of these disqualifications. Generally, an even more effective approach is to foster a change in anxious thinking within a state of emotional arousal by engaging the client in a behavioral experiment that allows the anxiety-provoking belief to be tested.

Even when the above steps are taken, accurate thinking may not necessarily lead to an immediate cessation of anxiety. This is particularly true with anxiety disorders where the beliefs of threat are more diffuse (e.g., generalized anxiety). In this case more than one "hot thought" may be involved and require identification and change through the aforementioned procedures. Furthermore, some people report that changes in their emotions seem to lag behind changes in their thoughts and behavior. This can, of course, lead to discouragement if not addressed by the therapist. The use of metaphor is often helpful in these situations to convey a realistic perspective on the process of therapeutic change. We have found two specific metaphors to be particularly helpful in dealing with discouragement at this stage of therapy.

"Courtroom of biased experience." It is explained to clients that the early stages of cognitive therapy are analogous to a courtroom where the jury (the clients' beliefs) have been biased by a lifetime of hearing a one-sided story. Now, despite the fact that a defense attorney is beginning to present conflicting evidence, the jury is not entirely convinced because of the relatively brief time spent with this new evidence (in contrast to a lifetime spent with the other). In fact, the social psychology literature provides a wealth of interesting findings that indicate that beliefs can often

persevere even after evidential discrediting (see Nisbett & Ross, 1980, pp. 175-183).

"Strokes on a canvas." Cognitive therapy is viewed as analogous to a painting. Each thought that is critically appraised and empirically tested is much like a stroke on a new canvas, where the client is attempting to paint a clearer picture. In the beginning the strokes do not look like much, but in time when they are all put together a beautiful picture can emerge.

It is beyond the scope of this chapter to provide a detailed description of all the techniques used in cognitive therapy. We have attempted to present some of the most frequently used procedures that illustrate the core process of cognitive therapy for anxiety. For more complete descriptions of cognitive therapy, the reader is referred to Beck, Emery, and Greenburg (1985), Beck, Rush, Shaw, and Emery (1979), Clark and Beck (in press), Clark and Salkovskis (in press), Burns (1980), Emery (1981, 1982), Young (1981), and Young and Beck (1982).

VIII. THE EFFICACY OF COGNITIVE THERAPY WITH ANXIETY DISORDERS

As can be seen from the preceding description, there are many ingredients to cognitive therapy as presented by Beck and his colleagues. At this time it is not empirically known which specific components are critical to treatment effectiveness. Although it is currently appropriate to refine treatment based on a well-developed model prior to embarking upon costly controlled trials, cognitive therapy for anxiety must eventually "pass the test" of empirical scrutiny. The first question that must be asked about cognitive therapy is this: "Does it work?"

Given the preceding descriptions of various procedures termed collectively as "cognitive therapy," it is apparent that viewing cognitive therapy as a generic treatment is not justified and could lead one to a misinterpretation of the literature. Unless these differences are taken into account, interpretations drawn from a review of the literature would be quite misleading. In fact, many evaluations of cognitive therapy treatments to date have been done with studies utilizing only one or two cognitive techniques rather than a comprehensive cognitive therapy program.

Treatment procedures that follow the style of Beck as described in this chapter and cognitive therapy manuals elsewhere (Beck, Rush, Shaw, & Emery, 1979) have been evaluated in several case studies. This type of cognitive therapy was shown to be effective in a case study (Hollon, 1980) as well as in a controlled study (Lindsay, Gamsu, McLaughlin, Hood, & Espie, 1987) in the treatment of generalized anxiety and a variety of nonphobic anxiety disorders (Clark & Beck, in press). More recently, several studies report results showing cognitive therapy to be effective for panic disorder (Clark, Salkovskis, & Chalkley, 1985; Salkovskis, Jones, & Clark, 1986; Sokol-Kessler & Beck, 1987; Waddell, Barlow, & O'Brien, 1984).

Evaluations of studies that have used other less complete cognitive therapies have recently been discussed in two major review articles. Miller and Berman (1983) conducted a meta-analytic quantitative review that attempted to evaluate the efficacy of cognitive-behavior therapies with anxiety disorders. The 48 studies included in this review encompassed a wide range of disorders and treatments. Studies were included if they fit the criterion of "treatments in which at least one component of therapy specifically focused on the patients' maladaptive beliefs." Excluded from the review were treatments that did not appear to require patients to challenge the validity of their beliefs. In 10 (21%) of the studies, the treatment of depression was involved; in 33 (69%) patients were treated for some form of anxiety (public speaking anxiety, test anxiety, neurotic anxiety, social anxiety, simple and complex phobias, assertiveness problems, stuttering, Type A behavior, and adaptation to college), and in the final five (10%) studies, the focus was on the alleviation of anxiety related to various somatic disorders. Notably absent from this review were other major DSM-III diagnostic categories of anxiety (generalized anxiety, panic disorder, and agoraphobia). Also, only 25% of the studies reviewed utilized clinical outpatients as subjects; 48% involved a student population and the remaining 29% involved volunteers from the community.

With these qualifications in mind, the findings of the meta-analysis indicate that, on the average, subjects treated with cognitive-behavior therapy obtained scores on outcome that were over three-quarters of a standard deviation greater than comparable scores of untreated patients. These treatment effects were comparable to effects from systematic desensitization procedures and were maintained at follow-up (range: 1-26 weeks). Miller and Berman (1983) concluded that cognitive-behavior therapies were superior to no treatment, were not consistently superior to the comparison psychotherapies (systematic desensitization procedures), were not more effective than primarily cognitive approaches, and appeared to be effective equally across the diagnostic categories reviewed.

Patient characteristics such as age, sex, and education as well as therapist experience and length of treatment were unrelated to outcome. However, a restricted range with most of those variables warrants caution when interpreting these results. The subjects were predominantly young (mean age = 26.6) and well educated (mean = 13.5 years); therapists were generally inexperienced (mean = 1.5 years); and the treatment was relatively brief (mean = 5.9 weeks).

Differences in size of treatment effect were not significant for diagnosis (e.g., depression, anxiety, or somatic disorders) or for the relative emphasis given to behavioral procedures in the cognitive-behavioral treatments. The authors interpreted this latter finding to indicate that an emphasis on behavioral techniques does not enhance the effectiveness of a primarily cognitive approach. Of course, the alternative hypothesis—that cognitive treatments that include any behavioral component capitalize on treatment effects due to that behavioral component—is equally plausible.

In contrast, Latimer and Sweet (1984), in a separate review, conclude that the efficacy of cognitive therapy (excluding behavioral components) has not been demonstrated in clinical populations and that cognitive therapy added to behavior therapy does not add anything to established behavioral methods used alone. These authors argued that, to evaluate the relative efficacy of cognitive therapy, and to determine whether it adds anything above and beyond behavioral treatments, it would be necessary to provide (a) comparisons of cognitive therapy alone to behavioral treatments alone or (b) comparisons of behavior therapy and combination treatments.

While argument (a) appears experimentally sound, pragmatically this may be a moot point, because cognitive therapies include behavioral procedures in typical practice, while, conversely, behavioral strategies most likely capitalize on cognitive factors. That is, it could be argued that there is no such thing in reality as "pure" cognitive or "pure" behavior therapy, but, instead, that the two are hopelessly confounded from an experimental perspective and optimally combined in effective therapy.

While cognitive therapists agree that behavioral techniques assume an important role, behavioral scientists often neglect to assess possible cognitive mediation of effects attributed to changes in overt behavior. A notable exception is the work of Bandura and colleagues (Bandura, 1977; Bandura & Adams, 1977; Bandura, Adams, & Beyer, 1977; Bandura, Reese, & Adams, 1982), which proposes that the perceptions of self-efficacy cognitively mediates behavioral change and that the most effective way to increase self-efficacy is through successful performance. However, there are situations where self-efficacy and successful performance do not lead to decreases in other domains of anxiety (e.g., emotional or psychological).

This, of course, is not a new phenomenon and has been termed desynchrony (Lang, 1968; Rachman, 1978; Rachman & Hodgson, 1974) or discordance (Michelson, 1984). Concordance of change across the various response systems of anxiety (behavioral, cognitive, emotional, and physiological) has been espoused as the optimal therapeutic outcome and is supported by data showing that "concordant" patients exhibited statistically superior outcomes relative to "discordant" patients (Michelson & Mavissakalian, 1985; Michelson, Mavissakalian, & Marchione, 1985).

The following case example illustrates the independent contribution of cognitions to the emotional experience of anxiety despite successful behavioral performance: Pat, 35 years old, reported difficulty saying "no" to requests from intimate friends. Initially, the therapist worked with Pat within an assertion training paradigm. Although she reported discomfort saying "no" in a socially appropriate manner during role-play, she agreed to say "no" to a friend that weekend to begin exposure therapy.

Despite several successful assertive occasions, the anxiety associated with this behavior did not abate. The therapist subsequently asked Pat to note thoughts and images that accompanied this anxiety. Pat was quite surprised to discover that the images had nothing to do with rejection from friends or letting people down. Rather, she reported, "If I say 'no' I might later decide it was the wrong decision. Then I'd kick myself for days about this mistake and feel miserable."

Once this cognition was identified, the therapist was able to help Pat learn to combat self-criticism over mistakes. Pat had little difficulty saying "no" after this cognitive intervention. For this patient, behavioral practice and exposure did not relieve the anxiety; instead, the underlying idiosyncratic meaning and consequences of the behavior had to be addressed. For Pat, these were primarily cognitive.

Another example of cognitive mediation of behavioral change is provided by Holroyd et al. (1984), who examined the role that frontal EMG biofeedback can play in decreasing headache activity. It had previously been assumed that teaching patients to decrease the physiological consequence of anxiety (increased forehead muscle activity) was responsible for headache decreases. In their study, the authors utilized a 2 × 2 design where half of the patients were given biofeedback to assist in lowering EMG activity and the other half biofeedback to raise EMG activity. Within each of these two conditions half were told they were successful and half were told they were not. The results showed greater headache reductions in patients who were led to believe they were successful at the biofeedback task, regardless of changes in EMG levels. It, therefore, seems that it was the *perceived* success at the biofeedback task, or the *perception* that the patient had learned to control a response that should help alleviate headaches, that was the factor responsible for headache relief.

Given that cognitive and behavior therapies are not mutually exclusive, as is often assumed, attempting to compare behavior therapy "alone" with cognitive therapy "alone" is not feasible. Furthermore, in clinical practice cognitive therapy incorporates behavioral components. Therefore, rather than asking the question: "Is cognitive therapy *or* behavior therapy the most effective treatment for anxiety?" the more useful question is this: "Can cognitive therapy procedures potentiate traditional behavioral treatments for anxiety?" Latimer and Sweet (1984) cite five studies utilizing a design comparing a traditional behavioral treatment alone to that treatment with cognitive procedures added. They conclude that none demonstrated a clinically significant contribution for the cognitive procedures (Emmelkamp and Mersch, 1982; Emmelkamp, Van der Helm, Van Zanten, & Plochy, 1980; Jacobs & Cochran, 1982; Stravynski, Marks, & Yule, 1982; Wolfe & Fodor, 1979). However, as these authors point out, several methodological issues are important to consider when interpreting these findings.

First, many of the studies reviewed were extremely brief (mean = 8 hours; range = 4-11 hours), and they utilized inexperienced therapists (graduate students) in all but one study (Biran & Wilson, 1981). These methodological factors may underestimate the efficacy of cognitive therapies under more ideal and usual circumstances.

Second, small sample size (mean = 18; range = 3-27) and failure to measure treatment compliance in the studies reviewed by Latimer and Sweet (1984) represent the most serious methodological problems. As these authors point out, Goldsmith (1979) has shown that a compliance rate of 50% can require a quadrupling of the sample size otherwise needed to detect a clinically significant effect. Because 50% compliance is not uncommon in various types of clinical outcome studies (Dunbar, 1980), when considered with the small sample size utilized in the reviewed studies, serious questions must be raised regarding the statistical power obtained in these studies to detect any changes.

Furthermore, Latimer and Sweet failed to mention other important aspects of some of the studies they critically reviewed, which, when examined more closely, place cognitive therapy in a more favorable light. For example, while Emmelkamp and Mersch (1982) reported that prolonged in vivo exposure and a combined exposure/self-instructional training was significantly superior to cognitive restructuring on the target behaviors (i.e., phobic anxiety and avoidance) at posttest, many of these effects were no longer significant at the one-month follow-up. Thus, although the short-term effects were similar to results reported by Emmelkamp, Kuipers, and Eggeraat (1978), in the long run cognitive modification was about equally effective. Furthermore, cognitive restructuring was the only treatment that led to significant improvement in depression, locus of control, and assertiveness. (Assertiveness was the only group difference that was significant at follow-up.) These results suggest that the eight, two-hour, cognitive restructuring treatments produced delayed effects that led not only to improvements on the target behaviors (i.e., phobic anxiety and avoidance) but to generalized behavior changes. Finally, it appears that Latimer and Sweet did not include one study that met their inclusion criteria but that showed a more favorable outcome for cognitive therapy. Woodward and Jones (1980) showed that an eight-week, ten-hour combined cognitive restructuring and imaginal desensitization treatment was superior to either component alone with a clinical generalized anxiety population. These results continued to be significant at one-month follow-up. This study may have been excluded from the Latimer and Sweet (1984) review because they did not consider imaginal desensitization to be a behavioral treatment.

If imaginal desensitization is considered to be a cognitive treatment, it would be interesting to compare its effects to in vivo desensitization. A review of the literature suggests that while there is evidence that in vivo exposure is superior to imaginal exposure at posttreatment (Sherman, 1972; Emmelkamp & Wessels, 1975) these results are sometimes no longer significant at later follow-up (Chambless, Foa, Groves, & Goldstein, 1982; Mathews et al., 1976; Wieselberg, Dyckman, & Abramowitz, 1979). It has been suggested this is particularly true when a circumscribed phobia (i.e., snake phobia) results in a low likelihood of encountering the feared stimulus following treatment, hence precluding the possibility of in vivo practice following treatment (Wieselberg, Dyckman, & Abramowitz, 1979).

IX. SUGGESTIONS FOR FUTURE RESEARCH

Several critical questions emerge from this review of the literature on cognitive therapy for anxiety. For each question, relevant data are reviewed and recommendations are made for future research.

A. Does Adding Cognitive Therapy to Behavior Therapy Minimize Dropout Rates?

Reviewing the literature from a large number of studies indicates that the median dropout rate from exposure-based treatments for agoraphobia is 12%, with rates from 25% to 40% reported when drugs are added to exposure-based treatments (Jansson & Ost, 1982; Zitrin, Klein, & Woerner, 1978, 1980). Furthermore, it appears that intensive in vivo exposure, administered over a short period of time, produces a dropout rate considerably higher than the median 12% (e.g., Emmelkamp & Ultee, 1974; Emmelkamp & Wessels, 1975; Michelson, Mavissakalian, & Marchione, 1985). In contrast, a more gradual, self-initiated program of exposure, implemented over a longer period of time with a cooperative partner, produces a very low dropout rate (e.g., Barlow, O'Brien, & Last, 1984; Jannoun, Munby, Catalan & Gelder, 1980; Mathews, Teasdale, Munby, Johnston, & Shaw, 1977). It has also been shown that continued improvement after treatment has been terminated does not occur with intensive, therapist-assisted in vivo exposure and that relapse rates are higher than with less intensive treatments (Hafner, 1976; Jansson & Ost, 1982).

An important question for future research to address is whether or not the addition of cognitive therapy to behavior therapies for agoraphobia reduces dropout rates. Furthermore, an important concern in any treatment is the amount of therapist time required to initiate an acceptable treatment response. Because therapist-assisted graduated exposure requires additional therapist time to travel to and from in vivo exposure assignments, factors that add to the efficacy of self-directed exposure would be advantageous from a perspective of cost-effectiveness.

B. Does Cognitive Therapy Improve Maintenance and Generalization of Change?

Does cognitive therapy prevent relapse at follow-up relative to exposure- or drug-based treatments? With depression, there is some evidence that cognitive therapy produces lower relapse rates than drug treatments (Blackburn, Eunson, & Bishop, in press; Simmons, Murphy, Levine, & Wetze, 1986). Given that cognitive therapy seeks to provide general skills that can be subsequently applied to a variety of specific situations, one could predict that this would lead to greater maintenance and generalization of change with anxiety disorders as well. Preliminary findings suggest that this may indeed be true with regard to generalization of treatment effects to nontarget behaviors (Emmelkamp & Mersch, 1982).

C. How Does Cognitive Therapy Compare with Drug Treatment?

This will be an important comparison, particularly with panic disorders, because it has been proclaimed that phenelzine and tricyclic antidepressants are the treatment of choice for this disorder (Quality Assurance Project, 1985). Several studies have supported the efficacy of imipramine for blocking panic attacks (Klein, Zitrin, & Woerner, 1977; Sheehan, 1982) as well as benzodiazepines (especially alprazolam).

However, pharmacological treatments of panic are not without shortcomings, the most serious being a high relapse rate, coupled with the need for indefinite continuation of medications. Habituation to the therapeutic effects of medication are common, to the extent that it is often necessary to raise dosages beyond the recommended range (Sheehan, 1986). In the absence of raised dosage and continued maintenance on medication, Sheehan (1986) found three-month relapse rates of 95% for alprazolam, 71% for phenelzine, 86% for imipramine, and 92% for combined alprazolam and imipramine. Taken with other side effects of panic medications, the importance of a nonpharmacological alternative to treating this disorder is obvious. Preliminary evidence has been reported showing a high success rate and low relapse rate for cognitive therapy applications to panic (Beck, 1987). Further comparisons between these medications and cognitive therapy will be important for future research to explore.

X. SUMMARY

In summary, we conclude that current evidence supports cognitive therapy as a promising approach to the treatment of anxiety. However, definitive conclusions regarding its efficacy must await large-scale, well-conducted, controlled trials that address the methodological shortcomings previously addressed. Furthermore, although there are many components to Beck's version of cognitive therapy, the critical ingredients are not known at this time. Despite the absence of data regarding this issue, we believe that future trials of cognitive therapy should include the following as core components: (a) identifying and modifying idiosyncratic anxiety-related beliefs, (b) using behavioral experiments to test those beliefs, and (c) utilizing well-trained therapists to administer treatment. This would provide a solid foundation from which to evaluate how cognitive therapy might add to the effectiveness of current behavioral treatments for anxiety disorders.

In addition, studies comparing treatment effectiveness of cognitive therapy, behavior therapy, and pharmacotherapy for anxiety would ideally include dropout rates, relapse rates, and generalization of changes made over time. The advantages of cognitive therapy approaches may not be evident in the short run because cognitive therapy may provide clients with a method for handling future environmental or internal stresses that might make this treatment approach more effective in the long-term amelioration of anxiety disorders.

REFERENCES

American Psychiatric Association. (1987). *Diagnostic and statistical manual of mental disorders* (3rd ed. rev.). Washington, DC: Author.

Bandura, A. (1977). Self-efficacy: Toward a unifying theory of behavioral change. *Psychological Review, 84*, 191-215.

Bandura, A. (1982). Self-efficacy mechanism in human agency. *American Psychologist, 37*, 122-147.

Bandura, A., & Adams, N. E. (1977). Analysis of self-efficacy of behavioral change. *Cognitive Therapy and Research, 1*, 287-308.

Bandura, A., Adams, N. E., & Beyer, J. (1977). Cognitive processes mediating behavioral change. *Journal of Personality and Social Psychology, 35*, 125-139.

Bandura, A., Adams, N. E., Hardy, A. B., & Howells, G. N. (1980). Tests of the generality of self-efficacy theory. *Cognitive Therapy and Research, 4*, 39-66.

Bandura, A., Reese, L., & Adams, N. E. (1982). Microanalysis of action and fear arousal as a function of differential levels of perceived self-efficacy. *Journal of Personality and Social Psychology, 43*, 5-21.

Barlow, D. H., O'Brien, G. T., & Last, C. G. (1984). Couples treatment of agoraphobia. *Behavior Therapy, 15*, 41-58.

Barlow, D., Vermilyea, J., Blanchard, E., Vermilyea, B., DiNardo, P., & Cerny, J. A. (1985). The phenomenon of panic. *Journal of Abnormal Psychology, 94*, 320-328.

Beck, A. T. (1967). *Depression: Clinical, experimental and theoretical aspects.* New York: Harper & Row.

Beck, A. T. (1970). Role of fantasies in psychotherapy and psychopathology. *Journal of Nervous and Mental Disease, 150*, 3-17.

Beck, A. T. (1976). *Cognitive therapy and the emotional disorders.* New York: International Universities Press.

Beck, A. T. (1986). Cognitive approaches to anxiety disorders. In B. F. Shaw, Z. V. Segal, T. M. Vallis, & F. E. Cashman (Eds.), *Anxiety disorders: Psychological and biological perspectives.* New York: Plenum.

Beck, A. T. (1987). Cognitive approaches to panic disorder: Theory and therapy. In S. Rachman & J. Maser (Eds.), *Panic: Psychological perspectives* (pp. 91-109). Hillsdale, NJ: Lawrence Erlbaum.

Beck, A. T., Emery, G., & Greenburg, R. L. (1985). *Anxiety disorders and phobias: A cognitive perspective.* New York: Basic Books.

Beck, A. T., Laude, R., & Bohert, M. (1974). Ideational components of anxiety neurosis. *Archives of General Psychiatry, 31*, 319-325.

Beck, A. T., Rush, A. J., Shaw, B. F., & Emery, G. (1979). *Cognitive therapy of depression.* New York: Guilford.

Beidel, D. C., Turner, S. M., & Dancu, C. V. (1985). Physiological, cognitive, and behavioural aspects of social anxiety. *Behaviour Research and Therapy, 23*, 109-117.

Bellack, A. S., & Hersen, M. (Eds.). (1979). *Research and practice in social skills training.* New York: Plenum.

Biran, M., & Wilson, G. T. (1981). Treatment of phobic disorders using cognitive and exposure methods: A self-efficacy analysis. *Journal of Consulting and Clinical Psychology, 49*, 886-889.

Blackburn, I. M., Eunson, K. M., & Bishop, S. (in press). A two-year naturalistic follow-up of depressed patients treated with cognitive therapy, pharmacotherapy, and a combination of both. *Journal of Affective Disorders.*

Brown, I., Jr., & Inouye, D. K. (1978). Learned helplessness through modeling: The role of perceived similarity in competence. *Journal of Personality and Social Psychology, 36*, 900-908.

Burns, D. D. (1980). *Feeling good: The new mood therapy.* New York: New American Library.

Butler, G., & Mathews, A. (1983). Cognitive processes in anxiety. *Advances in Behaviour Research and Therapy, 5*, 51-62.

Cacioppo, J. T., Glass, C. R., & Merluzzi, T. V. (1979). Self-statements and self-evaluations: A cognitive response analysis of heterosocial anxiety. *Cognitive Therapy and Research, 3*, 249-262.

Chambless, D. L., Caputo, G. C., Bright, P., & Gallagher, R. (1984). Assessment of fear in agoraphobics: The body sensations questionnaire and the agoraphobic cognitions questionnaire. *Journal of Consulting and Clinical Psychology, 52*, 1090-1097.

Chambless, D. L., Foa, E. B., Groves, G. A., & Goldstein, A. J. (1982). Exposure and communication training in the treatment of agoraphobia. *Behaviour Research and Therapy, 20*, 219-231.

Clark, D. M. (1986). A cognitive approach to panic. *Behaviour Research and Therapy, 24,* 461-470.

Clark, D. M., & Beck, A. T. (in press). Cognitive approaches. In C. Last & M. Hersen (Eds.), *Handbook of anxiety disorders.* New York: Pergamon.

Clark, D. M., & Hemsley, D. R. (1982). Effects of hyperventilation: Individual variability and its relation to personality. *Journal of Behavioral Therapy and Experimental Psychiatry, 13,* 41-47.

Clark, D. M., & Salkovskis, P. M. (in press). A cognitive-behavioural treatment for panic attacks. In W. Huber (Ed.), *Proceedings of the 2nd European Conference in Psychotherapy Research.* Louvain, Belgium: University of Louvain Press.

Clark, D. M., Salkovskis, P. M., & Chalkley, A. J. (1985). Respiratory control as a treatment for panic attacks. *Journal of Behavior Therapy and Experimental Psychiatry, 16,* 23-30.

Clark, J. V., & Arkowitz, H. (1975). Social anxiety and self-evaluation of interpersonal performance. *Psychological Reports, 36,* 211-221.

Curran, J. P. (1977). Skills training as an approach to the treatment of heterosexual-social anxiety. *Psychological Bulletin, 84,* 140-157.

Damas-Mora, J., Davies L., Taylor, W., & Jenner, F. A. (1980). Menstrual respiratory changes and symptoms. *British Journal of Psychiatry, 136,* 492-497.

Deffenbacher, J., & Hahloser, R. (1981). Cognitive and relaxation coping skills in stress-inoculation. *Cognitive Therapy and Research, 5,* 211-215.

Dunbar, J. (1980). Adhering to medical advice: A review. *International Journal of Mental Health, 9,* 70-87.

Ellis, A. (1962). *Reason and emotion in psychotherapy.* New York: Stuart.

Ellis, A. (1979). On Joseph Wolpe's espousal of cognitive behavior therapy. *American Psychologist, 34,* 98-99.

Ellis, A. (1984). Rational-emotive therapy. In R. J. Corsini, (Ed.), *Current psychotherapies.* Itasca, IL: F. E. Peacock.

Emery, G. (1981). *A new beginning: How to change your life through cognitive therapy.* New York: Simon & Schuster.

Emery, G. (1982). *Own your own life.* New York: New American Library.

Emery, G., & Tracy. (1987). Theoretical issues in the cognitive-behavioral treatment of anxiety disorders. In L. Michelson & L. M. Ascher (Eds.), *Anxiety and stress disorders.* New York: Guilford.

Emmelkamp, P. M. G., Kuipers, A. C. M., & Eggeraat, J. B. (1978). Cognitive modification versus prolonged exposure *in vivo*: A companion with agoraphobics as subjects. *Behaviour Research and Therapy, 16,* 33-41.

Emmelkamp, P. M. G., & Mersch, P. P. (1982). Cognition and exposure in-vivo in the treatment of agoraphobia: Short term and delayed effects. *Cognitive Therapy Research, 6,* 77-88.

Emmelkamp, P. M. G., Mersch, P. P., Vissia, E., & Van der Helm, M. (1985). Social phobia: A comparative evaluation of cognitive and behavioral interventions. *Behaviour Research and Therapy, 23,* 365-369.

Emmelkamp, P. M. G., & Ultee, K. A. (1974). A comparison of "successive approximation" and "self observation" in the treatment of agoraphobia. *Behavior Therapy, 5,* 606-613.

Emmelkamp, P. M. G., Van der Helm, M., Van Zanten, B. L., & Plochy, I. (1980). Treatment of obsessive-compulsive patients: The contribution of self-instructional training to the effectiveness of exposure. *Behaviour Research and Therapy, 18,* 61-66.

Emmelkamp, P. M. G., & Wessels, H. (1975). Flooding in imagination vs. flooding in-vivo: A comparison with agoraphobics. *Behaviour Research and Therapy, 13,* 7-15.

Evans, I. (1972). A conditioning model of common neurotic pattern: Fear of fear. *Psychotherapy: Theory, Research, and Practice, 9,* 238-241.

Farrell, A. D., Mariotto, M. J., Conger, A. J., Curran, J. P., & Wallander, J. L. (1979). Self-ratings and judges ratings of heterosexual social anxiety. *Psychological Bulletin, 84,* 140-157.
Fischetti, M., Curran, J. P., & Wessberg, H. W. (1977). A sense of timing: A skill deficit in heterosexual-socially anxious males. *Behavior Modification, 1,* 179-194.
Frankl, V. (1975). Paradoxical intention and deflection. *Psychotherapy: Theory, Research and Practice, 12,* 226-236.
Fremouw, W., & Zitter, R. (1978). A comparison of skills training and cognitive restructuring-relaxation for the treatment of speech anxiety. *Behavior Therapy, 9,* 248-259.
Girodo, M., & Roehl, J. (1978). Cognitive preparation and coping self-talk: Anxiety management during the stress of flying. *Journal of Consulting and Clinical Psychology, 46,* 978-989.
Glass, C., Gottman, J., & Shmurak, S. (1976). Response acquisition and cognitive self-statement modification approaches to dating skill training. *Journal of Counseling Psychology, 23,* 520-526.
Glass, C. R., Merluzzi, T. V., Biever, J. L., & Larsen, K. H. (1982). Cognitive assessment of social anxiety: Development and validation of a self-assessment questionnaire. *Cognitive Therapy and Research, 6,* 37-56.
Goldsmith, C. H. (1979). The effects of compliance distributions on therapeutic trials. In R. B. Haynes, D. W. Taylor, & D. L. Sackett (Eds.), *Compliance in health care.* Baltimore: Johns Hopkins University Press.
Goldstein, A. J., & Chambless, D. L. (1978). A reanalysis of agoraphobia. *Behavior Therapy, 9,* 47-59.
Hafner, R. J. (1976). Fresh symptom emergence after intensive behaviour therapy. *British Journal of Psychiatry, 129,* 378-383.
Heimberg, R. G., Becker, R. E., Goldfinger, K., & Vermilyea, J. A. (1985). Treatment of social phobia by exposure, cognitive restructuring and homework assignments. *Journal of Nervous and Mental Disease, 173,* 236-245.
Hibbert, G. A. (1984). Ideational components of anxiety: Their origin and content. *British Journal of Psychiatry, 144,* 618-624.
Hollon, S. D. (1980). Cognitive-behavioral treatment of drug-induced pansituational anxiety states. In G. Emery, S. D., Hollon, & R. C. Bedrosian (Eds.), *New directions in cognitive therapy: A case book.* New York: Raven.
Holroyd, K. A., Penzien, D. B., Hursey, K. G., Tobin, P. L., Rogers, L., Holm, J. E., Marcille, P. J., Hall, J. R., & Chila, A. G. (1984). Change mechanisms in EMG biofeedback training: Cognitive changes underlying improvements in tension headache. *Journal of Consulting and Clinical Psychology, 52,* 1039-1053.
Hussain, R., & Lawrence, P. (1978). The reduction of test, state and trait anxiety by test-specific and generalized stress inoculation training. *Cognitive Therapy and Research, 2,* 25-37.
Jacob, R., & Rapport, M. (1984). Panic disorder. In S. Turner (Ed.), *Behavioral treatment of anxiety disorders.* New York: Plenum.
Jacobs, M. K., & Cochran, S. D. (1982). The effects of cognitive restructuring on assertive behavior. *Cognitive Therapy Research, 6,* 63-76.
Jannoun, L., Munby, M., Catalan, J., & Gelder, M. (1980). A home-based treatment program for agoraphobia: An evaluative review. *Clinical Psychology Review, 2,* 311-337.
Jansson, L., & Ost, L. (1982). Behavioral treatments for agoraphobia: An evaluation review. *Clinical Psychology Review, 2,* 311-337.
Jaremko, M. (1980). The use of stress inoculation training in the reduction of public speaking anxiety. *Journal of Clinical Psychology, 36,* 735-738.
Jaremko, M. (1983). Stress inoculation training for social anxiety, with emphasis on dating

anxiety. In D. Meichenbaum & M. Jaremko (Eds.), *Stress reduction and prevention*. New York: Plenum.

Klein, D. F., Zitrin, C. M., & Woerner, M. G. (1977). Imipramine and phobia. *Psychopharmacology Bulletin, 13*, 24-27.

Koriat, A., Melkman, R., Averill, J. R., & Lazarus, R. S. (1972). The self-control of emotional reactions to a stressful film. *Journal of Personality, 40*, 601-619.

Lader, M. H. (1967). Palmar skin conductance measures in anxiety and phobic states. *Journal of Psychosomatic Research, 11*, 271-281.

Lang, P. J. (1968). Fear reduction and fear behavior: Problems in treating a construct. In J. M. Shlien (Ed.), *Research in psychotherapy* (Vol. 3). Washington, DC: American Psychological Association.

Lang, P. J. (1977). Imagery in therapy: An information processing analysis of fear. *Behavior Therapy, 8*, 862-866.

Last, C. G., & Blanchard, E. B. (1982). Classification of phobic versus fearful non-phobics: Procedural and theoretical issues. *Behavioral Assessment, 4*, 195-210.

Last, C. G., O'Brien, G. T., & Barlow, D. H. (1985). The relationship between cognitions and anxiety: A preliminary report. *Behavior Modification, 9*, 235-241.

Latimer, P. R., & Sweet, A. A. (1984). Cognitive versus behavioral procedures in cognitive-behavior therapy: A critical review. *Journal of Behavior Therapy and Experimental Psychiatry, 15*, 9-22.

Lazarus, R. S., & Alfert, E. (1964). The short-circuiting of threat by experimentally altering cognitive appraisal. *Journal of Abnormal and Social Psychology, 69*, 195-205.

Lazarus, R. S., Opton, E. M., Nomikos, M. S., & Rankin, N. O. (1965). The principal of short-circuiting of threat: Further evidence. *Journal of Personality, 33*, 622-635.

Leary, M. R. (1983a). Social anxiousness: The construct and its measurement. *Journal of Personality Assessment, 47*, 66-75.

Leary, M. R. (1983b). *Understanding social anxiety: Social, personality, and clinical perspectives*. Beverly Hills, CA: Sage.

Ley, R. (1985a). Agoraphobia, the panic attack, and the hyperventilation syndrome. *Behaviour Research and Therapy, 23*, 79-81.

Ley, R. (1985b). Blood, breath, and fears: A hyperventilation theory of panic attacks and agoraphobia. *Clinical Psychology Review, 5*, 271-285.

Ley, R. (1987). Panic disorder: A hyperventilation interpretation. In L. Michelson & L. M. Ascher (Eds.), *Anxiety and stress disorders: Cognitive-behavioral assessment and treatment*. New York: Guilford.

Lindsay, W. R., Gamsu, C. V., McLaughlin, E., Hood, E. M., & Espie, L. A. (1987). A controlled trial of treatments for generalized anxiety. *British Journal of Clinical Psychology, 26*, 3-17.

Lum, L. C. (1976). The syndrome of habitual chronic hyperventilation. In O. W. Hill (Ed.), *Modern trends in psychosomatic medicine* (Vol. 3). London: Butterworths.

Luria, A. (1961). *The role of speech in the regulation of normal and abnormal behavior*. New York: Liveright.

Malleson, M. (1959). Panic and phobia: A possible method of treatment. *Lancet*, 225-227.

Marks, I. M. (1985). Behavioral treatment of social phobia. *Psychopharmacology Bulletin, 21*, 615-618.

Mathews, A. M., Johnston, D. W., Lancashire, M., Munby, M., Shaw, P. M., & Gelder, M. G. (1976). Imaginal flooding and exposure to real phobic situations: Treatment outcome with agoraphobic patients. *British Journal of Psychiatry, 129*, 362-371.

Mathews, A. M., Teasdale, J., Munby, M., Johnston, D., & Shaw, P. A. (1977). A home-based treatment for agoraphobia. *Behavior Therapy, 8*, 915-924.

Meichenbaum, D. (1972). Cognitive modification of test anxious college students. *Journal of Consulting and Clinical Psychology, 39*, 370-380.

Meichenbaum, D. (1977). *Cognitive-behavior modification: An integrative approach.* New York: Plenum.

Meichenbaum, D. (1985). *Stress inoculation training.* New York: Pergamon.

Meichenbaum, D. H., Gilmore, J. B., & Fedoravicius, A. (1971). Group insight versus group desensitization in treating speech anxiety. *Journal of Consulting and Clinical Psychology, 36,* 410-421.

Meichenbaum, D., & Goodman, J. (1971). Training impulsive children to talk to themselves: A means of developing self-control. *Journal of Abnormal Psychology, 77,* 114-126.

Michelson, L. (1984). The role of individual differences, response profiles, and treatment consonance in anxiety disorders. *Journal of Behavioral Assessment, 6,* 349-368.

Michelson, L. (1987). Cognitive-behavioral assessment and treatment of agoraphobia. In L. Michelson, & L. M. Ascher (Eds.), *Anxiety and stress disorders: Cognitive-behavioral assessment and treatment.* New York: Guilford.

Michelson, L., & Mavissakalian, M. (1985). Agoraphobia: Psychophysiological outcome of behavioral and pharmacological treatments. *Journal of Consulting and Clinical Psychology, 53,* 229-236.

Michelson, L., Mavissakalian, M., & Marchione, K. (1985). Cognitive and behavioral treatments of agoraphobia: Clinical, behavioral, and psychophysiological outcomes. *Journal of Consulting and Clinical Psychology, 53,* 913-925.

Miller, R. C., & Berman, J. S. (1983). The efficacy of cognitive behavior therapies: A quantitative review of the research evidence. *Psychological Bulletin, 94,* 39-53.

Nichols, K. A. (1974). Severe social anxiety. *British Journal of Medical Psychology, 74,* 301-306.

Nisbett, R., & Ross, L. (1980). *Human inference: Strategies and shortcomings of social judgment* (pp. 175-183). Englewood Cliffs, NJ: Prentice-Hall.

Nomikos, M. S., Opton, E. M., Jr., Averill, J. R., & Lazarus, R. S. (1968). Surprise versus suspense in the production of stress reaction. *Journal of Personality and Social Psychology, 8,* 204-208.

Okel, B. B., & Hurst, J. W. (1961). Prolonged hyperventilation in man: Associated electrolyte changes and subjective symptoms. *Archives of Internal Medicine, 108,* 157-162.

Peterson, J., Fischetti, M., Curran, J. P., & Arland, S. (1981). Sense of timing: A skill deficit in heterosocially anxious women. *Behavior Therapy, 12,* 195-201.

Quality Assurance Project. (1985). Treatment outlines for the management of anxiety states. *Australian and New Zealand Journal of Psychiatry, 19,* 138-151.

Rachman, S. (1978). Human fears: A three systems analysis. *Scandinavian Journal of Behavior Therapy, 7,* 37-245.

Rachman, S., & Hodgson, R. I. (1974). Synchrony and desynchrony in fear and avoidance. *Behaviour Research and Therapy, 12,* 311-318.

Rappee, R. M. (1985). Distinctions between panic disorder and generalised anxiety disorder: Clinical presentation. *Australian and New Zealand Journal of Psychiatry, 19,* 227-232.

Salkovskis, P., Jones, D., & Clark, D. (1986). Respiratory control in the treatment of panic attacks: Replication and extension with concurrent measures of behaviour and pCO_2. *British Journal of Psychiatry, 148,* 526-532.

Schlenker, B. R., & Leary, M. R. (1982). Social anxiety and self-presentation: A conceptualization and model. *Psychological Bulletin, 92,* 641-669.

Schunk, D. H. (1981). Modeling and attributional effects on children's achievement: A self-efficacy analysis. *Journal of Educational Psychology, 73,* 93-105.

Schwartz, R. M., & Garamoni, G. L. (1984). The internal dialogue and anxiety: Asymmetries between positive and negative coping thoughts. In L. Michelson (Chair), *Cognitive-Behavioral Assessment and Treatment of Major Anxiety Disorders: Current Strategies and Future Perspectives,* Symposium conducted at the meeting of the Association for Advancement of Behavior Therapy, Philadelphia.

Schwartz, R. M., & Garamoni, G. L. (1986). A structural model of positive and negative states of mind: Asymmetry in internal dialogue. In P. C. Kendal (Ed.), *Advances in cognitive-behavioral research and therapy* (Vol. 5). New York: Academic Press.

Schwartz, R. M., & Michelson, L. (1987). States of mind model: Cognitive balance in the treatment of agoraphobia. *Journal of Consulting and Clinical Psychology, 55*, 557-565.

Sewitch, T. S., & Kirsch, I. (1984). The cognitive content of anxiety: Naturalistic evidence for the predominance of threat-related thoughts. *Cognitive Therapy and Research, 8*, 49-58.

Sheehan, D. V. (1982). Panic attacks and phobias. *New England Journal of Medicine, 307*, 156-158.

Sheehan, D. V. (1986). Tricyclic antidepressants in the treatment of panic and anxiety disorders. *Psychosomatics, 27*, 10-16.

Sherman, A. R. (1972). Real-life exposure as a primary therapeutic factor in the desensitization treatment of fear. *Journal of Abnormal Psychology, 79*, 19-28.

Simmons, A. D., Murphy, G. E., Levine, J. L., & Wetze, R. D. (1986). Cognitive therapy and pharmacotherapy for depression: Sustained improvement over one year. *Archives of General Psychiatry, 43*, 43-48.

Sokol-Kessler, L., & Beck, A. T. (1987, May 14). *Cognitive treatment of panic disorder.* Paper presented at the American Psychiatric Association Annual Meeting, Chicago.

Speisman, J., Lazarus, R. S., Mordkoff, A., & Davidson, L. (1964). Experimental reduction of stress based on ego defense theory. *Journal of Abnormal and Social Psychology, 68*, 367-380.

Stampler, F. M. (1982). Panic disorder: Description, conceptualization, and implications for treatment. *Clinical Psychology Review, 2*, 469-486.

Stravynski, A., Marks, I., & Yule, W. (1982). Social skills problems in neurotic outpatients: Social skills training with and without cognitive modification. *Archives of General Psychiatry, 39*, 1378-1385.

Sweeney, G., & Horan, J. (1982). Separate and combined effects of uncontrolled relaxation and cognitive restructuring in the treatment of musical performance anxiety. *Journal of Counseling Psychology, 29*, 486-497.

Turner, S. M., & Beidel, D. C. (in press). Social phobia: Clinical syndrome, diagnosis, and co-morbidity. *Clinical Psychology Review.*

Turner, S. M., Beidel, D. C., Dancu, C. V., & Keys, D. J. (1986). Psychopathology of social phobia and comparison to avoidant personality disorder. *Journal of Abnormal Psychology, 95*, 389-394.

Waddell, M. T., Barlow, D. H., & O'Brien, G. T. (1984). A preliminary investigation of cognitive and relaxation treatment of panic disorder: Effects on intense anxiety vs. background anxiety. *Behaviour Research and Therapy, 22*, 393-402.

Weeks, C. (1977). *Simple, effective treatment of agoraphobia.* New York: Hawthorn.

Wieselberg, N., Dyckman, J. M., & Abramowitz, S. I. (1979). The desensitization derby: *In vivo* down the backstretch, imaginal at the wire? *Journal of Clinical Psychology, 35*, 647-650.

Wilson, G. T. (1978). Cognitive behavior therapy: Paradigm shift or passing phase? In J. Foreyt & D. Rathjen (Eds.), *Cognitive behavior therapy: Research and application.* New York: Plenum.

Wolfe, J. L., & Fodor, I. G. (1979). Modifying assertive behavior in women: A comparison of three approaches. *Behavior Therapy, 8*, 567-574.

Woodward, R., & Jones, R. B. (1980). Cognitive restructuring treatment: A controlled trial with anxious patients. *Behaviour Research and Therapy, 18*, 401-407.

Young, J. E. (1981). Cognitive therapy and loneliness. In G. Emery, R. C. Bedrosian, & S. Hollon (Eds.), *New directions in cognitive therapy.* New York: Guilford.

Young, J. E., & Beck, A. T. (1982). Cognitive therapy: Clinical applications. In A. J. Rush (Ed.), *Short-term psychotherapies for depression.* New York: Guilford.

Zitrin, C. M., Klein, D. F., & Woerner, M. G. (1978). Behavior therapy, supportive psychotherapy, imipramine, and phobias. *Archives of General Psychiatry, 35,* 307-321.

Zitrin, C. M., Klein, D. F., & Woerner, M. G. (1980). Treatment of agoraphobia with group exposure in vivo and imipramine. *Archives of General Psychiatry, 37,* 63-72.

MODIFICATION OF CHILDHOOD AGGRESSION

JOHN E. LOCHMAN
Duke University Medical Center

AUTHOR'S NOTE: The preparation of this chapter was partially supported by a grant from the National Institute of Mental Health to the author (MH 39989).

I. INTRODUCTION

Aggressive behavior in childhood has not only been found to be a stable behavioral pattern, but high levels of aggression in childhood have also been found to be predictive of a variety of adolescent difficulties, including substance abuse, criminal activity, and psychiatric symptoms (Achenbach, 1982; Kandel, 1982; Olweus, 1979; Robins, 1978). Because highly aggressive childhood behavior is not usually a transient problem, the need for treatment is particularly strong. Traditional forms of individual and group therapy have historically had little success in reducing the behavioral problems of aggressive children. However, behavioral treatments have had more reported improvements in children's aggressive behavior, and two of the approaches that have produced the most promises results are behavioral family therapy and cognitive-behavioral therapy (Kazdin, 1987).

These two treatment approaches share a common strength, which is that the treatment strategies are designed to have an impact on moderating processes in the family or in the child that maintain the aggressive behavior. Based on systematic observation of family interaction processes, behavioral family therapy focuses on reducing parents' high rates of aversive, controlling behavior and vague "beta" commands, while increasing the parents' use of social reinforcement, clear "alpha" commands, and accurate monitoring of children's behavior (e.g., Forehand & Long, in press; Patterson, 1986). Cognitive-behavioral therapy focuses on the deficient and distorted social-cognitive processes identified in aggressive children, including distortions in their recall and perceptions of others' behavior and their own behavior, biases in their attributions about the hostile intentions of others, and overreliance on nonverbal direct action solutions and underreliance on verbal assertion solutions as they think of alternative means of responding to social problems (Dodge, 1986; Lochman, 1987; Lochman & Lampron, 1986). In both of these treatment approaches, basic research findings have been integrated into the ongoing treatment programs, thus enriching both the research on basic processes and the research on treatment outcomes. This chapter will review the outcome research for behavioral family therapy and cognitive-behavioral therapy with aggressive children as well as the predictors of treatment effectiveness within each of these approaches and will suggest issues that can be addressed in the increasing number of studies examining such approaches. While variations unfortunately exist in how different investigators define aggression, *aggressive behavior* in this review will refer to high rates of noncompliance as well as high rates of verbally and physically abusive behavior. This review will be restricted to treatment of children and will not include studies that have used similar treatment procedures with adolescents (e.g., Alexander & Parsons, 1973; Feindler,

Ecton, Kingsley, & Dubey, 1986). Other behavioral treatment approaches have been effectively provided to aggressive children who have a variety of cognitive and physical handicaps (such as mental retardation, visual impairment, and deafness—e.g., Denkowski & Denkowski, 1985; Luiselli, 1984) and to disruptive and aggressive students by classroom teachers using contingency management procedures (e.g., Pfiffner, O'Leary, Rosen, & Sanderson, 1985). However, this review will be restricted to the studies of behavioral family therapy and cognitive-behavior therapy with aggressive children who are not mentally retarded or physically handicapped.

II. BEHAVIORAL FAMILY THERAPY

During the past two decades, a large number of empirical studies have reported on the effectiveness of behavioral family therapy approaches with children. These studies have initially examined whether or not children's behaviors and parents' behaviors would change systematically over time, following the families' involvement in behavioral treatment. These relatively simple pre-post designs were often expanded to include follow-up assessment to determine if generalization of behavioral change over time had occurred. The initial studies led to, and were accompanied in time by, more rigorous scientific studies in which groups of subjects receiving behavioral family therapy were contrasted to other no-treatment or alternative treatment conditions. Such comparisons were designed to rule out alternative causes for the observed behavioral changes, including maturation and instrument sensitization. Several studies compared treated groups to "normal" nonclinical samples to determine if differences existed at posttreatment. Relevant research in these areas will be reviewed in the following sections.

A. Change Over Time

In examining research on the effects over time of behavioral family therapy, we will first review studies from the two centers that have produced the most visible programmatic research: Gerald Patterson and colleagues at the Oregon Social Learning Center (OSLC) and Rex Forehand and colleagues at the University of Georgia. We will also review positive and negative findings from several other influential studies.

Gerald Patterson and John Reid's work at the OSLC has established the rationale for using behavioral family therapy with aggressive children. Starting in the 1960s, Patterson began trying out behavioral strategies with families of aggressive children. Patterson's (1986) account of how aggressive children develop in family systems and his treatment model serve as a backbone for most current behavioral family therapies. Patterson and Fleischman (1979) examined the maintenance of treatment effects for the first 114 families who were referred to OSLC. Children referred to the OSLC were between 5 and 12 years of age, and had primary referral problems of social aggression in the home setting, although some children's referral problems involved other low-base-rate behavior such as truancy, stealing, and fire-setting. Of this initial set of referrals, complete 12-month follow-up data were available for 50 families. Treatment had involved training parents in social learning skills, including accurate pinpointing and observation of behavior, use of point systems, use of contingent social reinforcement, and time-out. These treatment procedures have been detailed in Patterson, Reid, Jones, and Conger (1975). Two of the notable characteristics of the OSLC treatment model are that the therapists were trained staff rather than student therapists and that the treatment was not time limited, so that families could continue in treatment as long as necessary to achieve treatment goals.

The follow-up data reported by Patterson and Fleischman (1979) were derived from the home observation system and the parents' daily reports of symptom occurrence used in the OSLC studies. The observations were conducted in each family's home with all members present. Each family member was observed, and the behaviors were coded into 29 categories. Fourteen of the categories represent noxious behavior (e.g., yell, hit, humiliate) and are summed to create the total deviant (TD) score. In some of the research reports, this was referred to as the total aversive behavior (TAB) score. Interrater reliability was assessed and was adequate. Reduction in the total deviant score was found to continue from baseline to termination and to the 12-month follow-up, with 84% of the children functioning in a normal range at follow-up. The parents' daily reports (PDR) followed a similar pattern. On the PDR, parents received a semiweekly telephone call and were asked to report the occurrence of targeted child behavior problems (e.g., fighting, crying, throwing tantrums, not complying) during the previous 24 hours. Good psychometric properties have been reported for the PDR. Patterson and Fleischman (1979) concluded that the treated children had become less coercive and that the changes had persisted into the one-year follow-up period.

This same set of OSLC clients was included in another study of treatment follow-up effects, this time separating out the effects on the target children's behavior, mothers' behavior, and siblings' behavior (Horne & Van Dyke, 1983). This study followed up 56 families that had completed at least three treatment sessions. The average number of treatment sessions was 22, ranging from 3 to 85. Using data from the same home observation system described earlier, the aggressive behavior rates for the target child, mother, and siblings continued the pattern identified at posttesting, and were significantly lower at the one-year follow-up than at

baseline. Thus the results suggested that the mothers were able to continue using less aversive behavior in their interactions with their children,
and this reduced the likelihood that the previous levels of coercive behavior in the children would reemerge. These results also illustrate that treatment effects generalize to other, nontargeted siblings, decreasing their
aggressive behavior as well. Horne and Van Dyke (1983, p. 611) do appropriately caution, however, that, while aggressive behaviors were reduced into a "normal" range for the observational system, "the behavior
rate was still at the upper levels of 'normal' behavior rates."

Two efforts have been made by staff using the OSLC treatment procedures to replicate these behavioral changes over time with clinic-referred
families (Fleischman, 1981; Fleischman & Szykula, 1981). Fleischman
(1981) examined the outcome for 16 families that had been treated at the
Family Center of the Oregon Research Institute during a 14-month period by staff affiliated with Patterson. A total of 35 families had been seen
at the center during this period, but these 16 families were the only ones
that underwent at least five treatment sessions and had been willing to
participate in the one-year follow-up. This substantial attrition rate over
time is a methodological problem that weakens much of the follow-up research in the aggression-modification field.

The referred children were between 3 and 12 years of age (mean, 7.6),
and, unlike the original studies, included female as well as male target
children. Nearly half of the families had a single parent, and the families'
occupational levels were within a lower-middle- to middle-class range.
The staff made an effort to make treatment more standardized by reducing the number of treatment sessions to an average of 13.7 hours (versus
31.2 in the original Patterson study), and by eliminating therapist-
specific effects by not using Patterson or his colleagues as therapists or for
clinical supervision. The findings replicated the prior studies and found
that the total aversive behavior rates in the home observation had decreased, as had the parents' daily reports of problem behavior and the
parents' problem behavior checklist ratings.

In the other study, Fleischman and Szykula (1981) attempted to replicate the OSLC findings in a community treatment setting at the Family
Teaching Center in Helena, Montana. Of 100 families referred for treatment, 50 did not complete the intake process, terminated treatment before five sessions, or moved during treatment. The 50 treated families
had target children between the ages of 3 and 12, with an average age of
6.9 years. Attrition rates in data collection were again relatively high,
with home observations collected on 24 target children at termination of
treatment and 12 children at the one-year follow-up, and with parent
daily reports collected on 44 children at termination and 28 children at
the one-year follow-up. By the end of treatment, treated children had significant reductions in total aversive behaviors during home observations

and in parent ratings of negative child behaviors. These significant reductions from baseline were continued to the one-year follow-up, and the authors concluded that social learning treatment for aggressive children can be effectively implemented in other settings.

In another programmatic set of studies, Rex Forehand and colleagues at the University of Georgia have evaluated a systematic behavioral parent training program for noncompliant children. These samples of children are generally somewhat younger than the OSLC target children, and are referred to the University Clinic for the treatment of noncompliance to parental commands, aggressive behavior to others, destruction of property, and negative verbal behaviors. The treatment program for parent-child pairs consists of two phases. In the first phase, mothers were instructed to become more effective reinforcing agents by increasing the contingent use of social rewards and attention and by decreasing competing verbal behavior, such as commands and criticisms. In phase two, parents were taught to give clear, concise commands which were labeled "alpha" commands), to allow the child sufficient time to comply with the command, to reward compliance with attention, and to use a three-to-five-minute time-out procedure if the child did not comply in five seconds (Baum & Forehand, 1981). Training took place in clinic playrooms with the therapist using a bug-in-the-ear device to give feedback to parents who interacted with their children in free-play situations and in parent-structured situations. Training with a family is typically conducted by a pair of graduate student therapists, one of whom has experience in the treatment program. The dependent measures for these studies have usually included (a) a behavioral observation of parent-child interaction that yields scores for maternal social rewards, maternal contingent attention, maternal "beta" commands (vague, unclear commands), child compliance, and child deviant behavior, and (b) the Parent's Attitude Test (PAT) to assess parent's attitudes toward and perception of children's behavior.

In one of the early studies, Forehand and King (1977) reported changes following treatment and at a three-month follow-up for 11 children. The children ranged in age from 3 1/2 to 7 1/2, averaging five years, two months, for the sample. Ten of the children were boys, and the families were predominantly middle class. The behavioral observations were conducted in clinic settings, and the mothers were found to decrease their commands and to increase their rewarding behavior by the end of treatment. Consequently, the children became more compliant to commands. The parents' ratings of the children's behavior and home attitude also became more positive, and both the observational and the parent rating improvements were maintained at the follow-up period. Forehand and King (1977) also selected 11 nonclinic mother-child pairs as a "normal" group, and compared the treated families with this group. The treated families were equivalent at posttreatment and at follow-up to the nonclinic group on the parent ratings (PAT), and the treated group surprisingly displayed more maternal reward and more child compliance following treatment than did the nonclinic group. While this comparison suggests that the treated group was functioning within a "normal" or higher range after treatment, the strength of findings involving only normal comparison groups has certain limitations.

A later study in this line has documented that the target children's siblings' behavior also improves following behavioral parent training, in a manner similar to Patterson's results. Humphreys, Forehand, McMahon, and Roberts (1978) examined pre-post changes in the observed home behavior of an untreated sibling of a treated target child. The mean age of the 8 target children was 6 years, 5 months, and the mean age of the untreated siblings was 5 years. Following an average of 5.6 treatment sessions, the siblings had become more compliant. In addition, the mothers' behavioral changes had clearly generalized to their interactions with these untargeted siblings, as the mother emitted higher rates of rewards and contingent attention and lower rates of beta commands.

Other studies have found that the target child's home behavior also improves, and that such change in home behavior persists into follow-up periods. Subsequent to parent training, a sample of 15 target children (average age of 4 years, 10 months) were found to be more compliant and to exhibit less deviant behavior during home observation. Mothers of the target children were more rewarding and gave more contingent attention and fewer beta commands (Forehand, Wells, & Griest, 1980). Comparison of this target group to a nonclinic comparison group of 15 children (mean age of 5 years, 4 months) indicated that the target children and their families were initially worse than nonclinic families at the pretreatment observations, but that the target children's compliance was not significantly different than nonclinic children by posttreatment. Similar to Forehand and King (1977), the target children's mothers were found to be more rewarding and attentive than nonclinic mothers at posttreatment. While several subjects were lost to attrition, these behavioral improvements were maintained at a two-month follow-up. Baum and Forehand (1981) found essentially identical behavioral changes for target children over a more extended follow-up period. After attempting to contact 40 mother-child pairs who had completed training at least one year earlier, 20 parents agreed to participate in follow-up observations and 34 parents completed the parent questionnaires (PAT). The follow-up interval ranged from 1 to 4.5 years, and significant behavior improvements were maintained in both child and parent behavior. In these two studies, as well as in a study by McMahon, Tiedemann, Forehand, and Griest (1984), the parents have been found to report a high degree of consumer satisfaction with the parent training at both posttreatment and follow-up periods. Such assessment of parents' satisfaction with the treatment program, the therapists, the teaching format, and the specific parenting skills that were taught is a useful effort to document the social validity of the program (Kazdin, 1977; McMahon & Forehand, 1983).

In the most lengthy follow-up attempted, Forehand and Long (in press) contacted previously treated children during their early adolescent years (ages 11 to 14). The average follow-up interval was 7 years, 7 months, and ranged from 4.5 to 10.5 years. Of 43 families who had been recipients of the program, 21 agreed to participate in this follow-up. A nontreated "normal" comparison group of 21 families was drawn from a pool of 155 families in another study, and were equated on age, gender, and socioeconomic status to the treated group. Using a broad array of parent and teacher ratings, the parent training subjects were not significantly different from the normal comparison groups on most measures of externalizing and internalizing child behavior problems and of parenting skills. However, the parent trained children had more reported conflicts with parents, more teacher-rated attention, more anxiety and withdrawal problems, and lower perceived cognitive competence and grade-point average. The parent-trained mothers reported higher levels of marital adjustment, and fathers reported less interparental conflict. Forehand and Long (in press) found these results to be generally encouraging, although they did caution that the families that agreed to this follow-up assessment had higher baseline levels of child compliance and marital satisfaction than did the families who did not agree to the follow-up, and this may have exaggerated the follow-up effects. In addition, while mean differences existed between the groups on many variables, most of the differences were not significant with this sample size. This study provides suggestive evidence that the treated group had been brought into a normal range at follow-up.

Several other research studies outside of the Patterson and Forehand programs have attempted to document behavioral changes resulting from parent training. These, however, have produced mixed results. Webster-Stratton (1985) used a parent training program that was based on a two-stage model similar to Forehand's training program. Parents met weekly for nine two-hour sessions. The children ranged in age from 3 to 8 and averaged 5 years, 2 months. The children lived in lower-middle- to lower-class families, and were referred to a conduct disorder program in a psychiatric and behavioral clinic in a pediatric hospital. The 32 children who continued through follow-up (only two families dropped out) were rated on checklists on a range of behavior problems that are typical for clinical samples. Using home observation and behavior checklist ratings, Webster-Stratton replicated the prior results. She found at posttreatment and at one-year follow-up that children were more compliant and less deviant, mothers were less critical, and mothers rated children as having fewer behavior problems.

Similarly, Strain, Steele, Ellis, and Timm (1982) found, in an extended follow-up study, that treatment effects appeared to be maintained over time. Observations in the home and school settings were conducted three to nine years following treatment for 40 families. Because the follow-up measures had not been used at earlier assessment points, the results are only suggestive, however. The treated children's school behavior was not significantly different from the behavior of a group of randomly selected classmates. Home observations indicated that treated children complied with parental commands, demands, and requests 82% of the time, and that parents generally used contingent social reinforcement as they had been instructed during parent training. In contrast to these positive replications, other researchers have either not found posttreatment gains, or the posttreatment gains have faded during follow-up. Eyberg and Johnson (1974) developed a 12-session parent training program that focused on contingency contracting for children's behavioral problems at home. Parents of 17 children (mean age 7.4 years, range of 4 to 11) completed treatment with graduate student therapists. Another 13 families had terminated treatment during the program. By posttreatment, parents rated their children as being less problematic on checklists and, according to parent observation, they were generally satisfied with treatment. However, children did not significantly improve on total deviant behaviors during home observations and did not significantly improve in standard laboratory situations. Ferber, Keeley, and Shemberg (1974) also reported negative findings on home observations following 10 weeks of parent training with seven children seen at a university clinic. Therapists for four of these cases were doctoral-level psychologists, while the other three cases were seen by the psychologists and trained undergraduate behavioral analysts. The training program and dependent measures were based on Patterson's program. Three of the families had positive posttreatment changes on multiple measures, but only one family had substantial long-term improvement at the one-year follow-up.

Wahler's (1980) parent training program produced reductions in mothers' aversive behaviors and in children's oppositional behaviors by the end of treatment, but these negative behaviors returned to baseline levels by the end of the one-year follow-up period. Parents treated in this program had a lower income level (less than $5,000) and lower educational level (less than high school degree) than parents treated in the other programs. The treatment program was implemented by graduate student therapists, who focused on interrupting the "coercion trap" identified by Patterson and on training in time-out. The children had been referred to the clinic for treatment of problems, such as noncompliance, verbal abuse, fighting, and stealing. The average age of the 18 treated boys was 8 years of age (range of 4 to 10).

The overall thrust of this series of studies indicated that families that complete behavioral parent training generally display significant changes in children's and parents' behavior observed in the home. These changes usually persist into follow-up periods and bring the families close to "normal" functioning. However, several reservations must be noted. First, the normal comparison group design is not a conclusive measure of treatment effects. This design, like simple pre-post/follow-up designs, does not control for alternative explanations for the treatment effects, such as maturation, sensitization to measures, and families' potential abilities to present themselves in a positive light during behavioral observation (e.g., by knowingly constricting aversive behavior during the posttreatment observation periods). Second, the treatment and follow-up results may be inflated because of the fairly high dropout and attrition rates. Finally, while the Patterson and Forehand treatment programs have been consistently able to replicate treatment effects, some other researchers have found these behavioral training procedures to be ineffective, at least during follow-up periods. Such variability in treatment results does not appear to be simply due to the training level of the therapists or to treatment length, given that the Forehand program has produced significant changes with graduate student therapists who often see families for 10 to 12 sessions. Other factors, such as low socioeconomic status (e.g., Wahler, 1980), or kind of training for therapists may be important variables.

B. Comparison with Untreated Controls and Alternative Treatments

In an effort to eliminate alternative explanations for the changes noted in pre-post studies, research has compared the effects of behavioral parent training with untreated control conditions and with alternative treatment conditions. In the earliest of these studies, Wiltz and Patterson (1974) compared six families who had received behavioral parent training with six other families who served as a wait-list control condition. All families had been referred because of sons' aggressive behavior, and the treatment condition received five weeks of group sessions, using Patterson and Gullion's *Living with Children*. The sons' average age was 9. Treated children had a significant decrease in targeted deviant behaviors during home observation. While the control children did not display a reduction over time in deviant behavior, the two conditions were not statistically compared with each other.

In a subsequent study, Patterson, Chamberlain, and Reid (1982) contrasted 10 families that had received an average of 17 hours of treatment at the OSLC to a waiting list comparison group of nine families. All of the waiting list families were referred for interim services to other professionals in the community. Because these families received an average of 11 hours of treatment from the community professionals, this group served as a methodologically more rigorous nonspecific alternative treatment condition rather than as a simple untreated control condition. Boys and girls had been referred for social aggression and ranged in age from 3 to 11 (mean of 6.8). The OSLC experimental condition produced a significant reduction in children's total deviant behavior during home observations, in comparison with the pre-post changes of the comparison groups. The parent training group had a 63% reduction in the mean rate of children's deviant behavior. However, the parent's daily report (PDR) results indicated that children in both the treatment and the comparison conditions had reductions in parent-reported problem behaviors, and the treatment condition was not more effective in producing PDR improvements than the comparison conditions. Thus, while treatment effects were apparent on measures of direct observation of behavior, the results from parents' reports of behavior change were more equivocal.

In a controlled study of the effects of the Forehand program on compliance training, Peed, Roberts, and Forehand (1977) trained the parents of six children (average age of 5 years, 4 months) who had been referred because of their noncompliant behavior. These parents received 9.5 treatment sessions (range of 7 to 12). In comparison to pre-post changes in a waiting list control group of 6 children, the treated children had significant increases in compliant behavior during observation sessions. Their parents displayed significantly more attending and rewarding behavior, more alpha commands, and fewer beta commands. Significant treatment effects were also evident on parents' ratings of children's behavior, in contrast to the results of the Patterson, Chamberlain, and Reid, (1982) study.

Forehand, et al. (1979) explored the generalization of parent training effects to children's school behavior. In the first part of this study, Forehand et al. (1979) documented that training with a sample of 10 parents generalized over time, with children being more compliant at a one-year follow-up. In the second part of the study, the school behavior of a treated group of eight children was compared to an untreated group of randomly selected classmates. The treated parents received 7.8 training sessions, and the children's home behavior had improved by the posttreatment observation. The treated and comparison groups were only compared on the observations of school behavior, and there were no significant differences between groups at either the pre- or posttreatment assessment. Therefore, the significant gains in children's home behavior did not generalize to the school setting.

In addition to the Patterson and Forehand programs, several other researchers have also reported positive results for behavioral parent training relative to untreated control groups. Karoly and Rosenthal (1977) presented a ten-session training program to nine families and compared their progress to a wait-list control group of eight families. Both sets of children had been referred to a psychiatric clinic because of their behavior problems. The average age of the sample was 7.5 years. Treatment was provided by doctoral-level psychologists and other clinic staff. The treatment group had a significant reduction in targeted deviant behavior during home observation. Treated parents' ratings indicated that problem behaviors had decreased, and that family cohesion had increased. The control group did not improve on these measures. Adesso and Lipson (1981) have also replicated these treatment effects, although their sample did not consist of only noncompliant or aggressive children. In the latter study, 12 parents who had received a nine-session behavioral training program were compared with four families in a nontreatment control group. The treated group had significant relative improvements in target behavior during home observation. This improvement was maintained during a three-month follow-up period.

In the only two controlled studies with a longer-term follow-up of at least nine months, the results concerning longer-term efficacy of behavioral parent training have been more mixed. Kent and O'Leary (1976) developed a multicomponent behavior modification program for second-, third-, and fourth-grade children who had been identified by teachers as having conduct problems. The treatment program was implemented by doctoral-level psychologists and included an eight-hour behavioral school intervention component as well as seven sessions of behavioral parent training. Children were randomly assigned to the treatment condition or to the untreated control condition, with 16 children in each condition. At the posttreatment assessment, treated children had significant reductions in independently observed disruptive classroom behavior and in teachers' ratings of students' aggressive behavior, in comparison with the untreated control condition. However, these group differences were no longer apparent at the nine-month follow-up, because the control group subjects displayed improvement in their observed and teacher-rated classroom behavior during that time. Because no observational data were collected in the home setting, it was not apparent whether behavioral improvements had occurred or been maintained in the home.

Finally, Bernal, Klinnert, and Schultz (1980) implemented a 10-session behavioral parent training program, with graduate students as therapists, to children referred to a clinic because of conduct problems. Children ranged in age from 5 to 12 years (mean age, 8.4 years) and generally came from middle-class families. The 36 children were randomly assigned to three conditions: behavioral treatment, client-centered treatment, and a waiting list control group. The behavioral parent training was based in part on Patterson and Gullion's *Living with Children*. The client-centered treatment focused on family members' feelings, attitudes, and experiences and used material from Ginott's *Between Parent and Child*. At posttreatment, the parents in the behavioral condition rated their children as having fewer behavior problems in daily telephone interviews, and on the Becker Adjective checklist, in comparison with the client-centered and untreated control conditions. There were no significant group effects on home observation variables. No group differences were evident on the direct observational variables or on parent rating measures at the one- or two-year follow-up assessments. The behavioral parent training condition was not different from the other two conditions at follow-up.

The most common finding from this series of controlled studies is that behavioral parent training can produce significant improvements in children's behavior by the end of treatment and that these improvements in behavior are not found in untreated and alternative treatment control groups. However, some mixed findings were evident. It is not clear that the effects of behavioral parent training generalize into other settings, such as the school classroom. In two of the studies that did examine follow-up, the results of behavioral parent training also did not generalize well over time. When effects were not found between treatment and comparison groups on certain variables collected at posttreatment (e.g., Forehand et al., 1979) or at follow-up, the lack of significant results was often due to the control conditions showing improvement over these periods. These findings confirm that the results of uncontrolled studies with the pre-post/follow-up design need to be interpreted with some caution and that further controlled research is warranted.

III. PREDICTORS OF EFFECTIVENESS OF BEHAVIORAL FAMILY THERAPY

In the last several years, the most active focus for research in the area of behavioral family therapy with aggressive children has been on the family, the child, and the treatment characteristics that are most predictive of successful treatment outcome. This line of research has developed in large part because of the recognized inability to produce behavioral change in all clients of behavioral family therapy (e.g., Griest & Wells, 1983; Wahler & Graves, 1983), as the prior review illustrates.

A. Family and Child Characteristics as Predictors of Outcome

1. SOCIAL SETTING

In a recent effort to develop a causal model of factors predicting outcome effects, Dumas (1986) clustered predictor variables into three groups of socioeconomic setting events, parental setting events, and child setting events. Dumas (1986) implemented a six- to ten-session treatment program with 109 families referred for out-of-control, noncompliant, aggressive behavior. Children ranged in age from 2 to 16 (mean age, 7.3 years). Therapy was provided by experienced behavior therapists using elements from Patterson's treatment program. Treatment outcome was determined by reviewing records to determine whether families had completed the two major phases of the program, whether the parents had made adaptive changes in their parenting skills, and whether the family had needed additional services during the year following treatment. Treatment involvement was assessed by examining the rate of parents' attendance at sessions and their compliance with treatment requirements, such as completing homework assignments. In the LISREL causal modeling procedure, the outcome and involvement variables constituted an overall construct for treatment involvement and outcome. The socioeconomic setting events were the only significant predictors of this overall construct. Thus poorer outcomes were found to occur in families that had lower incomes, smaller family size, and lower educational attainment by mother and father and had been referred by agencies rather than being self-referrals. In a subsequent study of 82 of those 109 families who actually completed the treatment program, Dumas and Albin (1986) found that treatment outcome was also strengthened when a father or stepfather lived in the home.

Webster-Stratton (1985) classified the 34 families that had received behavioral parent training, as described previously, into responders and nonresponders at posttreatment and at follow-up. Responders met a criterion of having at least a 50% reduction in their baseline rate of deviant behavior. Predictors of treatment outcome included several parental characteristics, as well as a cluster of variables indicating socioeconomic disadvantage (e.g., family income, maternal education, marital status, and source of referral). Of the variables investigated, socioeconomic disadvantage was the clearest predictor of the children's and mother's observed behavioral changes at both posttreatment and follow-up. Poorer response to treatment occurred in families having greater socioeconomic disadvantage; by follow-up, the marital status variable was the strongest of these predictors. This finding supports the Dumas and Albin (1986) finding, and suggests that in single-parent families "the lack of social support seems to be an important predictor of success and failure" (Webster-Stratton, 1985, p. 239).

The importance of parents' social supports in predicting outcome for behavioral parent training has also been emphasized in Wahler's (1980) study of the insularity of mothers. In this case, the focus is not on whether the mothers have a husband or husband figure, but on the number and quality of the mothers' daily social interactions with friends, relatives, and agency workers. Wahler (1980) carefully analyzed the relationship between the mothers' and children's daily behavior and the kinds of interchanges that the mother had with other adults on those days. On "low friendship" days, mothers interacted primarily with agency representatives and relatives rather than friends in a manner typical of "insular" mothers. The nonfriend contacts were generally rated as more aversive by the mothers then contacts with friends. During "low friendship" days, mothers were found to be more aversive with their children—and their children were more oppositional—than on "high friendship" days. Wahler and Graves (1983) provide a descriptive case study of this process, indicating how aversive contacts between a mother and her own mother led to sharp, aversive behavioral changes during subsequent mother-child interactions. Wahler and Graves (1983) described how these "social network setting events" (e.g., contacts with a grandmother) produce affective responses in the mother, and that these affective responses then become transferred to the child through prior conditioning. Such social setting events appear to be an important mediator of the maintenance of treatment effects over time. While Wahler (1980) had found that observed changes in treated families' behavior was no longer apparent at follow-up in general, he did find that "child improvement during treatment did continue into the follow-up phase during the mothers' high friendship days" (Wahler, 1980, p. 217), when the mothers interacted most frequently with friends.

While the link between treatment outcome and social supports inside and outside of the home appears to be clear, the relationship between outcome and other specific socioeconomic variables, such as family income, is less clear. Dropouts from treatment have variously been found to have lower socioeconomic status (McMahon, Forehand, Griest, & Wells, 1981), higher socioeconomic status (Horne & Van Dyke, 1983), or equivalent income levels (Lochman & Brown, 1980) than parents who complete treatment. Similarly, Rogers, Forehand, Griest, Wells, and McMahon (1981) found that families' socioeconomic levels did not affect observed behavioral outcomes following individual parent training. Other studies have found that parents having lower incomes report poorer goal attainment and less satisfaction following group parent training (Lochman & Brown, 1980; Rinn, Vernon, & Wise, 1975). The latter discrepancies may indicate that low-income parents have less success in groups than in individual parent training. Parents' income level does appear to be associated with parents' perceptions of the acceptability of different behavioral management interventions. While both low-income and middle-income parents have positive perceptions of response cost and positive reinforcement procedures, and are relatively less accepting of spanking and medication use, they have significantly different perceptions of time-out (Heffer & Kelley, 1987). Low-income parents do not perceive time-out to be a very acceptable child management technique, and thus may have more difficulty successfully complying with such training unless their perceptions are also addressed. While the results are mixed, the overall findings suggest that lower-income parents may be more at risk of not having successful outcomes following parent training.

Negative life experiences or stressors that happen to the parents can also be conceptualized as social setting events. Webster-Stratton (1985) found that higher levels of maternal negative life events significantly predicted higher levels of improvement in observed mother and child behaviors. This finding was in the opposite direction of what was anticipated. To further confuse the results, higher rates of negative life events were also found to predict mothers' ratings that children's problem behaviors became worse following treatment. These finding are difficult to interpret, but it does not yet appear that maternal negative life experiences have been documented as predicting treatment failure.

2. FAMILY SETTING

The two primary family setting events that have been investigated as predictors of outcome involve parents' psychopathology and marital discord. Dumas (1986) included variables tapping both of these sets of family factors into his construct of parental setting events. In the LISREL model, these parental setting events tended to affect the parents' perception at intake of how deviant the child was, but the parental setting events did not have a direct impact on the construct assessing treatment involvement and outcome. Parental setting event variables were correlated with the outcome variables, but they were also highly related to the social setting events variables, and the latter emerged as the best predictors of outcome.

When parental psychopathology and marital discord variables are examined separately, evidence for their role as predictors of outcome are mixed. Dumas and Albin (1986) found that presence of maternal psychopathological symptoms that required treatment was strongly related to negative outcomes from treatment. This finding supported earlier results from behavioral parent training that found parental depression to be related to treatment failure and dropout (McMahon, Forehand, Griest, & Wells, 1981) and that also found mothers to become less depressed following parent training (Forehand, Wells, & Griest, 1980); Webster-Stratton, 1985). However, Webster-Stratton (1985) did not find maternal depression to be predictive of behavioral outcomes in discriminant analyses. As with the Dumas (1986) results, such a lack of independent prediction of outcome appeared to be due to the strong relationship between maternal depression and the socioeconomic disadvantage variables. While maternal depression may have been correlated with outcome, maternal depression did not separately add to the strong predictive power of socioeconomic disadvantage.

Marital discord does not appear to influence the immediate effects of behavioral parent training but may moderate the longer-term maintenance of these effects. Dadds, Schwartz, and Sanders (1987) did not find any differences between couples with marital discord and without marital discord in observed child and mother behavior in the home or in parents' ratings of children's problems following child management training. Such a lack of immediate effects for marital discord on treatment replicates Brody and Forehand (1985). However, by the six-month follow-up period, only the families without marital discord had maintained their reductions in maternal aversive behavior and in child deviance (Dadds, Schwartz, & Sanders, 1987).

Two other family setting factors that have been implicated as potential predictors of treatment outcome are the aggressiveness of siblings and the parents' resistance or noninvolvement in therapy. Horne and Van Dyke (1983) found that target children have more reductions in aggressive behavior during treatment and at follow-up when their siblings have relatively low pretreatment rates of aggressive behavior. With regard to parental involvement in the treatment process, Dumas and Albins (1986) found that parents' rate of attendance at treatment sessions and their compliance in completing homework assignments did not predict the success of treatment outcome for parents who completed treatment. However, while these general indications of parental involvement have not been found to relate to outcome, Chamberlain, Patterson, Reid, Kavanagh, and Forgatch (1984) note that more molecular indications of observed behavioral resistance during treatment sessions (e.g., interruptions, challenge, own agenda, parents not tracking toward therapists) are correlated with dropping out from treatment and with lower therapist ratings of outcome.

3. CHILD CHARACTERISTICS

In contrast to the growing knowledge about family and social setting characteristics that predict outcome, there have been few investigations of the type of children who benefit most and least from behavioral parent training. Horne and Van Dyke (1983) found that children with school problems as well as home difficulties were not as likely to have improvements in their aggressive behavior at posttreatment and at follow-up in comparison with children without school problems. This finding suggests that children whose aggressive behavior is widespread and cross-situational may be less amenable to behavioral parent training and may account for the findings of lack of generalization of behavioral treatment effects to the school setting (Forehand et al., 1979).

In contrast, the degree of behavioral disturbance that children show in the home setting does not appear to be related to treatment outcome. Dumas (1986) found that parents reported more negative children's behavior at intake when the children had lower intellectual abilities, when they had been born prematurely (e.g., weighed less than 2,500 grams), and when they were male rather than female. However, the parents' reports of the frequency of children's problem behavior did not affect their degree of success in the treatment program (Dumas & Albin, 1986).

B. Treatment Characteristics as Predictors of Outcome

1. KNOWLEDGE OF SOCIAL LEARNING PRINCIPLES

Behavioral parent training programs vary in the degree to which they train parents in basic principles of social learning theories, in addition to training in specific, concrete behavioral skills. To determine if teaching social learning principles enhances generalization, McMahon, Forehand, and Griest (1981) assigned 20 mother-child pairs to two conditions: technique alone parent training (TA) and social learning principles training plus parent training (SL). The two conditions were comparable with respect to age of child (just over 5 years), sex of child, and marital status (90% married). Children had been referred to the clinic for noncompliance and oppositional behavior. The families were seen in treatment for five weeks, and a follow-up assessment was conducted approximately eight weeks later. At posttreatment, the SL parents had acquired more knowledge of social learning principles, but there were no differences between conditions on home observations. However, in comparison with the TA families at the follow-up assessment, children in the SL families were significantly more compliant during home observations, and SL parents tended to provide more contingent attention and rewards. Indications that the SL condition assisted the generalization of treatment effects over time were supported in a subsequent study using the same sample (McMahon, Tiedemann, Forehand, & Griest, 1984). At the follow-up, mothers who had received training in social learning principles maintained their satisfaction with the treatment better than mothers who did not have this adjunctive training.

2. PARENT SUPPORT TRAINING

Because of the potential relationship between parental depression and marital discord as well as (a) children's aggressive behaviors and (b) families' response to behavioral parent training, researchers have explored the possibility of including adjunctive training focusing on these parental factors in addition to behavioral parent training. Griest et al. (1982) found that parent training plus parent enhancement training produced higher levels of child compliance and of parents' child management techniques at posttreatment and at the two-month follow-up. Parent enhancement training included clarifying parents' expectations for their children, cognitive restructuring of parents' moods, such as depression, and developing conflict resolution skills for marital conflict. Dadds, Sanders, Behrens, and James (1987) replicated this finding by providing four families with a treatment program that included both child management training (CMT) (five to eight sessions) and parent support training (PST) (four sessions). Results were assessed with a multiple baseline design. Deviant child behavior and maternal aversive behavior decreased by the end of the CMT phase, but the parents' aversive behavior toward each other and their problem-solving behavior did not improve until they received PST.

Results of a study by Dadds, Schwartz, and Sanders (1987) indicate that PST may be particularly useful in helping to maintain treatment effects over time when parents are experiencing marital discord. PST focused on assisting with parents' marital conflict, communication, and problem solving and was similar to Griest et al.'s (1982) parent enhancement training and to Wahler and Graves's (1983) review training. Of 24 families referred for assistance with child behavior problems, half were also identified as experiencing marital discord while half were not. Both sets of families were then randomly assigned to CMT only or to CMT plus PST. The generality of the results are somewhat limited because the first author acted as the therapist for all families. All four conditions improved by posttreatment on home observations and parent rating measures. All conditions maintained these gains at the six-month follow-up (except for the marital discord parents who received CMT only), thus indicating the role that PST can play in enhancing generalization for maritally discordant parents.

3. PARENTS' PERCEPTIONS OF PARENTING
SKILLS AND TRAINING METHODS

McMahon and Forehand (1983) concluded that the social validity of behavioral parent training should be assessed. This assessment should include parents' perceptions of the various skills taught during parent training and parents' perceptions of the teaching methods used with the parents and children. In a study with 20 mothers who had received parent training, McMahon, Tiedemann, Forehand, and Griest (1984) found that at posttreatment mothers rated rewards as being significantly more useful than ignoring—and as being less difficult to implement than attending, ignoring, alpha commands, or time-out. The follow-up ratings were similar, except that mothers had begun to rate time-out and alpha commands as being more useful than at posttreatment. In two other studies of the perceptions of nonreferred mothers, Cross Calvert and McMahon (1987) found that strategies used to increase deficit behavior (e.g., rewards, commands, attends) were rated as being more acceptable than strategies used to reduce behavioral excesses (e.g., time-out, ignoring), while Heffer and Kelley (1987) found that positive reinforcement and response cost procedures were rated as being more acceptable than time-out, spanking, or medication. Heffer and Kelley (1987) also found that these ratings of acceptability were mediated by the parents' income level. The general pattern that emerges across these studies is that time-out and extinction are not initially regarded very positively, and these perceptions of the acceptability of procedures could limit parents' compliance with training. In an exploratory study of the comparative usefulness of time-out training versus training of parents in problem-solving skills with their children, Olson and Roberts (1987) found that mothers' ratings of sibling aggression were reduced more by time-out training than by the other conditions. Thus, as suggested by the McMahon, Tiedemann, Forehand, and Griest (1984) findings, parents may overcome initial reservations and find time-out more acceptable over time after they have begun to successfully implement the procedure.

Treated parents in the McMahon et al. (1984) study indicated at follow-up that they had found practice of the parenting skills with the child in the clinic to be more useful than other teaching strategies (e.g., therapist demonstration, written materials). Cross Calvert and McMahon (1987) assessed mothers' preferred methods of introducing behavioral procedures to children. Mothers preferred to be instructed in how to explain the rationale for the procedure to the child rather than merely learning about the techniques themselves. Some investigators have begun to explore other effective means of implementing behavioral techniques with children. For example, Hamilton and MacQuiddy (1984) found that when a Signal Seat was used with the time-out procedure, children's behavioral problems decreased, and their compliance increased. When the child was placed on the Signal Seat during time-out, the seat would buzz if the child got up before the end of the required three-minute time-out period.

4. TREATMENT FORMAT

The effects of group versus individual parent training and the relative effectiveness of including the father as well as the mother in training have recently been examined. While several research reports have indicated that successful behavioral change could occur following group treatment of parents (e.g., Rinn, Vernon & Wise, 1975; Wiltz & Patterson, 1974), few direct comparisons between group and individual training of parents have been made. Eyberg and Matarazzo (1980) evaluated the effects of group and individual parent training with a sample of 29 children (aged 4 to 9) who had been in a summer speech and language program. Because the sample was not selected for aggressive problems, the effects are only suggestive for more disturbed children. Individual training focused on the mother-child interaction and was more effective than the didactic group training in increasing children's compliance, mothers' facilitative behavior, and mothers' satisfaction. Examining a different aspect of individual versus group training, Webster-Stratton, Kolpacoff, and Hollingsworth (1988) found that teachers' ratings of children's behavioral difficulties were most improved after their parents received 10 parent training sessions, using either group discussions or group discussions plus videotape modeling, rather than 10 sessions of individually administered videotape modeling. Fathers' behavioral ratings of children improved most following either type of videotape modeling, while mothers' ratings were equally affected by all three conditions.

Adesso and Lipson (1981) assigned 16 two-parent families to mother training, father training, couple training, and no-treatment control conditions. Children averaged 6.2 years of age (range 2 to 10 years) and were referred for noncompliance, fighting, and other nonaggressive problems (e.g., eating problems, spinning). As with the previous study, generality of results to samples of aggressive children is limited. Following the nine-week treatment program there were no differences between the three treatment conditions on observational measures. All treatment conditions had declines in target program behavior in comparison with the control group. Thus parent training appears to be equally effective whether mothers, fathers, or couples are treated. If marital discord were present, these results may be less likely to hold.

5. THERAPIST BEHAVIOR

Two studies have begun to indicate how therapists' behavior can have differential impact on families' resistance during sessions and on outcome following treatment. Patterson and Forgatch (1985) found, in a two-part study, that directive therapist behavior (e.g., confront, teach) elicited immediate resistance or noncompliance from the parent (e.g., interrupt, confront, own agenda, not tracking), while therapist support and facilitative behaviors led to decreases in noncompliance. In a second phase of the study, therapist behavior was purposefully altered in an ABAB design to increase their teaching and confrontation. These behaviors causally produced more parent noncompliance.

Alexander, Barton, Schiavo, and Parsons (1976) obtained supervisor ratings of therapists' skills and then examined these therapists' success in reducing recidivism and in improving families' communication from 21 families of delinquents. Therapists who had higher levels of structuring (e.g., directiveness, self-confidence) and relationship skills (e.g., warmth, humor, affect-behaviors integration) had more successful treatment outcomes. These two studies indicate that therapist behaviors have substantial effects on the outcome of behavioral therapy with families.

IV. COGNITIVE-BEHAVIORAL THERAPY

The effectiveness of cognitive-behavioral therapy with aggressive children has not been examined as extensively as the behavioral family therapy approaches, but research has developed during the past decade. Cognitive-behavior programs can include training in self-instructions, social problem solving, perspective-taking, imagery, or relaxation, and most programs consist of a combination of several of these techniques. All of these techniques have in common a focus on children's cognitions during frustrating or provocative situations. The results of the early pre-post studies will be reviewed first in this section, followed by controlled studies with children.

A. Change Over Time

After early studies had begun to demonstrate that cognitive-behavioral treatment could help impulsive children behave less impulsively on impersonal problem-solving tasks (e.g., Meichenbaum & Goodman, 1971), researchers began to examine whether similar techniques could also be useful in treating children's aggressive behavior. Goodwin and Mahoney (1975) used modeling, coaching, and behavioral rehearsal to modify the coping self-statements that three boys used when they were being teased by peers. The children ranged in age from 6 to 11 and had been referred to a clinic because of their impulsive, hyperactive behavior. After two group sessions, in which the boys were taught to use covert self-statement during a verbal taunting game, the boys displayed marked increases in coping responses on the verbal taunting game. Independent observers found that the boys had also improved their levels of nondisruptive classroom behavior.

Robin, Schneider, and Dolnick (1976) developed a program for self-control of children's aggression that emphasized relaxation training and social problem-solving training rather than focusing only on self-statements. Eleven elementary school aged children, who had been identified as highly aggressive by teachers in classes for the emotionally disturbed, were trained in the Turtle Technique. During three to eight weeks of daily instruction by teachers, these children learned to imagine they were pulling back into their "shell" when they were anger aroused, where they could consider alternative means of responding to social provocations. Significant reductions were found in these children's independently observed aggressive behavior in the classroom.

In another study with positive preliminary findings, Lochman, Nelson, and Sims (1981) developed an anger control program for 12 children who had been referred by teachers because of high rates of physical and verbal aggression and disruptive classroom behavior. The children ranged in age from 7 to 10 years. All were Black and lived in single-parent families in a low-income area. The children met with a graduate student therapist in group sessions twice a week for 12 sessions. The program used structured activities (role-playing and videotapes to develop children's social problem-solving skills; inhibitory self-statements and awareness of psychological arousal when angered) as a cue to begin using coping skills. By the end of the program, the children tended to have reductions in teachers' ratings of their acting-out behavior, using the Walker Program Behavior Identification Checklist, and had significant improvements in the teachers' daily ratings of on-task behavior and aggressive behavior.

B. Comparison with Untreated Controls and Alternative Treatments

While these pre-post studies indicate that children's aggressive and disruptive behaviors changed following cognitive-behavioral treatment, controlled studies have produced mixed results about treatment effectiveness. Three studies have not found effects on aggressive behavior following treatment (Camp, Blom, Herbert, & Van Doorninck, 1977; Coats, 1979; Dubow, Huesmann, & Eron, 1987), even though two of the interventions did produce changes in the cognitive and social-cognitive processes that were assumed to mediate the behavior. Such a lack of congruence between behavioral and cognitive results indicates that cognitive-behavioral research should examine both areas of functioning. Thus, while a well-designed study with a no-contact control group can potentially demonstrate that problem-solving skill training can increase young aggressive children's abilities to think of relevant solutions to in vivo problems with frustrating peer confederates (Vaughn, Ridley, & Bullock, 1984), it is not possible to conclude that this kind of intervention is effective if no assessment is made of actual behavior in the child's natural environment.

In an evaluation of the Think Aloud Program, Camp, Blom, Herbert, and Van Doorninck (1977) randomly assigned 12 aggressive boys to the experimental program and 10 boys to the control condition. These second-grade boys had been identified by teacher ratings as highly aggressive. The Think Aloud Program was administered individually to children in daily 30-minute sessions for six weeks and included structured activities to develop coping self-statements and social problem solving. By the end of treatment, boys were less impulsive on the Matching Familiar Figures Test and better able to focus their attention on the Mazes subtest of the WISC-R. In comparison with the control condition, the treated boys were also able to generate more alternative solutions on a problem-solving measure. However, as they became freer in their problem solving, treated boys also thought of significantly more aggressive, as well as nonaggressive, solutions. More important, despite the cognitive gains, teachers did not rate the boys as significantly less aggressive, although teachers did perceive improvement in the treated boys' needs for achievement.

Using an attention control condition and a similar program that developed children's problem solving on both impersonal as well as interpersonal tasks, Coats (1979) found that eight boys who had received self-instructional training used less verbal aggression. They were also able to wait longer to obtain a valued object when posttested in a "staged" problematic situation with a confederate peer. However, there were no significant differences in improvement between the treatment and control conditions on observational measures of inappropriate and off-task behavior in the classroom or on teachers' ratings of aggression on Connors's behavioral checklist. These children had been identified for the study by teachers' ratings of students' aggression and impulsivity, and the self-instructional training had been conducted in eight 30-minute sessions over two weeks.

Dubow, Huesmann, and Eron (1987) identified 104 children who had been placed in self-contained Behavior Disorders classrooms because of their aggressive behavior. The children were assigned to cognitive, behavioral, cognitive-behavioral, or attention/play conditions. Cognitive training included self-instruction training, perspective-taking, and social problem solving. Behavioral training focused on prosocial skills such as sharing. The attention/play condition provided modeling, coaching, and discussion about improving game strategy in dyadic play with peers in board and card games. All conditions were provided in the one-hour group session over five weeks. On teacher ratings, which were the only dependent measure used, the attention/play condition produced more reduction in aggression and improvement in prosocial behavior than the cognitive and the behavioral conditions at posttesting and in all three treatment conditions by a six-month follow-up. Because there were no process assessments of cognitive or social skills, it was not evident whether the interventions failed to have their intended impact on these processes or whether the treatments' effects failed to generalize to teachers' ratings.

Other studies generally have had more positive, although still mixed, behavioral results than were evident in the three studies just reviewed. Forman (1980) evaluated cognitive restructuring, response cost, and placebo control conditions with 18 children (aged 8 to 11) who had been referred to school psychologists for aggressive behavior. The cognitive restructuring treatment was conducted by graduate student therapists in half-hour group sessions that met twice weekly for six weeks and emphasized self-instruction training for interpersonal provocations. In the response cost procedure, students lost two minutes of activity time for each aggressive act that teachers recorded. Significant, but different, outcome effects were evident for the two groups in comparison with the control condition. Cognitive restructuring produced significant reductions in independent observations of inappropriate classroom behavior, while response cost treatment produced significant reductions in teachers' recordings of aggressive behavior and in teacher ratings of classroom disturbance on a behavioral checklist. Because teachers were more actively involved in the response cost procedures, teachers' ratings may have been more subject to bias in this condition.

Kettlewell and Kausch (1983) assigned 10 aggressive day-camp children to a cognitive-behavioral program (which included both social problem-solving skill training and self-instruction training) and 21 other children to a no-treatment control. The children ranged in age from 7 to 12. It is possible that many of the aggressive children were only mildly disturbed; hence, this study may have limited generalization for more aggressive populations. The treatment group met for eight group sessions and four individual sessions during a four-week period. In comparison with the control condition, children in cognitive-behavioral treatment had developed more coping responses on the verbal taunting game, self-reported less anger, received fewer time-out restrictions and generated more solutions on a social problem-solving measure. However, as in the Camp, Blom, Herbert, and Van Doorninck (1977) findings, the treated children also increased their rate of aggressive solutions on the social problem-solving measure, and they did not have relative improvement on counselor and peer ratings of aggression.

Using a markedly different cognitive intervention with 30 teacher-referred aggressive children (ages 8 to 11), Garrison and Stolberg (1983) assigned the children to affective imagery training, attention control, or untreated control conditions. The affective imagery training was offered in three sessions (30 to 40 minutes) during one week, and emphasized awareness of physiological states with different affects and labeling of affective states. The children in the treatment condition became more proficient in accurately identifying situations that evoke mixed affective responses ("compound anger") on the Affect Questionnaire, and their aggression during teacher observations tended to decrease. These changes were modest, but the magnitude of the change may have been affected by the brevity of the treatment.

The strongest treatment effects have been evident in a study by Kazdin, Esveldt-Dawson, French, and Unis (1987b) and in studies of the Anger Coping Program. Kazdin et al. (1987b) placed psychiatric inpatient children who had been referred because of their antisocial behavior into three conditions: program-solving skills training (PSST), relationship therapy (RT), and treatment-contact control. Children ranged in age from 5 to 13. The sample consisted of 47 children by posttesting and 42 by the one-year follow-up. The treatment conditions were provided two to three times weekly in 45-minute sessions, for a total of 20 sessions, and were conducted by experienced clinicians. Similar results were found at posttesting and at the one year follow-up, with PSST children having greater reductions in parents' and teachers' ratings of aggressive behavior than did children in the other conditions. A similar pattern of results was reported in another study by Kazdin, Esveldt-Dawson, French, and Unis (1987a). Inpatient psychiatric patients received an intervention that included both problem-solving skill training and parent management training. Significant posttest and follow-up gains were obtained on parents' and teachers' ratings of aggressive behavior in relation to a contact-control condition.

In addition to generalized improvements in parents' and teachers' behavioral ratings, as in the Kazdin et al. (1987b) study, the controlled outcome research on the anger coping program has also found that improvements in independently observed classroom behavior can result from cognitive-behavioral treatment. Lochman, Burch, Curry, and Lampron (1984) identified 76 aggressive boys on the basis of teachers' ratings on the Missouri Children's Behavior Checklist, and randomly assigned the boys to anger coping (AC), goal-setting (GS), anger coping plus goal-setting (AC-GS), or untreated control (UC) conditions. The boys ranged in age from 9 to 12 years old, with 53% being of minority racial status. The anger coping program was based on the earlier anger control program (Lochman, Nelson, & Sims, 1981) and focused on perspective-taking, awareness of physiological cues when angry, coping self-statements, and especially on social problem-solving skills training. Boys met in weekly group sessions (45-60 minutes) in their schools for 12 weeks, and each of the groups was co-led by an outpatient clinic staff member or advanced trainee and a school counselor. Goal setting was conceptualized as a minimal treatment condition and included eight group sessions in which boys set weekly goals for classroom behaviors and received contingent reinforcements for goal attainment. In comparison with the GS and UC groups, the two anger coping conditions at posttesting produced significant reductions in independently observed disruptive classroom behavior and in parents' ratings of boys' aggression as well as producing trends for improvement in self-esteem. Treatment effects were not found on teacher and peer ratings. The treatment effects tended to be strongest in the AC-GS condition, indicating that generalization of cognitive-behavioral effects can be enhanced by including behaviorally based goal setting in the intervention.

These treatment effects were replicated in another controlled study in which 32 teacher-identified aggressive boys with an average age of 11 years were assigned to anger coping, anger coping plus teacher consultation, and an untreated control cell (Lochman, Lampron, Gemmer,

Harris, & Wyckoff, in press). In this study the two anger coping conditions lasted for 18 sessions but otherwise were identical to the prior groups. In contrast to the control condition at posttesting, the two anger coping conditions produced significant reductions in disruptive classroom behavior and improvements in perceived social competence as well as a trend for a reduction in teachers' ratings of aggressive behavior.

In an initial effort to examine generalization of anger coping intervention effects over time, Lochman and Lampron (1988) conducted a partial follow-up of the Lochman, Burch, Curry, and Lampron (1984) sample in four of the eight schools. In the follow-up sample, 21 of the boys had been in the two anger coping conditions and 10 had been in the untreated control condition. When classroom behavior was examined seven months following treatment, the anger coping boys had significant improvement in on-task classroom behavior and significant reductions in passive off-task classroom behavior. The significant improvements in disruptive off-task classroom behavior were not maintained for the AC condition. Indeed, the follow-up subsample had weaker pre-post improvement in disruptive off-task behavior than had the non-followed-up portion of the original Lochman, Burch, Curry, and Lampron (1984) sample.

A long-term, three-year follow-up study of the preventive effects of the anger coping program has recently been completed (Lochman, 1988a). Based on aggression status assessed from peer sociometric ratings collected at the time of the anger coping intervention, groups of anger coping, untreated comparison aggressive, and nonaggressive boys were identified. Of the original pool of 345 boys, 28% could not be contacted at follow-up. Of the remaining boys, 66% consented to the follow-up. Boys who were followed-up on were highly similar on peer aggression nominations and social status ratings to boys who were not available for follow-up. In comparison with the untreated aggressive group, the anger coping boys had lower rates of marijuana and drug involvement and lower rates of alcohol use. Also, they maintained their previously noted improvements in self-esteem and in social problem-solving skills. The self-esteem and problem-solving skill gains appeared to moderate the anger coping boys' substance use behavior. In all of these areas, the anger coping boys were functioning in the same range as the nonaggressive boys at follow-up. Treatment effects were not found for overall self-reported delinquency rates. Improvements in classroom behavior and parents' ratings were not maintained. However, a subset of anger coping boys who had received a second-year booster treatment tended to maintain their gains in passive off-task classroom behavior and in parents' ratings of aggression (Lochman, 1988b), suggesting that a longer treatment period may be necessary to enhance the maintenance of behavioral change. These results indicate that cognitive-behavioral interventions could serve as useful secondary prevention programs in reducing later substance use by high-risk aggressive children. While this set of controlled studies has produced mixed results about the efficacy of cognitive-behavioral treatment, several factors may be related to obtaining stronger or weaker findings. The clearest treatment effects occurred in more recent studies with the longer treatment program (at least 8 to 12 weeks), and length of treatment rather than number of sessions appeared to be related to successful outcome. Longer treatment periods conceivably allow for more time to rehearse the cognitive-behavioral skills and to be monitored and reinforced for their use. In addition, more positive treatment outcomes have tended to occur in studies that have used direct observation of behavior rather than relying on behavioral ratings only, although certain exceptions exist (e.g., Coats, 1979; Kazdin, Esveldt-Dawson, French, & Unis, 1987a). Several studies have indicated that cognitive-behavioral treatment effects may generalize across settings and have an impact on parents' ratings and that treatment effects may generalize across time to follow-up periods, although here again some mixed results are evident. In contrast to the behavioral parent training research, relatively few of these studies to date have examined longer-term outcome effects, and the degree of long-term maintenance is still not firmly determined.

V. PREDICTORS OF EFFECTIVENESS OF COGNITIVE-BEHAVIORAL THERAPY

Research examining factors that affect outcome for cognitive-behavioral treatment has been less extensive than in the behavioral parent training studies. Because there have been efforts to examine correlates for self-instructional training outcomes with impulsive and normal children, these results will be briefly noted for heuristic purposes, along with the several studies of aggressive children.

A. Child Characteristics as Predictors of Outcome

In a secondary analysis of the Lochman, Burch, Curry, and Lampron (1984) anger coping intervention, Lochman, Lampron, Burch, and Curry (1985) found that approximately three-quarters of the untreated control children had higher levels of disruptive and aggressive behavior in the classroom and in parents' ratings by the end of the school year. Untreated aggressive children who had lower levels of social problem-solving skills and of self-esteem were most likely to have increased levels of behavioral difficulties during the course of the school year. Thus problem-solving skills and self-esteem partially moderate spontaneous changes in boys' disruptive and aggressive behavior. When the two anger coping conditions were examined, the most consistent predictor of behavioral improvement in parents' ratings of boys' aggression was, again, problem-solving skills. Boys who initially had the poorest abilities to generate a number of alternative solutions to social problems had the greatest reductions in parent-rated aggression. Because this correlation was in the opposite direction to the pattern for untreated control boys, the results suggest that the boys who were least likely to display spontaneous remission in their behavioral problems were those who made the most treatment gains. Other predictors of improvement on parent ratings were more tentative as they emerged only in one of the two treatment cells. However, these correlations did suggest that aggressive boys with initially higher levels of somatizing and anxiety symptoms, and who were more disliked by their peers, made greater behavioral improvements during intervention. The boys in the anger coping condition who had the greatest reduction in disruptive off-task classroom behavior were those who initially were the most disruptive, although this may have been an artifact of regression to the mean.

In a meta-analysis of three self-instruction studies with teacher-identified impulsive children, Braswell, Kendall, and Urbain (1982) found that children coming from families with lower-socioeconomic status performed more poorly at pretesting on tasks of cognitive impulsivity, social problem solving, and perspective-taking than those from families with higher-socioeconomic status. However, both upper- and lower-class children displayed similar levels of improvement at posttesting and at follow-up on teachers' ratings of impulsivity, hyperactivity, and social impulsivity-aggression and on the cognitive and social-cognitive measures. Because these children were identified on the basis of a lack of self-control in their classwork and classroom behavior, it has not yet been determined whether the same results would emerge with children identified primarily because of their aggressive behavior. In studies using samples of nondisturbed children, Nichol, Cohen, Meyers, and Schlesser (1982) found that children who have attained a Piagetian level of concrete operations are more likely than preoperational children to benefit from self-instruction. Copeland and Hammel (1981) found that greater reductions in impulsive behavior on the Porteus Maze task following self-instruction training were seen for children who had greater verbal skills on the Peabody Picture Vocabulary Test, more internal causal attributions for success, more vocalization during free play, and higher therapist ratings of subjects' involvement and cooperation. Such characteristics, tapping levels of cognitive and verbal development, and socioeconomic status, warrant further investigation in research with aggressive children.

B. Treatment Characteristics as Predictors of Outcome

In the previous review of outcome effects, it was noted that stronger treatment effects were obtained on behavioral outcome measures when the anger coping program was augmented by including a behavioral goal-setting procedure (Lochman, Burch, Curry, & Lampron, 1984) and a six-session booster group during a second school year (Lochman, 1988b). The effects of variations in treatment length and the additions of certain treatment components to the basic anger coping program have also been examined.

1. TREATMENT LENGTH

In a quasi-experimental study, Lochman (1985) compared an 18-session version of the anger coping program with the 12-session groups evaluated in the Lochman, Burch, Curry, and Lampron (1984) study. Through teacher ratings, 22 boys were identified as aggressive. In the 18 group sessions they received additional training in perspective-taking, more playing, and more group discussion of concurrent anger-arousing difficulties than was possible in the 12-session program. The 18-session groups produced significantly more on-task classroom behavior and less passive, off-task behavior than did the 12-session program. The study's conclusion that longer treatment lengths are important for cognitive-behavioral intervention is consistent with the relationship noted in the previous section between degree of behavioral improvement and treatment length.

2. ADDITIONAL TREATMENT COMPONENTS

Two studies have indicated that including additional self-instruction training for nonsocial tasks and adjunctive teacher consultation have not led to stronger anger coping effects. Lochman and Curry (1986) assigned 20 teacher-identified aggressive boys (average age, 10 years, 3 months) to either anger coping (AC) or anger coping plus self-instruction training (AC-SIT) conditions. Both conditions lasted for 18 weekly sessions. In the AC-SIT condition, the first six sessions used a fading procedure to internalize self-instructions on academic kinds of tasks. Both conditions produced significant improvements in boys' on-task classroom behavior and their self-esteem as well as significant reductions in their parent-rated aggression. While the AC-SIT condition tended to produce stronger reductions in passive off-task classroom behavior than the AC condition, as hypothesized, the AC groups surprisingly produced more significant reductions in disruptive off-task behavior. These results suggest that, if the primary goal is to reduce socially disruptive behavior, time-limited cognitive behavioral interventions are more effective if they primarily restrict their focus to self-statements and program solving about social conflicts.

Lochman, Lampron, Gemmer, Harris, and Wyckoff (in press) compared the effects of an anger coping plus teacher consultation (ACTC) with anger coping and untreated control conditions. The teacher consultation component included six hours of consultation offered to small groups of teachers and emphasized how teachers can use problem-solving skills training and contingency management with their students. In comparison with the untreated control conditions, the two anger coping conditions had improvements in disruptive classroom behavior, teacher ratings of aggression, and boys' reports of self-esteem. However, there were no significant differences between the two anger coping conditions. Thus this level of teacher consultation did not augment the existing effectiveness of the intervention.

In samples of impulsive but not necessarily aggressive children, self-instructional training provided in a group format produced posttest improvements that were similar to a one-to-one treatment format (Kendall & Zupan, 1981). Both approaches had lasting effects at a one-year follow-up, although the group format was more successful in producing sustained improvements in teachers' ratings of self-control, while the individual format had the greatest effect on teachers' ratings of hyperactivity and children's memory of the training material (Kendall, 1982). In addition, more successful treatment outcomes with impulsive children have been found (a) when self-instruction training has provided children with conceptual self-instructions that can be used in any problem situation rather than concrete self-instructions (Kendall, 1981; Kendall & Wilcox, 1980), and (b) when children can generate their own self-instructions through a Socratic directed discovery procedure rather than receiving only didactic training (Schlesser, Meyers, Cohen, & Thackwray, 1983). These treatment characteristics have been found to interact with certain child characteristics in critical ways, with concrete-operational children having stronger treatment effects following discovery training in comparison to preoperational children (Nichol, Cohen, Meyers, & Schlesser, 1982). Apparently this occurred because concrete operational children were better able to note and understand the process of generating and adapting strategies to fit different tasks and hence made better use of discovery training.

VI. ISSUES TO BE ADDRESSED IN THE NEXT STAGE OF RESEARCH

The major conclusion to be drawn from the array of reviewed studies is clearly an encouraging one. In working with aggressive noncompliant children who have not responded well to most forms of psychological treatment, both behavioral family therapy and cognitive-behavioral therapy have been able to produce significant behavioral changes in the children. Behavioral family therapy studies have used strong observational methods to show that target children's behavior, siblings' behavior, and parents' behavior can change following treatment. Many of these studies have also included follow-up probes. Most cognitive-behavioral therapy studies have documented that treatment effects on at least some outcome measures can occur in comparison with untreated and alternatively treated conditions. Kazdin (1987) has concluded that both of these approaches are promising treatment strategies for conduct-disordered children, although behavioral family therapy approaches have produced more observed behavioral change in the current research.

However, several caveats about these encouraging conclusions should also be included. Even though significant changes can be found in most of these studies, the results *may not* be clinically significant (Kazdin, 1987). Even more troubling are the mixed outcome results that are evident for both behavioral family therapy and cognitive-behavioral therapy. The treatment of choice for aggressive children, or for subtypes of aggressive children, has not yet been documented. To make more definitive conclusions about these therapies' effects, research in this area will have to move to a new qualitative stage in which key design, sample, treatment procedure, measurement, and analyses steps will be required. While many methodological issues could be raised, the following points summarize specific methodological concerns that emerged in this research review.

A. Design

The most critical need is for treatment studies that include (a) a sample large enough so that the children and families are representative, which will allow the results to be generalized to other populations; (b) untreated and/or alternative treatment control conditions, so that alternative explanations for behavior change (such as maturation and sensitization to measures) can be eliminated; and (c) long-term follow-up. Despite the behavioral changes evident in most behavioral family therapy studies, no studies have yet included all of these design elements. The study that most closely approximates these conditions did not find significant treatment effects (Bernal, Klinnert, & Schultz, 1980). While comparison groups consisting of nondisturbed children and families are important to include to clarify the meaningfulness and social validity of the findings, it is also important for studies not to rely only on this kind of comparison group. This latter kind of design attempts to prove, rather then disprove, the null hypotheses of group differences, making this design highly sensitive to the effects of small sample sizes. Because larger sample sizes increase the power of tests and make it more likely that significant group differences will be found, a small sample size works in favor of researchers' hypotheses in this case by making it more difficult to find differences between treated and nondisturbed "normal" groups.

A logical extension of the current research in this area will be to develop multicomponent treatment studies for aggressive children that will include a cognitive-behavioral therapy component for the children and a behavioral family therapy component for parents. In addition, this design could include a more intensive treatment component combining both forms of therapy, as in Kazdin, Esveldt-Dawson, French, and Unis's (1987a) study, and contrast the more intensive combined treatment with the two treatment procedures provided separately. This kind of combined treatment package would address the need for broad-based interventions when working with children who have chronic difficulties that surface across settings and in multiple aspects of the child's functioning (Kazdin, 1987).

B. Sample

Recent studies in this area have generally included adequate information about how samples were identified (including the degree of behavioral disturbance), using behavioral checklists and behavioral observation systems with normative information. However, attrition of the sample over time is not always reported, even though such attrition may gravely affect generalizability of the findings. It is crucial to know whether families and children who drop out of treatment, or who do not consent to follow-up assessments, are different from subjects who remain in follow-up groups. For example, it is plausible to suggest that cases lost to follow-up represent the least cooperative and most mobile families, and these families may also have been least likely to respond to treatment. If so, follow-up results can be biased in an overly positive direction, unless adequate control conditions are used. It is also important to know whether the initially referred group is representative of aggressive children in general, or whether the referred population unknowingly, but systematically, has omitted certain types of aggressive children. Thus children and families who came to outpatient and inpatient settings probably do not include all of the families who have been referred, given that some families fail to follow through with referrals. Families who are seen in clinic settings may be more motivated to seek behavioral changes than the families of children seen in captive settings, such as in schools. When one identifies aggressive children from large group settings, such as school classrooms, there is the advantage of being able to document whether certain types of aggressive children are frequently evident in families that are not seen in behavioral family therapy or in cognitive-behavioral therapy.

C. Treatment Delivery

Kazdin (1987) has argued convincingly for outcome research to use high-strength interventions and to recognize that antisocial behavior in children follows a "chronic disease" pattern. In essence, treatments for aggressive children should be highly intensive. The previous review suggests that treatment effects are likely to be stronger in studies that have used experienced clinicians and in which treatment is provided over a longer period of time. However, these effects are somewhat complex. Thus the amount of experience that a clinician or trainee has received with a particular treatment approach appears to be more critical than their professional level or professional degrees. The total length of the treatment period appears to be more related to outcome than the number of sessions. An intensive treatment program would use experienced clinicians and would provide treatment over a relatively long period of time, potentially including booster treatments that continue into subsequent years. Outcome research also should include viable assessments of treatment integrity (Kazdin, 1987) to ensure that procedures are actually being provided as planned. Audiotaping of sessions, as well as the use of close supervision, could assist in ensuring treatment integrity.

D. Measurement

Two important measurement issues involve the need to use multimethod behavioral assessment measures and to assess generalization of behavioral changes across settings. Results from direct observation of behavior do not always correspond to the results of behavioral ratings provided by parents or teachers. Future research, especially on cognitive-behavioral treatment, should include observational measures as well as behavioral ratings by significant others. Behavioral ratings have the advantage of assessing behavior that is emitted outside of the specific situation being observed, while "blind" observational measures are less likely to be affected by biased perceptions of the person providing the behavioral information. Generalization of behavioral change across settings has not been conclusively demonstrated by either treatment procedure, although more evidence of generalization across settings has been evident in cognitive-behavioral research. Multimethod behavioral measures should be collected in both home and school settings to assess setting generalization.

E. Analysis: Processing Outcomes

To make substantial gains in treatment effectiveness, research will need to further address the characteristics of children, of families, and of the treatment process itself that are predictive of successful and unsuccessful outcomes. A growing body of research on correlates of improvement in behavioral family therapy has emerged, although relatively little is known about child characteristics that are related to this treatment outcome. Less effort has been made to process the outcomes of cognitive-behavioral therapy, and further research is needed in this area. For both forms of treatment, more sophisticated research can also begin to document that changes in behavior during treatment are related to changes in the social-cognitive and family processes that are assumed to mediate the problem behavior.

REFERENCES

Achenbach, T. M. (1982). *Developmental psychopathology* (2nd ed.). New York: John Wiley.

Adesso, V. J., & Lipson, J. W. (1981). Group training of parents as therapist for their children. *Behavior Therapy, 12*, 625-633.

Alexander, J. F., Barton, C., Schiavo, R. S., & Parsons, B. V. (1976). Systems-behavioral intervention with families of delinquents: Therapist characteristics, family behavior, and outcome. *Journal of Consulting and Clinical Psychology, 44*, 656-664.

Alexander, J. F., & Parsons, B. V. (1973). Short-term behavioral intervention with delinquent families: Impact on family process and recidivism. *Journal of Abnormal Psychology, 81*, 219-225.

Baum, C. G., & Forehand, R. (1981). Long term follow-up assessment of parent training by use of multiple outcome measures. *Behavior Therapy, 12*, 643-652.

Bernal, M. E., Klinnert, M. D., & Schultz, L. A. (1980). Outcome evaluation of behavioral parent training and client-centered parent counseling for children with conduct problems. *Journal of Applied Behavior Analysis, 13*, 677-691.

Braswell, L., Kendall, P. C., & Urbain, E. S. (1982). A multi-study analysis of the role of socio-economic status (SES) in cognitive-behavioral treatments with children. *Journal of Abnormal Child Psychology, 10*, 443-449.

Brody, G. H., & Forehand, R. (1985). The efficacy of parent training with maritally distressed and nondistressed mothers: A multi-method assessment. *Behaviour Research and Therapy, 23*, 291-296.

Camp, B. W., Blom, G., Herbert, F., & Van Doorninck, W. (1977). Think Aloud: A program for developing self-control in young aggressive boys. *Journal of Abnormal Child Psychology, 5*, 157-168.

Chamberlain, P., Patterson, G., Reid, J., Kavanagh, K., & Forgatch, M. (1984). Observation of client resistance. *Behavior Therapy, 15*, 144-155.

Coats, K. I. (1979). Cognitive self-instructional training approach for reducing disruptive behavior of young children. *Psychological Reports, 44*, 127-134.

Copeland, A. P., & Hammel, R. (1981). Subject variables in cognitive self-instructional training. *Cognitive Therapy and Research, 5*, 405-420.

Cross Calvert, S., & McMahon, R. J. (1987). The treatment acceptability of a behavioral parent training program and its components. *Behavior Therapy, 2*, 165-179.

Dadds, M. R., Sanders, M. R., Behrens, B. C., & James, J. E. (1987). Marital discord and child behavior problems: A description of family interactions during treatment. *Journal of Clinical Child Psychology, 16,* 192-203.

Dadds, M. R., Schwartz, S., & Sanders, M. R. (1987). Marital discord and treatment outcome in behavioral treatment of child conduct disorders. *Journal of Consulting and Clinical Psychology, 55,* 396-403.

Denkowski, G. C., & Denkowski, K. M. (1985). Community-based residential treatment of the mentally retarded adolescent offender: Phase 1, reduction of aggressive behavior. *Journal of Community Psychology, 13,* 299-310.

Dodge, K. A. (1986). A social information processing model of social competence in children. In M. Perlmutter (Ed.), *Cognitive perspectives on children's social and behavioral development.* Hillsdale, NJ: Lawrence Erlbaum.

Dubow, E. F., Huesmann, L. R., & Eron, L. D. (1987). Mitigating aggression promoting prosocial behavior in aggressive elementary schoolboys. *Behaviour Research and Therapy, 25,* 527-531.

Dumas, J. E. (1986). Parental perception on treatment outcome in families of aggressive children: A causal model. *Behavior Therapy, 17,* 420-432.

Dumas, J. E., & Albin, J. B. (1986). Parent training outcome: Does active parental involvement matter? *Behaviour Research and Therapy, 24,* 227-230.

Eyberg, S. M., & Johnson, S. M. (1974). Multiple assessment of behavior modification with families: Effects of contingency contracting and order of treated problems. *Journal of Consulting and Clinical Psychology, 42,* 594-606.

Eyberg, S. M., & Matarazzo, R. G. (1980). Training parents as therapists: A comparison between individual parent-child interaction training and parent group didactic training. *Journal of Clinical Psychology, 36,* 492-499.

Feindler, E. L., Ecton, R. B., Kingsley, D., & Dubey, D. R. (1986). Group anger-control training for institutionalized psychiatric male adolescents. *Behavior Therapy, 17,* 109-123.

Ferber, H., Keeley, S. M., & Shemberg, K. M. (1974). Training parents in behavior modification: Outcome of and problems encountered in a program after Patterson's work. *Behavior Therapy, 5,* 415-419.

Fleischman, M. J. (1981). A replication of Patterson's "Intervention for boys with conduct problems." *Journal of Consulting and Clinical Psychology, 49,* 342-351.

Fleischman, M. J., & Szykula, S. A. (1981). A community setting replication of a social learning treatment for aggressive children. *Behavior Therapy, 12,* 115-122.

Forehand, R., & King, H. E. (1977). Noncompliant children: Effects of parent training on behavior and attitude change. *Behavior Modification, 1,* 93-108.

Forehand, R., & Long, N. (in press). Outpatient treatment of the acting out child: Procedures, long term follow-up data, and clinical problems. *Journal of Child and Adolescent Psychology.*

Forehand, R., Sturgis, E. T., McMahon, R. J., Aguar, D., Green, K., Wells, K., & Breiner, J. (1979). Parent behavioral training to modify child noncompliance: Treatment generalization across time and from home to school. *Behavior Modification, 3,* 3-25.

Forehand, R., Wells, K., & Griest, D. L. (1980). An examination of the social validity of a parent training program. *Behavior Therapy, 11,* 488-502.

Forman, S. G. (1980). A comparison of cognitive training and response cost procedures in modifying aggressive behavior of elementary school children. *Behavior Therapy, 11,* 594-600.

Garrison, S. R., & Stolberg, A. L. (1983). Modification of anger in children by affective imagery training. *Journal of Abnormal Child Psychology, 11,* 115-130.

Ginott, H. G. (1965). *Between parent and child.* New York: Macmillan.

Goodwin, S. F., & Mahoney, J. J. (1975). Modification of aggression through modeling: An experimental probe. *Journal of Behavior Therapy and Experimental Psychiatry, 6,* 200-202.

Griest, D. L., Forehand, R., Rogers, T., Breiner, J., Furey, W., & Williams, C. A. (1982). Effects of parent enhancement therapy on the treatment outcome and generalization of a parent training program. *Behaviour Research and Therapy, 20,* 429-436.

Griest, D. L., & Wells, K. C. (1983). Behavioral family therapy with conduct disorders in children. *Behavior Therapy, 14,* 37-53.

Hamilton, S. B., & MacQuiddy, S. L. (1984). Self-administered behavioral parent training: Enhancement of treatment efficacy using a time-out Signal Seat. *Journal of Clinical Child Psychology, 13,* 61-69.

Heffer, R. W., & Kelley, M. L. (1987). Mothers' acceptance of behavioral interventions for children: The influence of parent race and income. *Behavior Therapy, 2,* 153-163.

Humprheys, L., Forehand, R., McMahon, R., & Roberts, M. (1978). Parent behavioral training to modify child noncompliance: Effects on untreated siblings. *Journal of Behavior Therapy and Experimental Psychiatry, 9,* 235-238.

Horne, A. M., & Van Dyke, B. (1983). Treatment and maintenance of social learning family therapy. *Behavior Therapy, 14,* 606-638.

Kandel, D. B. (1982). Epidemiological and psychosocial perspectives in adolescent drug abuse. *Journal of the American Academy of Child Psychiatry, 21,* 328-347.

Karoly, P., & Rosenthal, M. (1977). Training parents in behavior modification: Effects on perceptions of family interaction and deviant child behavior. *Behavior Therapy, 8,* 406-410.

Kazdin, A. E. (1977). Assessing the clinical or applied importance of behavior change through social validation. *Behavioral Modification, 1,* 427-452.

Kazdin, A. E. (1987). Treatment of antisocial behavior in children: Current status and future directions. *Psychological Bulletin, 102,* 187-203.

Kazdin, A. E., Esveldt-Dawson, K., French, N. H., & Unis, A. S. (1987a). Effects of parent management training and problem-solving skills training combined in the treatment of antisocial child behavior. *Journal of the American Academy of Child and Adolescent Psychiatry, 26,* 416-424.

Kazdin, A. E., Esveldt-Dawson, K., French, N. H., & Unis, A. S. (1987b). Problem-solving skills training and relationship therapy in the treatment of antisocial child behavior. *Journal of Consulting and Clinical Psychology, 55,* 76-85.

Kendall, P. C. (1981). One-year follow-up of concrete versus conceptual cognitive-behavioral self-control training. *Journal of Consulting and Clinical Psychology, 49,* 748-749.

Kendall, P. C. (1982). Individual versus group cognitive-behavioral self-control training: One-year follow-up. *Behavior Therapy, 13,* 241-247.

Kendall, P. C., & Wilcox, L. E. (1980). A cognitive-behavioral treatment for impulsivity: Concrete versus conceptual training in non-self-controlled problem children. *Journal of Consulting and Clinical Psychology, 48,* 80-91.

Kendall, P. C., & Zupan, B. A. (1981). Individual versus group application of cognitive-behavioral strategies for developing self-control in children. *Behavior Therapy, 12,* 344-359.

Kent, R. N., & O'Leary, K. D. (1976). A controlled evaluation of behavior modification with conduct problem children. *Journal of Consulting and Clinical Psychology, 44,* 586-596.

Kettlewell, P. W., & Kausch, D. F. (1983). The generalization of the effects of a cognitive-behavioral treatment program for aggressive children. *Journal of Abnormal Child Psychology, 11,* 101-114.

Lochman, J. E. (1985). Effects of different treatment lengths in cognitive behavioral interventions with aggressive boys. *Child Psychiatry and Human Development, 16,* 45-56.

Lochman, J. E. (1987). Self and peer perceptions and attributional biases of aggressive and nonaggressive boys in dyadic interactions. *Journal of Consulting and Clinical Psychology, 55,* 404-410.

Lochman, J. E. (1988a, August). *Cognitive-behavioral intervention with aggressive boys: Three year follow-up effects.* Paper presented at the American Psychological Association Annual Convention, Atlanta.

Lochman, J. E. (1988b, September). *Long-term efficacy of cognitive behavioral interventions with aggressive boys.* Paper presented at the World Congress on Behavior Therapy, Edinburgh, Scotland.

Lochman, J. E., & Brown, M. V. (1980). Evaluation of dropout clients and of perceived usefulness of a parent education program. *Journal of Community Psychology, 8,* 132-139.

Lochman, J. E., Burch, P. R., Curry, J. F., & Lampron, L. B. (1984). Treatment and generalization effects of cognitive behavioral and goal setting interventions with aggressive boys. *Journal of Consulting and Clinical Psychology, 52,* 915-916.

Lochman, J. E., & Curry, J. F. (1986). Effects of social problem-solving training and of self instruction training with aggressive boys. *Journal of Clinical Child Psychology, 15,* 159-164.

Lochman, J. E., & Lampron, L. B. (1986). Situational social problem-solving skills and self-esteem of aggressive and nonaggressive boys. *Journal of Abnormal Child Psychology, 14,* 605-617.

Lochman, J. E., & Lampron, L. B. (1988). Cognitive behavioral interventions for aggressive boys: Seven months follow-up effects. *Journal of Child & Adolescent Psychotherapy, 5,* 15-23.

Lochman, J. E., Lampron, L. B., Burch, P. R., & Curry, J. F. (1985). Client characteristics associated with behavior change for treated and untreated aggressive boys. *Journal of Abnormal Child Psychology, 13,* 527-538.

Lochman, J. E., Lampron, L. B., Gemmer, T. C., Harris, R., & Wyckoff, G. M. (in press). Teacher consultation and cognitive-behavioral interventions with aggressive boys. *Psychology in the Schools.*

Lochman, J. E., Nelson, W. M., III, & Sims, J. P. (1981). A cognitive behavioral program for use with aggressive children. *Journal of Clinical Child Psychology, 10,* 146-148.

Luiselli, J. K. (1984). Treatment of an assaultive, sensory-impaired adolescent through a multi-component behavioral program. *Journal of Behavior Therapy and Experimental Psychiatry, 15,* 71-78.

McMahon, R. J., & Forehand, R. (1983). Consumer satisfaction in behavioral treatment of children: Types, issues, and recommendations. *Behavior Therapy, 14,* 209-225.

McMahon, R. J., Forehand, R., & Griest, D. L. (1981). Effects of knowledge of social learning principles on enhancing treatment outcome and generalization in a parent training program. *Journal of Consulting and Clinical Psychology, 49,* 526-532.

McMahon, R. J., Forehand, R., Griest, D. L., & Wells, K. C. (1981). Who drops out of therapy during parent behavioral training? *Behavior Counseling Quarterly, 1,* 79-85.

McMahon, R.J., Tiedemann, G. L., Forehand, R., & Griest, D. L. (1984). Parental satisfaction with parent training to modify child noncompliance. *Behavior Therapy, 15,* 295-303.

Meichenbaum, D. H., & Goodman, J. (1971). Training impulsive children to talk to themselves: A means of developing self control. *Journal of Abnormal Psychology, 77,* 115-126.

Nichol, G., Cohen, R., Meyers, A., & Schlesser, R. (1982). Generalization of self-instruction training. *Journal of Applied Developmental Psychology, 3,* 205-215.

Olson, R. L., & Roberts, M. W. (1987). Alternative treatments for sibling aggression. *Behavior Therapy, 18,* 243-250.

Olweus, D. (1979). Stability of aggressive behavior patterns in males: A review. *Psychological Bulletin, 86,* 852-875.

Patterson, G. R. (1986). Performance models for antisocial boys. *American Psychologist, 41*, 432-444.

Patterson, G. R., Chamberlain, P., & Reid, J. B. (1982). A comprehensive evaluation of a parent training program. *Behavior Therapy, 13*, 638-650.

Patterson, G. R., & Fleischman, M. J. (1979). Maintenance of treatment effects: Some considerations concerning family systems and follow-up data. *Behavior Therapy, 10*, 168-185.

Patterson, G. R., & Forgatch, M. S. (1985). Therapist behavior as a determinant for client noncompliance: A paradox for the behavior modifier. *Journal of Consulting and Clinical Psychology, 53*, 846-851.

Patterson, G. R., & Gullion, M. E. (1968). *Living with children: New methods for parents and children.* Champaign, IL: Research Press.

Patterson, G. R., Reid, J. B., Jones, R. R., & Conger, R. E. (1975). *A social learning approach: Vol. 1. Families with aggressive children.* Eugene, OR: Castalia.

Peed, S., Roberts, M., & Forehand, R. (1977). Evaluation of the effectiveness of a standardized parent training program in altering the interaction of mothers and their noncompliant children. *Behavior Modification, 1*, 323-350.

Pfiffner, L. J., O'Leary, S. G., Rosen, L. A., & Sanderson, W. C., Jr. (1985). A comparison of the effects of continuous and intermittent response cost and reprimands in the classroom. *Journal of Clinical Child Psychology, 14*, 348-352.

Rinn, R. C., Vernon, J. C., & Wise, M. J. (1975). Training parents of behavioral-disordered children in groups: A three years' program evaluation. *Behavior Therapy, 6*, 378-387.

Robin, A. L., Schneider, M., & Dolnick, M. (1976). The Turtle Technique: An extended case study of self-control in the classroom. *Psychology in the Schools, 73*, 449-453.

Robins, L. N. (1978). Sturdy childhood predictors of adult antisocial behavior: Replications from longitudinal studies. *Psychological Medicine, 8*, 611-622.

Rogers, T. R., Forehand, R., Griest, D. L., Wells, K. C., & McMahon, R. J. (1981). Socioeconomic status: Effects on parent and child behaviors and treatment outcome of parent training. *Journal of Clinical Child Psychology, 10*, 98-101.

Schlesser, R., Meyers, A. W., Cohen, R., & Thackwray, D. (1983). Self-instruction interventions with non-self-controlled children: Effects of discovery versus faded rehearsal. *Journal of Consulting and Clinical Psychology, 51*, 954-955.

Strain, P. S., Steele, P., Ellis, T., & Timm, M. A. (1982). Long-term effects of oppositional child treatment with mothers as therapists and therapist trainers. *Journal of Applied Behavior Analysis, 15*, 163-169.

Vaughn, S. R., Ridley, C. A., & Bullock, D. D. (1984). Interpersonal problem-solving skills training with aggressive young children. *Journal of Applied Developmental Psychology, 5*, 213-223.

Wahler, R. G. (1980). The insular mother: Her problems in parent-child treatment. *Journal of Applied Behavior Analysis, 13*, 207-219.

Wahler, R. G., & Graves, M. G. (1983). Setting events in social networks: Ally or enemy in child behavior therapy? *Behavior Therapy, 14*, 19-36.

Webster-Stratton, C. (1985). Predictors of treatment outcome in parent training for conduct disordered children. *Behavior Therapy, 16*, 223-243.

Webster-Stratton, C., Kolpacoff, M., & Hollingsworth, T. (1988). Self-administered videotape therapy for families with conduct-problem children: Comparison with two cost-effective treatments and a control group. *Journal of Consulting and Clinical Psychology, 56*, 558-566.

Wiltz, N. A., & Patterson, G. R. (1974). An evaluation of parent training procedure designed to alter inappropriate aggressive behavior of boys. *Behavior Therapy, 5*, 215-221.

PHARMACOLOGICAL AND BEHAVIORAL TREATMENT FOR CIGARETTE SMOKING

SHARON M. HALL
University of California, San Francisco and
San Francisco Veterans Administration
Medical Center

ROBERT G. HALL
Palo Alto Veterans Administration Medical Center and
Stanford University School of Medicine

DOROTHY GINSBERG
University of California, San Francisco

AUTHORS' NOTE: Work on this chapter was in part supported by Research Scientist Development Award KO2 DA00065, by grants RO1 DA02538 and RO1 DA03082, from the National Institute on Drug Abuse, and grant RO1 HL39201 from the National Heart, Lung and Blood Institute. Abbreviated versions of sections of this chapter appeared in A. S. Bellack, M. Hersen, & A. E. Kazdin (Eds.), *International Handbook of Behavior Modification and Therapy*, New York: Plenum (1988).

I. INTRODUCTION

The purpose of this chapter is to discuss the state of the art of behavioral and pharmacological treatments for tobacco dependence. The discussion focuses largely on nicotine, which is most likely the psychoactive component of tobacco. Our discussion proceeds along the outlines of the 1988 *Report of the Surgeon General* (U.S. Public Health Service [PHS], 1988), which includes consideration of cigarette smoking as highly controlled behavior and nicotine as a psychoactive drug and as a positive reinforcer. We then discuss some effects of cigarettes that smokers may perceive as beneficial and that are important for both clinical and theoretical reasons. These include suppression of body weight, regulation of negative affect, and perhaps improved cognitive functioning.

One benefit in working clinically and experimentally with smoking cessation is that there is a useful technology for measuring severity of the problem and successful outcome. This technology is discussed in the section on measurement of dependence. From this foundation, we examine the efficacy of treatment techniques and issues specific to different techniques. The behavioral techniques evaluated are aversive smoking, self-management procedures, and relapse-prevention strategies. We assume that most readers of this chapter will be less familiar with the models of pharmacological treatment than with behavioral models. Therefore, we include an overview of pharmacological models in drug dependencies. Four classes of pharmacological treatments of tobacco dependence are then considered. These are (1) over-the-counter treatments, (2) nicotine fading, (3) nicotine gum, and (4) other drug treatments. Finally, we considered some implications of the increasing interest in pharmacological treatments.

II. TOBACCO USE AS DRUG DEPENDENCE

Nicotine, the active component of cigarettes, has actions that are perceived as beneficial by smokers. It aids memory, concentration, alertness, and relaxation. It suppresses weight, a desirable effect for many smokers. In tolerant users, it produces pleasure and even euphoria. Unfortunately, nicotine is inhaled in tobacco smoke, which is not benign. Tobacco also includes tars and other carcinogenic substances. Also, the carbon monoxide in the smoke has harmful effects on the heart. Finally, nicotine itself is cardiotoxic (Gilman, Goodman, Rall, & Murad, 1985).

A question of clinical and legal interest is whether nicotine is an addicting drug. Investigators in the field who were aware of the relevant data have long been convinced that it is. However, the impact of these data was greatly increased by the 1988 *Report of the Surgeon General* on tobacco and health (U.S. PHS, 1988). This influential report focused on the pharmacology of tobacco addiction. The authors concluded that tobacco use is addicting and that nicotine is the drug in tobacco that causes addiction. Similarities between tobacco addiction and other addictions, including heroin and cocaine, were described. The 1988 report presents voluminous, convincing evidence of the addictive properties of tobacco that contribute to use despite the existence of well-documented and widely recognized health hazards.

The criteria used by the Surgeon General to evaluate tobacco as pharmacologically addicting are as follows:

1) that highly controlled or compulsive patterns of drug taking occur, 2) that a psychoactive or mood-altering drug is ingested by use of the substance and is involved in the resulting patterns of behavior, and 3) that the drug is capable of functioning as a reinforcer that can directly strengthen behavior leading to further drug ingestion. Addicting drugs can be characterized by other properties that include the following: They can produce pleasurable effects in users, they can cause tolerance and physical dependence, and they can have adverse or toxic effects. (p. 149, preliminary version)

A. Cigarette Smoking as a Highly Controlled Behavior

The automatic and stereotypic features of cigarette smoking are illustrated by consistencies in smoking patterns across and within users. For example, novice smokers gradually increase their cigarette intake until they reach a level of daily use and a smoking routine that remains stable over time. Also, tolerant smokers maintain a constant blood level of nicotine and cotinine (a metabolite of nicotine). This occurs even when changes are made in the number of cigarettes smoked or in the (machine-estimated) nicotine yield of the cigarettes. Smokers tend to thwart attempts to reduce nicotine intake by blocking filter holes in ventilated cigarettes, smoking more cigarettes, spending a greater proportion of time puffing, taking more puffs, or taking larger puffs.

Experimental manipulations of tobacco or nicotine dose have also provided evidence that smokers regulate nicotine intake. For example, increasing the nicotine yield per cigarette, slowing the rate of nicotine excretion through alkalinization of the urine, and increasing exposure to tobacco smoke may result in decreases in cigarette smoking.

Investigations have been conducted to determine whether the actions of nicotine are responsible for the patterns of smoking behavior. Theoretically, if nicotine is responsible, then pretreatment with nicotine should produce decreases in the amount taken from smoking behavior. Nicotine pretreatment has included nicotine polacrilex gum, oral nicotine, and intravenous nicotine. The results provide evidence for the specific effects of nicotine on smoking. Regardless of the form of administration, nicotine pretreatment tends to result in decreased smoking (U.S. PHS, 1988).

B.   Nicotine as a Psychoactive Drug

The pharmacological properties of nicotine are analogous to other psychoactive drugs such as morphine, cocaine, and alcohol. Nicotine produces unique identifiable effects that animals and humans can discriminate from placebos and other psychoactive drugs. Also, the stimulus properties of nicotine are mediated in the central rather than in the peripheral nervous system, the hallmark of drug psychoactivity (U.S. PHS, 1988).

C.   Nicotine as a Positive Reinforcer

Nicotine functions as a positive reinforcer in humans and animals. Nicotine presentation strengthens behavior leading to nicotine use. Studies indicate that nicotine is more reinforcing when intermittently delivered (which is similar to human smoking behavior) and when nicotine drug-associated environmental stimuli are presented.

Under some conditions, particularly large doses or in nontolerant users, aversive effects have also been demonstrated. Throat irritation, dizziness, or bitter taste may influence the total amount of cigarette smoking or determine when a cigarette is discarded (U.S. PHS, 1988).

Two characteristics usually considered indicative of the physical component of addiction are tolerance (the need for increasing amounts of the drug to obtain the same effects) and dependence (the experience of withdrawal symptoms and craving when drug use is terminated). Nicotine meets both of these criteria (Gilman, Goodman, Rall, & Murad, 1985).

Tolerance does occur. For example, the daily doses most smokers tolerate are much greater than the doses they would have tolerated when beginning to smoke. As Jarvik and Henningfield (1988) have noted, even within a single day, tolerance is lost and gained. Tolerance decreases during sleep, so that the first cigarette of the day provides the strongest effect. Smokers often report little subjective effect of evening and afternoon cigarettes. Over longer periods, they may increase nicotine dose by switching to brands with greater nicotine content, increasing the number of cigarettes smoked, or changing smoking behavior so that more nicotine is ingested.

The evidence for dependence is similarly convincing. In a series of studies, Hatsukami, Hughes, and their colleagues (Hatsukami, Hughes, & Pickens, 1985) demonstrated that an uncomfortable syndrome exists when smokers quit. The most consistent components are decreased heart rate and increased eating, sleep disturbance, confusion, and craving for cigarettes. Other difficulties reported include increased irritability, anxiety, poor concentration, restlessness, and a variety of somatic complaints. Evidence for the physical basis of these symptoms is found in data showing that craving, confusion, and sleep disturbances are correlated with blood nicotine and cotinine levels or other measures of smoke exposure. However, the network of relationships is not simple. Some withdrawal symptoms are not reduced by administration of nicotine in gum form as they should be if nicotine is the active agent in producing dependence.

It is unclear how many smokers show evidence of withdrawal when they quit smoking. Hughes, Gust, and Pechacek (1987) used two criteria for withdrawal, those of DSM-III, and their own empirically derived criteria—21% of their sample of 1,006 smokers met the DSM-III criteria, 46% met Hughes, Gust, and Pechacek criteria. Agreement between the two diagnostic systems was poor. These data suggest there is work to be done to describe withdrawal.

The acknowledgment that nicotine is an addicting drug, and that smokers could become dependent upon tobacco, is a new one. For many years, smoking was considered a simple habit. The realization that physical dependence plays a role in smoking has focused attention away from psychological and behavioral factors to biological and pharmacological ones.

Although physical dependence is important in tobacco addiction, it does not explain all the variance in quitting smoking and relapse. Behavioral and psychological variables must be considered, as they must in any addiction. There is a large literature on the relationships between these variables and cigarette smoking (Tunstall, Ginsberg, & Hall, 1984). However, these studies have not been based on a model so compelling or consistent as the nicotine dependence model. Nor are they overwhelmingly consistent. Hence, they have not had the impact of recent studies of nicotine dependence.

III. PERCEIVED BENEFITS OF NICOTINE THAT
MAY PROMOTE CIGARETTE SMOKING

The Surgeon General's report discusses three "positive" effects of cigarette smoking that may play an important role in maintaining smoking for some subgroups of smokers. Thus they need to be considered when treatment programs are developed. These perceived benefits are weight regulation, affect regulation, and enhancement of cognitive functioning. These effects are probably in part produced by nicotine, but more data are needed to establish the precise role played by the drug.

A. Weight Regulation

The most thoroughly studied of these phenomena is weight regulation. Of the 28 studies that have examined the phenomenon, 25 (89%) found that smokers weigh less than nonsmokers. Also, of the 43 studies examining weight changes following smoking initiation or cessation, 37 (83%) found that smoking and weight were inversely correlated. That is, quitting smoking produces weight gain and beginning smoking produces weight loss. The cause of this phenomenon is not yet known (U.S. PHS, 1988).

Those few studies that have examined physical activity as a cause of weight change have found no difference in activity levels following quitting smoking (Hall, McGee, Tunstall, Duffy, & Benowitz, 1988; Rodin, 1987). Changes in energy output also have been studied. Two variables have been studied: basal metabolic rate—the amount of energy used by the body when it is at rest—and thermogenesis—the total amount of heat emitted by the body. The data are inconsistent. Glauser, Glauser, Reindenberg, Rusy, and Tallarida (1970) and Dallosso and James (1984) found a decrease in basal metabolic rate after quitting smoking. Hofstetter, Schutz, Jequier, and Wahren (1986) did not. However, this group found that thermogenesis increased after quitting. Others also have found no change in metabolic rate (Burse et al. 1982; Robinson & York, 1986; Stamford et al. 1984). Some of the inconsistency may be because of weak methods. Studies used small samples, often did not control for diet, and measured metabolic changes *after* weight gain occurred. Because weight is known to influence metabolic level, postgain measurements are confounded (U.S. PHS, 1988).

The most consistent findings have been changes in the number of calories eaten. Hatsukami, Hughes, Pickens, and Svikis (1984), Robinson and York (1986), and Hall, McGee, Tunstall, Duffy, and Benowitz (1988) found increased calories after smoking cessation. Dallaso and James (1984) reported a small but nonsignificant increase. It is interesting to determine which nutrients contribute to this increase, because the particular nutrient increased may indicate which physiological mechanisms underlie the change. In a series of laboratory studies, Grunberg (1985) has shown increased consumption of sweet foods in laboratory animals after termination of chronic nicotine infusions. He links this increase to an increase in blood insulin and a decrease in blood glucose that followed cessation of nicotine administration. In a short-term study with humans, Grunberg showed that deprived smokers ate more "sweet" foods than nondeprived smokers or nonsmokers (Grunberg, Bowen, Maycock, & Nespor, 1985). However, the actual nutrient content of the foods was not determined. Also, smokers were deprived of cigarettes for only a few hours. It is unclear whether findings from such a short deprivation period generalize to the long-term weight gain that accompanies quitting smoking. Field studies produced mixed evidence. Rodin (1987) studied self-selected quitters and found that those who gained weight were likely to increase their intake of sugar. Hall, McGee, Tunstall, Duffy, and Benowitz (1988) randomly assigned smokers to early or late quit dates one month apart and studied their eating behavior at the time when subjects in one condition were smoking and the others were abstinent or smoking at low rates. The results indicated an increase in sucrose intake after quitting. The results for total sugars were inconsistent. Sucrose may be a better indicator of sweet taste than total sugars, given that some sugars do not taste sweet. Also, fat intake increased significantly. Protein and nonfat carbohydrates showed no change. Changes in calories were correlated with later weight gain, especially for women. At six months postquitting changes in intake returned to baseline level, but the weight gain continued. It was not clear which nutrient caused the weight gain. Controlled studies are needed to determine whether it is increases in fats or in sweet foods that are most closely related to the weight gained after quitting smoking.

These data suggest that a major change in the biological systems that regulate weight occurs after quitting smoking. For the ex-smoker, this is not good news. Changes in metabolic rate can be offset by exercise. However, if the weight gain is linked to changes in appetite that are biologically driven, behavior changes to prevent weight gain may be difficult to achieve.

How this weight gain affects quitting smoking is not clear. While smokers are aware of the weight-suppressing effects of nicotine, and report concern about weight gain when quitting smoking, the two studies that have examined the effects of weight gain on quitting have produced surprising findings. Hall, Ginsberg, and Jones (1986) examined the weight of men and women smokers who had been abstinent for six months and their smoking status six months later. Weight gain during the six months of abstinence predicted continued abstinence, not relapse. Comparable results were reported by Gritz, Carr, and Marcus (1988). Whether these findings reflect the action of biological mechanisms that enhance the reinforcing properties of food deprivation (Carroll & Meisch, 1984), or because more motivated smokers ignore weight gain and concentrate on maintaining abstinence, is not known. Also, smokers who greatly fear weight gain may relapse early, because significant weight gain appears within three weeks of quitting. They may thus select themselves out of samples that examine long-term abstinence and weight gain. These data do suggest that clinicians should take care in prescribing weight loss strategies for those attempting to quit, because use of these strategies may hinder, rather than help, abstinence. At present, attitudinal interventions may be the most effective ones. Clinicians need to counsel patients that the health costs of weight gain are substantially outweighed by the costs of continued smoking.

B. Affect Regulation

Smokers reporting high levels of affective distress fail to quit smoking and fail to maintain abstinence. A cluster of psychological characteristics, including sadness, anxiety, low self-esteem, and anger, consistently predict failure in quitting smoking. McArthur et al. (1958) and Guilford (1966) reported that smokers who were able to quit smoking were less "neurotic" than those who were unable to quit. Schwartz and Dubitsky (1968) found that abstinence five years after treatment was related to good adjustment, low chronic illness, low anxiety, and evidence of less chronic habitual smoking. Jacobs (1972) reported that male relapsers were more distressed, guarded, isolated, and defiant than abstainers. Benfari and Eaker (1984) reported similar findings at four years in the Multiple Risk Factor Intervention Trial. Low "personal security" (Knutson, 1952) and high "life stress" (Holmes & Rahe, 1967) predicted relapse.

Although questions have been raised about the methodology of these studies (e.g., Coan, 1967; Kozlowski, 1979), most reviewers agree that the evidence is consistent enough to support the idea of a relationship between self-report of affective distress and inability to abstain (U.S. PHS, 1980, 1988).

Our data support those of earlier investigators. In our study of chronically ill smokers, we found that *consistently* high (elevated at each of two assessments) mood disturbance predicted relapse at follow-up (Hall, Bachman, Henderson, Barstow, & Jones, 1983).

Theoreticians (e.g., Leventhal & Cleary, 1980) have long argued that negative affect plays a predominant role in relapse. Tompkins (1966) proposed a topology of smoking that included smoking in response to affect. However, scales derived from that topology have been poor predictors of treatment outcome (Flaxman, 1978; Hall, Bachman, Henderson, Barstow, & Jones, 1983).

Retrospective evidence suggests that negative affect plays a role in relapse. Marlatt and Gordon (1980) found that 43% of smokers reported
negative affect as a determinant of relapse. In a sample studied by
Lichtenstein, Antonuccio, and Rainwater (1977), 20% of subjects did so.
Callers to a "hot line" for smokers who had relapsed, or who feared they
might, reported that 71% of smoking-related crises were preceded by negative affect, including anxiety (42%), anger (26%), and depression (22%;
Shiffman, 1982). In a prospective study, Pomerleau, Adkins, and
Pertschuk (1978) found that variables indicating the strength of dependence or habit (number of years smoked, number of cigarettes per day)
predicted cessation. However, abstinence at one year was related to
negative-affect-induced smoking. Only 26% of smokers who said they
smoked in response to negative effect were abstinent at one year, compared with 50% of those who were not negative-affect smokers.

It is unlikely that the dysphoria noted results from social pressure on
smokers because the relationship between smoking and affect was noted
before smoking became socially disfavored (e.g., Jacobs, 1972). Also, the
dysphoria is likely to be an enduring rather than situation-specific characteristic, because the relationship is present with both trait and state measures and has been found in both cross-sectional studies of smokers *versus*
nonsmokers and ex-smokers as well as longitudinal evaluations of smoking treatment outcome.

Recently, Glassman et al. (1988) reported that 61% of the smokers who
entered a smoking treatment trial had histories of major depressive disorder and that these smokers relapsed at higher rates than those without this
history. The rate for major depressive disorder in the general population
is about 7% to 10%. These data, if reliable, raise questions about whether
smokers with psychiatric disorders have always been so heavily overrep-
resented among smoking treatment clients. Another issue is discovering
the mechanisms by which depression and smoking covary. These findings
suggest that mood management strategies, especially those designed to
prevent negative affect, may be useful in preventing relapse.

C. Cognitive Function

Smokers frequently report that smoking enhances work and academic
activities. Studies of attention- and state-dependent learning tend to support this perception, but those of memory and learning do not (U.S. PHS,
1988). Many studies fail to use nonsmokers as controls. Thus, differences
found could be because of withdrawal symptoms in deprived smokers.
However, some studies that administered nicotine to nonsmokers found
increments in some tasks. Independent of which view is correct, there are
few methods currently available to assist the quitting smoker regain the
perceived loss in cognitive function (U.S. PHS, 1988). Clinicians can

work with clients to suggest other methods to increase efficiency. Examples are better time management, better study skills, better organizational skills, and better management of coworkers and employees.

IV. MEASUREMENT OF DEPENDENCE

Traditional measures of tobacco dependence fall into two categories: biochemical and self-report. Biochemical measures are indices of how much nicotine a smoker routinely ingests. While some might argue that constituents of tobacco other than nicotine have psychoactive effects, nicotine is the most important active substance in cigarette smoke. Potential biochemical measures are the levels of nicotine or nicotine metabolites found in the brain. Because brain measures of nicotine levels are not possible in human subjects, researchers measure these substances in body fluid that are assumed to reflect brain levels. The most common fluids used are blood, saliva, and urine.

Nicotine itself is a poor indicator of amount smoked. Nicotine has a short half-life (about two hours). Thus levels are unduly influenced by recency of smoking (Benowitz et al., 1983). A better measure of dependence is cotinine, a nicotine metabolite. Cotinine has a longer half-life (about 20-40 hours), so it remains in the system two to three days after the last cigarette was smoked. The long half-life means that levels are less likely to fluctuate because of recently smoked cigarettes (Benowitz et al., 1983). Cotinine levels have been found to predict treatment outcome (Hall, Herning, Jones, Benowitz, & Jacob, 1984) and responsivity to nicotine gum treatment (Hall, Tunstall, Rugg, Jones, & Benowitz, 1985).

There are other biochemical indicators of *smoking*, including carbon monoxide, carboxyhemoglobin, and thiocyanate. These are measures of the by-products of the smoke inhaled. Amount of smoke inhaled and amount of nicotine ingested do not correlate well. For example, while smoke inhalation in a smoker of very low-nicotine cigarettes might be greater than that of a smoker who smoked a high-nicotine cigarette, the smoker of high-nicotine cigarettes is actually inhaling more nicotine per cigarette. While he or she might have lower carbon monoxide levels, he or she would have higher blood cotinine levels.

There are two self-report measures of nicotine dependence. The first, and oldest, is number of cigarettes smoked per time unit. This is widely considered a poor measure of nicotine intake, because both smoking behavior and nicotine content of cigarettes vary widely. Also, self-report is not always accurate. It has been shown that self-report of number of cigarettes smoked is frequently subject to rounding error. Most smokers report daily consumption in figures that end with a zero, representing either a pack or a half pack of cigarettes. The second self-report measure of nicotine dependence is the Tolerance Scale (Fagerstrom, 1978). The scale includes items about actual smoking behavior, including number and brand of cigarettes smoked, inhalation patterns, time of first cigarette of the day, and the constancy of the need for cigarettes. In correlates moderately well with cotinine (Hall, Tunstall, Rugg, et al., 1985), and has been useful in predicting responsivity to nicotine gum (Hall, Tunstall, Ginsberg, Benowitz, & Jones, 1987).

These unidimensional measures of dependence are appealing because of their simplicity. However, they do not completely describe the range of nicotine dependence. For example, recent definitions of nicotine dependence describe a phenomenon with multiple manifestations. Therefore, measurement of nicotine dependence should not use a simple linear model. Consider, for example, a 50-year-old smoker who smokes 15 cigarettes each day and suffers from emphysema, which will certainly get worse if he does not quit smoking. Compare him with a 40-year-old chain-smoker of 40 cigarettes per day who has yet experienced no adverse health consequences. Both have tried unsuccessfully to quit, and both have gradually increased smoking over the years. While the smoker of more cigarettes would probably score higher on traditional measures of dependence, such as number of cigarettes smoked per day, both would be diagnosed as moderately nicotine-dependent according to current diagnostic schemes, such as DSM-III-R. At present, there is no instrument that characterizes severity of nicotine dependence in its entirety. Ratings derived from clinical interviews are perhaps the only way to obtain a rough estimate of severity.

V. BEHAVIORAL TREATMENT TECHNIQUES

The span of behavioral and psychological treatment techniques used to treat nicotine dependence is broad. In this chapter, we concentrate on those behavioral and psychological techniques that are the most promising. These are also the techniques that have been used in combination with pharmacological treatments. These are aversion, self-management, and relapse-prevention programs, usually combined with aversion.

A. Aversive Smoking

"Aversion" encompasses a variety of techniques including rapid smoking (e.g., Danaher, 1977a; Hall, Sachs, & Hall, 1979; Hall, Sachs, Hall, & Benowitz, 1984); warm smoky air (e.g., Lichtenstein, Harris, Birchler, Wahl, & Schmahl, 1973); stimulus satiation or saturation (e.g., Best, Owen, & Trentadue, 1978); smoke holding or taste satiation (e.g., Tori,

1978); covert sensitization (e.g., Barbarin, 1978); and shock therapy (e.g., Berecz, 1979).

The most effective aversion procedures are those that use cigarette smoke as the aversive stimulus (Schwartz, 1987). Of these, rapid smoking has generated the most research. In the standard procedure, smokers are instructed to inhale from a cigarette every six seconds to the point of physical discomfort (nausea or dizziness) or until a time limit is reached, whichever occurs first.

In early studies, abstinence rates of 100% at treatment termination (e.g., Harris & Lichtenstein, 1971; Schmahl, Lichtenstein, & Harris, 1972) and 60% at six-month follow-up were reported (Lichtenstein, Harris, Birchler, Wahl, & Schmahl, 1973; Schmahl, Lichtenstein, & Harris, 1972). Later research produced variable results. In Danaher's (1977b) review of 22 rapid-smoking studies, abstinence rates ranged from 0%-81% at three-month follow-up and 6.7%-55% at six-month follow-up. In 10 of 14 studies permitting comparison with placebo control or alternative treatments, rapid smoking produced higher abstinence rates at three- to six-month follow-up (Danaher, 1977b). However, these differences were not statistically significant. In most of these studies abstinence rates were based on unverified self-reports or incomplete samples (subjects who completed treatment or responded to follow-up).

Since Danaher's review, there have been several rapid-smoking studies that used biochemical verification of abstinence and included dropouts in outcome analyses (Danaher, 1977a, 1977b; Danaher, Jeffery, Zimmerman, & Nelson, 1980; Glasgow, 1978; Hall, Rugg, Tunstall, & Jones, 1984; Hall, Sachs, & Hall, 1979; Hall, Sachs, Hall, & Benowitz, 1984; Hall, Tunstall, Ginsberg, Benowitz, & Jones, 1987; Norton & Barske, 1977; Raw & Russell, 1980). Some studies compared rapid smoking to control conditions or other aversive smoking procedures. Others compared rapid smoking alone with rapid smoking in multicomponent programs. These studies produced mixed results about the effectiveness of rapid smoking compared with the nonspecific components of the treatment or other aversive smoking procedures. Most produced lower abstinence rates than the original Lichtenstein studies. Deviations from the original method may be the cause (Danaher, 1977a, 1977b; Hall, Herning, Jones, Benowitz, & Jacob, 1984). These studies have restricted or controlled the number of sessions (Raw & Russell, 1980); conducted treatment in groups (Hall et al., 1984; Hall et al., 1987; Norton & Barske, 1977; Raw & Russell, 1980); added other components or booster sessions (Danaher, 1977a, 1977b; Hall et al., 1984; Hall et al., 1987); or had clients rapid smoke at home (Danaher, Jeffery, Zimmerman, & Nelson, 1980).

Rapid smoking has continued to be a popular smoking intervention. In recent years it has usually been used in conjunction with other smoking cessation procedures. Schwartz (1987) reviewed 49 rapid-smoking trials and found only 4 trials after 1977 that employed rapid smoking without additional procedures. Modifications of rapid smoking that are of only moderate effectiveness alone may be more successful when combined with other procedures. Schwartz (1987) reported that 17% of the studies using rapid smoking alone produced abstinence rates of at least 33% at one-year follow-up; 50% of those using combined treatments did so. Although many of these studies had weak methodology, rapid smoking and other aversive smoking procedures used in multicomponent programs produce quit rates that are among the highest in the literature.

Before selecting rapid smoking, the health of the patient should be carefully assessed. Evidence suggests that rapid smoking among healthy smokers does not present a health risk greater than that of normally paced smoking (Sachs, Hall, & Hall, 1978). However, caution should be used in selecting rapid smoking for patients with cardiopulmonary disease (Hall & Hall, 1987; Hall, Sachs, Hall, & Benowitz, 1984). Compared with normally paced smoking, rapid smoking produces increases in heart rate, blood nicotine levels, carboxyhemoglobin, and other blood gases (Hall, Sachs, & Hall, 1979; Miller, Schilling, Logan, & Johnson, 1977; Russell, Raw, Taylor, Feyerabend, & Saloojee, 1978; Sachs, Hall, & Hall, 1978). Concerns that rapid smoking might lead to nicotine poisoning have not been substantiated (Russell et al., 1978). Guidelines are available concerning screening procedures and the safe use of rapid smoking (Hall & Hall, 1987; Lichtenstein & Glasgow, 1977).

B. Self-Management Procedures

Self-management programs include (1) the recording of one's own smoking behavior, (2) changes in the antecedent consequences of one's smoking response, and (3) developing awareness of and changing cue-elicited smoking patterns (Schwartz, 1987).

Because awareness of stimuli that control smoking behavior is central to this approach, self-monitoring is a basic element in all self-management procedures. Smokers may monitor behaviors such as the number of cigarettes smoked, nicotine intake, and the time, place, activity, and mood when smoking each cigarette (e.g., Abrams & Wilson, 1979; Foxx & Axelroth, 1983; McFall & Hammen, 1971; Moss, Prue, Lomax, & Martin, 1982).

Self-management procedures combined with self-monitoring include gradual reduction and stimulus control techniques. Gradual reduction is use of goals to gradually reduce the number of cigarettes smoked. This technique is frequently used in combination with a stimulus control procedure, in which the number of situations in which smoking occurs is gradually reduced.

Other self-management procedures include contingency management and relaxation. Contingency management involves use of a contract to specify treatment goals and to enhance motivation for quitting (e.g., Lando & McCullough, 1978; Paxton, 1980; Stitzer & Bigelow, 1982). Contracts typically include monetary deposits or social contracts with peers. Relaxation techniques may be taught to smokers under tape-recorded or therapist direction. Relaxation techniques may be used (1) to reduce the stress generated by quitting or (2) as a substitute for smoking in anxiety-producing situations.

The most effective use of self-management approaches is in multi-component programs, especially in combination with aversive smoking. Self-management procedures alone have not produced results better than the generally expected rates of 20%-30% abstinence at follow-up (Pechacek & McAlister, 1980).

C. Relapse Prevention

Almost all interventions for tobacco dependence have relapse prevention as a goal. However, a few interventions evaluated specific components that are designed to decrease relapse. Those aimed at relapse can be partitioned by whether they are based on a theoretical model or whether they are empirical. Several studies have examined the effects of nonspecific continued support from a theoretical perspective. However, there are theoretically derived interventions that are based on cognitive-behavioral models emphasizing coping skills (Hall, 1980; Marlatt & Gordon, 1979).

A straightforward method to prevent relapse is to provide some kind of social support after treatment. Usually, this takes the form of continued group meetings. Several studies have evaluated such support. Evidence for continued nonspecific support is mixed. Some studies find an effect (e.g., Tiffany, Martin, & Baker, 1986). Most do not, or find an effect only while groups continue to meet (e.g., Brandon, Zelman, & Baker, 1987).

More theoretically interesting and promising are interventions that are provided either during treatment, or immediately afterwards to teach skills and ways of thinking that are specifically designed to prevent relapse. Several such programs have been evaluated. The first of these was a "self-control" program developed by Danaher (1977a, 1977b) that included self-management skills before providing aversive smoking for cessation. The training was found to produce lower abstinence rates than a nonstructured discussion control. However, both the timing and the content of the self-management intervention may have operated against success. Before quitting, most smokers have difficulties in thinking about anything other than quitting. Relapse prevention seems of secondary importance. Second, the program itself was complex and multifaceted. An overly complex program may be too difficult to learn.

Davis and Glaros (1986) compared a multicomponent smoking relapse-prevention program based on Marlatt and Gordon's (1980) model of relapse with controls that received only Pomerleau and Pomerleau's (1977) smoking program or received the Pomerleau and Pomerleau program and discussed high-risk situations. There were no differences in abstinence rates. However, subjects in the relapse-prevention condition took longer to relapse and smoked fewer cigarettes when they did relapse.

A targeted-skill-training-based relapse-prevention intervention based on a cost-benefit model (Hall, 1980) was reported by Hall and her colleagues (Hall, Rugg, Tunstall, & Jones, 1984; Hall, Tunstall, Rugg et al., 1985). Subjects were taught relapse-prevention skills through role-playing and cognitive rehearsal. Using this intervention program, substantial abstinence rates have been obtained. However, these rates have fluctuated considerably from study to study. These fluctuations could not be attributed to differences in the sample, in therapists, or in the treatment. It is possible that they may reflect the large confidence intervals that occur when moderate sample sizes are used with dichotomous variables such as abstinence.

In summary, specific, targeted interventions appear promising. Most have solid theoretical underpinnings, derived from relapse-specific models (Hall, 1980; Marlatt & Gordon, 1980). None has yet shown robust, replicable effects on smoking.

VI. PHARMACOLOGICAL TREATMENT

A. Pharmacological Models

Pharmacological treatments of nicotine dependence include any that use nicotine or other drugs to reduce cigarette consumption. Pharmacological approaches that have been evaluated include replacement therapy, pharmacological aversion, detoxification, antagonists, and symptom relief.

A widely studied treatment for nicotine dependence is replacement therapy. Replacement therapies provide the same or a related drug to reduce self-administration (Henningfield & Jasinski, 1988). For example, in methadone maintenance, methadone is substituted for heroin. Replacement therapies help by reducing withdrawal symptoms, by attenuating the reinforcing properties of the abused drug, and by reducing ingestion of the problem drug. However, they may not reduce craving (Jasinski & Henningfield, 1988). Many clients and practitioners question the desirability of replacement therapy. Some feel that the ideal state is a "drug-free" state. This may be naive. Many who consider themselves drug-free ingest some drugs on a regular basis. Examples are caffeine, alcohol, and over-the-counter painkillers. However, to be "drug-free" is a widely held value and, therefore, a factor in treatment acceptability. It must be considered seriously because of that.

Drugs can be used to produce aversion to the abused drug. The pairing of alcohol and disulfiram to produce nausea is an example. One can also conceptualize rapid smoking as a pharmacological treatment that produces a mild nicotine toxicity that is paired with the sight, taste, and smell of cigarettes, and, by repeated pairings, produces an aversion. Detoxification is gradual reduction of level of the abused drug. Detoxification is a common treatment for heroin addiction. In some instances, supportive medication may be used. The rationale is that gradual reduction produces less intense withdrawal symptoms than rapid withdrawal.

Antagonists are drugs that block the effect of the abused drug. The ideal antagonist does not produce any aversive side effects of its own. For example, the opiate antagonist, naltrexone, is known to block the effects of heroin without producing pleasurable or aversive effects of its own. Disulfiram is an alcohol antagonist, but has more side effects. One of these is a constellation of symptoms that occur if alcohol is ingested. These include flushing, vomiting, and rapid heartbeat. In this case, the side effects may also serve as a punishment for alcohol ingestion. A common problem with antagonist treatment is compliance: Many patients refuse to take them for extended times.

Symptom relief is often a goal of pharmacotherapy. Included is prescription of benzodiazepines to reduce the anxiety associated with withdrawal from some psychoactive drugs.

B. Pharmacological Treatment Programs

We group pharmacological treatments for nicotine dependence into five classes. The first is over-the-counter programs. These include both a putative replacement drug (lobeline sulfate), a drug that produces an aversive reaction to smoking (silver acetate), and a fading procedure (Water Pik filters). The remaining treatments are clinic based. They include nicotine fading, a detoxification procedure; nicotine replacement, which at this time is mostly nicotine gum; and a few trials of antagonists and symptom-relief medication.

Few of these strategies have been studied without the inclusion of some behavioral techniques. However, the range of the behavioral techniques is sometimes small. Few studies have considered the optimal kind or amount of behavioral intervention. Usually, partitioning the amount of variance attributable to each is not possible. The exception is studies of nicotine gum. From its introduction in this country, both Merrell-Dow, the marketers of the gum, and the treatment community have been interested in how much and what kinds of behavioral treatments should be included with nicotine gum. Several studies provide data relevant to the question of how much and what kind of behavioral support is optimal when nicotine gum is used.

C. Over-the-Counter Treatments

Over-the-counter preparations for quitting smoking have been generally ineffective. Three products (lobeline sulfate, silver acetate, and the Water Pik filters) have been studied well enough to permit conclusions about their effectiveness. Lobeline sulfate (sold under the trade names of Bantron, Nikoban, and Lobidan) is said to be a nicotine substitute because it produces effects similar to those of nicotine. However, reviews of studies of its effectiveness (e.g., Schwartz, 1987) concluded that it was no better than a placebo for quitting smoking.

Silver acetate produces an unpleasant metallic taste in the mouth after smoking. It also has little empirical support as an aid to quitting smoking. For example, in a large study (Malcom, Currey, Mitchell, & Keil, 1980) 285 subjects were randomly assigned to either silver acetate or placebo control conditions. Subjects were told how to use the gum containing either silver acetate or placebo, met with the experimenters three times, and were told to set a quit day. On the third visit a raffle was announced for all subjects who attended the four-month follow-up. At four months abstinence rates were 11% for the silver acetate condition and 4% for the placebo, a nonsignificant difference.

Hymowitz, Lasser, and Safirstein (1982) studied the efficacy of the graduated filter system (One Step at a Time) marketed by Teledyne Water Pik. A group of 130 subjects were randomly assigned to quit smoking on their own, to placebo filters, or to the graduated filter system. Subjects were seen five or more times over the year. At 12 months there was a significant difference between the abstinence rates of the three groups—the group that quit on their own obtaining the highest abstinence rate.

D. Nicotine Fading

In nicotine fading, under the supervision of a professional therapist, smokers change the brand of cigarettes they smoke to a brand lower in tar and nicotine (Foxx & Brown, 1979). After baseline they reduce nicotine consumption by 30%, 60%, and 90% in successive weeks and then quit. Foxx and Brown found a 50% abstinence rate at six months for a combined nicotine fading and self-management group. This exceeded self-management only, a nicotine fading only group, or an educational format control. At the two-and-a-half-year follow-up, the abstinence rate remained 50%. Nicki, Remington, and McDonald (1984) reported comparable outcomes in a four-group comparison. Treatment conditions were (1) nicotine fading and self-management (NF/SM), (2) NF/SM and self-talk, (3) NF/SM and self-efficacy, and (4) NF/SM, self-talk, and self-efficacy. The two groups that included self-efficacy reported the highest 12-month rates. The quit rate for the group including all three components was 46%. The self-efficacy group without self-talk reported a 25% quit rate at one year. Nicki, Remington, and McDonald concluded that the differences found in the quit rates of other studies were because of changes in self-efficacy.

However, most other studies have reported lower rates. Foxx and Axelroth added a period of cigarette fading (reducing the number of cigarettes each week) for smokers who were unable to quit at the end of the nicotine fading procedure. They reported a 33% quit rate at the end of one year. They did not report the number who required the additional cigarette fading. Subjects reported reducing nicotine intake by 81.6%. They reduced the number of cigarettes per day by 28.1%. Prue, Davis, Marden, and Moss (1983) developed a self-help manual for nicotine fading. They supplemented it with brief telephone contacts each week. At six months, 23% of the subjects in the experimental group were abstinent. None of the subjects in a waiting list control was abstinent. Bowers, Winett, and Fredericksen (1987) compared nicotine fading with fading plus a maintenance procedure and a behavioral contracting procedure. The study does not report abstinence rates. Brown, Lichtenstein, McIntyre, and Harrington-Kostur (1984) reported two studies. The first, a single-group design, examined the effect of self-efficacy and nicotine fading combined. They reported 46% abstinent at six months. The authors then assessed the importance of the individual elements. They compared nicotine fading and relapse prevention, nicotine fading and group discussion, and relapse prevention alone. There were no differences between groups. In this attempted replication, the combined treatment group had a quit rate of 19% at one year. The authors concluded that a change in the treatment manual that increased the clients' work load was responsible. Lando and McGovern (1985) randomly assigned smokers either to oversmoking, nicotine fading, nicotine fading and smoke holding, or to a control group. The combined nicotine fading and smoke holding group produced the highest abstinence rate at three and six months. These differences did not last to one year.

In summary, the evidence for nicotine fading is mixed, at best. It is unclear how much "fading" really occurs. Benowitz et al. (1983) have shown that smokers' blood cotinine levels are not closely related to FTC machine-determined nicotine levels of cigarettes. Thus reducing the amount of nicotine purposely ingested by changing to cigarettes with lower nicotine yields, as measured by the FTC, may have a net result in ingesting more nicotine. This lack of relationship probably occurs because blood cotinine level is influenced by depth of inhalation, number of puffs per cigarette, and other smoking behavior variables. This may result in a titration effect, so that smokers actually ingest as much nicotine from low-nicotine cigarettes as from high-nicotine cigarettes.

E. Nicotine Gum

Nicotine polacrilex gum was approved by the FDA in 1984 as a prescription treatment for tobacco dependence. Trademaked as Nicorette, it is distributed by Lakeside Pharmaceutical, a subsidiary of Merrell-Dow Pharmaceutical. Nicotine gum was designed to provide an alternative source of nicotine to smokers who want to quit. Theoretically, the gum prevents abrupt withdrawal from nicotine and provides an oral substitute for cigarettes. Once the smoker has learned to cope with the psychological aspects of the addiction, nicotine withdrawal presumably is easier. After three to six months the smoker gradually tapers off the gum. Nicotine gum is contraindicated for smokers with serious cardiovascular disease, active ulcers, and temporomandibular joint disease and for pregnant or nursing women.

It is useful to compare outcome results of the smoking-clinic-based nicotine gum studies with the dispensing of nicotine chewing gum in minimal treatment such as physician's prescription for nicotine gum. Such treatments provide a "lower limit" of effectiveness against which other treatments can be compared. They are appropriate as a lower limit because not only is the nonpharmacological treatment minimal, the population is probably not as motivated to quit smoking as clinic patients are. In such studies, abstinence rates of 8% to 14% have been reported. In the British Thoracic Society study, smokers were randomly assigned to four conditions, including combinations of advice, information, and nicotine chewing gum. At one year 10%-14% of 1,550 patients remained continuously abstinent among the four treatment groups. The gum was found to be no better than advice alone.

Russell, Merriman, Stapleton, and Taylor (1983) evaluated 1,938 smokers who were randomly assigned to one of three groups: (a) nonintervention controls, (b) advice plus booklet, and (c) advice, booklet, and offered nicotine chewing gum. The success rates for the three groups were 3.9%, 4.1%, and 8.8% (p < .001) at one year. Although the absolute abstinence rate was not high, nicotine chewing gum was more effective than advice alone.

A study by Schneider et al. (1983) provides suggestive data on the role of counseling apart from motivations. These investigators studied 60 subjects who were randomly assigned to nicotine chewing gum or a placebo and provided "clinic support." Clinic support consisted of meeting individually with an experimenter and discussing the subject's problems and progress. In a second study, 36 subjects were randomly assigned, double blind, to nicotine chewing gum or placebo and merely dispensed the gum. At one year 30% of "clinic support" subjects who received nicotine chewing gum were abstinent versus 20% of "clinic support" subjects who received placebo. In the dispensary study 13% of the placebo gum users quit versus only 8% for the nicotine chewing gum. The two studies, clinic and dispensary, are not a definitive comparison because subjects were not randomly assigned to either dispensary or clinic. The two studies were done sequentially. However, the dispensary condition suggests that motivated subjects given only pharmacological treatment have abstinence rates in the same range as those seen in a physician's office.

There has been considerable research on the effectiveness of nicotine gum in smoking-clinic settings. Several early studies in Europe showed short-term decreases in cigarette smoking while chewing nicotine gum compared with placebo gum. Ohlin and Westling (1972) conducted a double-blind randomized trial in which 92 subjects received either four-milligram nicotine gum or placebo. During the first week of treatment, tobacco consumption was significantly less in the active than in the placebo group. A second double-blind trial was conducted in which 44 subjects received either four-milligram nicotine gum or placebo (Brantmark, Ohlin, & Westling, 1973). At the end of two weeks the active treatment group had consumed less tobacco than the placebo group, although differences were not statistically significant. In the second trial, the results were reported only for the 35 subjects who completed treatment. Russell, Wilson, Feyerabend, and Cole (1976) conducted a double-blind placebo-controlled crossover trial in which 43 smokers were randomly assigned to receive either two-milligram nicotine gum or placebo gum for two days and were then switched to the other gum for two days. During the first week subjects were instructed to smoke "as inclined." During the second week subjects were instructed to attempt smoking cessation and the crossover procedures were repeated. When subjects were smoking as inclined, tobacco consumption decreased significantly more in the nicotine gum group than in the placebo group. However, when subjects attempted smoking cessation, the difference between the active and placebo group was no longer significant.

Later studies found nicotine gum to be more effective than placebo gum in producing cessation at long-term follow-up. At least 13 randomized placebo-controlled double-blind trials have been conducted that include long-term (4- to 24-month) follow-up (British Thoracic Society, 1983; Christen, McDonald, Olson, Drook, & Stookey, 1984; Fagerstrom, 1982; Fee & Stewart, 1982; Hall, Tunstall, Ginsberg, Benowitz, & Jones, 1987; Hjalmarson, 1984; Jamrozik, Fowler, Vessy, & Wald, 1984; Jarvis, Raw,

Russell, & Feyerabend, 1982; Malcolm, Sillett, Turner, & Ball, 1980; Puska, Björkquist, and Koskela, 1979; Schneider et al., 1983; Tonnesen et al., 1988). In 11 of 13 trials, the active gum was superior to placebo. However, these differences were not always statistically significant. Five trials reported significant differences at short-term follow-up at one to three months (Christen et al., 1984; Tonnesen et al., 1988; Jarvis et al., 1982; Hjalmarson, 1984; Fagerstrom, 1982). Eight trials showed significant differences at long-term (4- to 24-month) follow-up (Christen et al., 1984; Fagerstrom, 1982; Hall et al., 1987; Hjalmarson, 1984; Jarvis et al., 1982; Puska et al., 1979; Schneider et al., 1983; Tonnesen et al., 1988). The two trials producing negative results dispensed gum with little support or follow-up (British Thoracic Society, 1983; Schneider et al., 1983).

Researchers, practitioners, and Merrell-Dow all agree that the gum should be administered in conjunction with therapeutic support. Across studies, the highest quit rates are found when the gum is combined with behavioral treatment. In studies with at least one-year follow-up, nicotine gum with behavior therapy resulted in abstinence rates of 12%-49% (median = 29%; Schwartz, 1987), as compared with the 8%-10% abstinence rates that are found when less support is offered.

Although nicotine gum is recommended as an adjunct to behavioral treatment, the optimal type and amount of therapeutic support for use with the gum remains unclear. Studies comparing the effectiveness of nicotine gum with varying levels of clinic support are few and inconclusive. We found four randomized trials that compared nicotine gum plus behavioral treatment with low-contact nicotine gum control groups (Ginsberg, Hall, Rosinski, 1988; Hall, Tunstall, Rugg, et al., 1985; Killen, Maccoby, & Taylor, 1984). These studies were conducted in smoking-cessation clinics and produced mixed results.

Some of them showed nicotine gum plus behavioral treatment to be superior to low-contact nicotine gum controls. Hall, Tunstall, Rugg, Jones, and Benowitz (1985) compared three interventions: intensive behavior treatment, nicotine gum in a low-contact treatment, and intensive behavioral treatment plus nicotine gum (combined treatment). The combined treatment resulted in higher abstinence rates than did the other conditions through one-year follow-up. However, differences were no longer significant at one-year follow-up. Abstinence rates for combined, low-contact, and behavioral treatments were 44%, 37%, and 28% at one year. Similarly, Killen, Maccoby, and Taylor (1984) compared nicotine gum, skills training, and nicotine gum plus skills training (combined treatment). Throughout the 10.5-month follow-up period the combined treatment produced higher abstinence rates than nicotine gum alone. However, differences were not statistically significant. Abstinence rates for combined, nicotine gum, and skills training groups were 50%, 23%, and 30% at 10.5-month follow-up.

In contrast, other randomized trials conducted in smoking clinics showed combined treatments to have lower abstinence rates than low-contact nicotine gum control groups. Hall et al. (1987) used a 2 × 2 factorial design to compare nicotine versus placebo gum and intensive behavioral treatment versus low-contact treatment. Contrary to prediction, low-contact nicotine gum treatment produced slightly higher abstinence rates than nicotine gum plus intensive behavioral treatment throughout the one-year follow-up period. For example, abstinence rates for the intensive plus gum and low-contact plus gum were 34% and 50% at one year. Ginsberg, Hall, and Rosinski (1988) used an incremental design to compare three treatments: nicotine gum only, nicotine gum plus psychological treatment, and nicotine gum plus psychological treatment and partner support. As in the previous study, low-contact nicotine gum only produced slightly higher abstinence rates at one year than the comparison groups, although not significantly. Abstinence rates for gum only, gum plus psychological treatment, and gum plus psychological treatment and partner support were 40%, 33%, and 27% at one year.

Two other randomized trials were conducted in general medical practices. They too produced mixed results. Lando, Kalb, and McGovern (in press) compared nicotine gum and behavioral self-help materials with nicotine gum and a control pamphlet containing factual information. Contrary to prediction, smokers who received self-help booklets did no better than smokers receiving the comparison pamphlets. Fagerstrom (1984) employed a 2 × 2 factorial design to examine nicotine gum versus no gum and short versus long follow-up. Smokers provided nicotine gum plus long follow-ups had the highest abstinence rates throughout the one-year follow-up period. There were significant main effects favoring both nicotine gum and longer follow-up, although by one-year long follow-up was not significantly better than short follow-up.

In summary, controlled randomized trials have not identified the nature of the support or guidance necessary for optimal use of nicotine gum. The six trials that used randomization high-contact or behavioral treatments failed to produce significantly higher abstinence rates at long-term (10- to 12-month) follow-up. Explanations for these negative results may include minimal differences between comparison groups (Lando, 1986; Fagerstrom, 1984) and small sample sizes. Furthermore, most of the low-contact treatments in the clinic studies included at least four group sessions that may have provided sufficient support (Hall, Tunstall, Rugg et al., 1985; Hall, Tunstall, Ginsberg et al., 1987; Killen, Maccoby, & Taylor, 1984). The optimal level of support to supplement nicotine gum may vary by sex and level of psychological dependence. Evidence suggests that women benefit from clinic support more than do men (Ginsberg, Hall, & Rosinski, 1988).

Some studies have compared the effectiveness of nicotine gum to behavior therapy. Most of these studies combined nicotine gum with behavioral or educational interventions. For example, Raw, Jarvis, Feyerabend, and Russell (1980) compared nicotine gum in a withdrawal clinic to psychological treatment alone. Nicotine gum resulted in significantly higher abstinence rates at one-year follow-up than psychological treatment (38% compared with 14%). DeWit and Camic (1986) compared the effectiveness of behavioral treatment plus nicotine gum with behavioral treatment alone but reported the opposite results. The behavioral treatment alone resulted in significantly higher abstinence rates at termination. However, it is unclear whether group differences were related to treatment method or to other factors. Neither study used random assignment to comparison groups, and the behavioral treatments were conducted two to three years before the nicotine gum groups were conducted.

Well-controlled randomized studies show that nicotine gum is a useful adjunct to behavior therapy. Killen, Maccoby, and Taylor (1984) reported that nicotine gum plus skills training (combined treatment) resulted in higher abstinence rates than skills training alone throughout a 10.5-month follow-up period. Abstinence rates for combined treatment and skills training alone were 86% and 55% at 6 weeks, 73% and 45% at 15 weeks, and 50% and 30% at 10.5 months. However, differences were statistically significant only at six-week follow-up. Similarly, Hall, Tunstall, Rugg et al. (1985) reported that intensive behavioral treatment plus nicotine gum (combined) resulted in higher abstinence rates throughout a one-year follow-up period than intensive behavioral treatment alone. Abstinence rates for combined treatment and behavioral treatment alone were 95% and 78% at week 3, 73% and 47% at week 12, 59% and 31% at week 26, and 44% and 28% at one year.

Another unresolved issue is length of administration of gum use. Many quitters return to smoking when the gum is discontinued. Longer use of the gum improves quit rates. As a result, some investigators have recommended that the gum be used for six months to one year following cessation (Russell, Raw, & Jarvis, 1980). This is in contrast to the manufacturer, who advises patients not to use the gum for more than six months. Extended use has raised concern about addiction to the gum. However, difficulty giving up the gum is infrequent. Among smokers who used the gum to help them quit, gum use one to two years later generally has not exceeded 5% (e.g., Hjalmarson, 1984). Factors that may decrease the dependence potential of nicotine gum include availability by prescription only, unpleasant taste, the necessity of active chewing to extract the nicotine, slow nicotine uptake, and weak reinforcing effects (U.S. PHS, 1988). While there are disadvantages to use of the gum, the health risks and dependence potential are less than those of smoking cigarettes.

Evidence also indicates that the gum is more helpful to smokers who are highly dependent on nicotine (e.g., Fagerstrom, 1982; Hall, Tunstall, Rugg et al., 1985; Jarvik & Schneider, 1984). One method for evaluating a smoker's level of nicotine dependence is the Fagerstrom Tolerance Scale (Fagerstrom, 1978; Hall, Tunstall, Ginsberg et al., 1987). Blood cotinine may also be useful in this way (Hall, Tunstall, Rugg, et al., 1985).

F. Other Drug Treatment

Nicotine gum is the only nicotine replacement drug approved for that use in this country. Other drug and nicotine preparations have been studied. Russell, Jarvis, Feyerabend, and Ferno (1983) have evaluated a nicotine nasal gel. They found that the gel did produce greater and more rapid absorption of nicotine than that obtained from nicotine gum. They reasoned that such an absorption pattern would be more acceptable to smokers because it would more closely mimic the nicotine absorption pattern of cigarettes. Jarvis (1986, as cited in the *Report of the Surgeon General*, U.S. PHS, 1988) reported decreased craving in 26 smokers treated at the Maudsley Smokers Clinic. About two-thirds of the subjects quit smoking. One-third remained abstinent at one year. Others have suggested that transdermal nicotine patches may be useful, but clinically relevant data are not yet available.

We found three other drugs that have been used in attempts to treat nicotine dependence. Each is based on a different pharmacological rationale. Two of these studied the effects of putative nicotine antagonists. Karas and Kane (1980) studied the effects of naloxone hydrochloride on smoking behavior over a short (three-hour) time period. The rationale was complex. Naloxone is a known opiate antagonist. Its effects are opposed to that of opiates, and it will not only block the effects of opiates but produce withdrawal symptoms if given to an opiate addict. Some have suggested this occurs because it reduces levels of beta endorphin. Karas and Kane suggest that smoking may also elevate endorphin levels. Therefore, naloxone would decrease the positive effects derived from cigarettes. They found that number of puffs, the weight of the amount of cigarettes smoked, and the number of trials in which cigarettes were smoked decreased when smokers were given naloxone. There have been no clinical studies of naloxone's effectiveness. However, naloxone also suppresses intake of food, water, and ethanol. Such nonspecific effects seem to cast doubt on the investigators' causal hypothesis.

Mecamylamine is known to be a centrally acting nicotine antagonist. Tennant, Tarver, and Rawson (1983) studied mecamylamine in smoking treatment. While some subjects did stop smoking when given mecamylamine, the side effects were unpleasant enough that one-half of the subjects dropped out of the treatment.

A final rationale is simple symptom relief. Glassman and his colleagues have studied the effects of clonidine hydrochloride, an antihypertensive agent, in smoking withdrawal. In a first study, Glassman, Jackson, Walsh, and Roose (1984) administered clonidine, placebo, or the benzodiazepine, alprazolam, to 15 heavy smokers who were abstaining from cigarettes. Both active drugs decreased anxiety, tension, irritability, and restlessness, but clonidine was more effective in reducing cigarette craving. In a second study, smoking treatment failures were assigned to either clonidine or placebo drug treatment for four weeks. Clonidine produced higher abstinence rates than the placebo drug at both four weeks and six months. The effect may have been greater for women, but the small number of men subjects may also explain the lack of effect in this subgroup. This study has been of interest to smokers and to the field. However, the meaning of the data is difficult to interpret for several reasons. Clonidine is assumed to ameliorate withdrawal in other addictions because it dampens the increased sympathetic activity that occurs. However, increased sympathetic activity is not a consistent feature of nicotine withdrawal. Therefore, there is no straightforward theoretical reason why clonidine should decrease craving. The methods of the study differed from those standard in smoking treatment, making interpretation of the data difficult. For example, subjects who failed to reduce smoking to 50% of baseline at the quit date were omitted from further consideration. Also, six-month outcomes were not biologically verified. If abstinence rates are recalculated with all subjects entering into the trial in the sample, the continuous abstinence rate at four weeks is 44% in the active drug group and 19% in placebo. While differences between conditions were statistically significant they do not differ greatly from those already in the literature. At six months, the self-reported abstinence rate was 24% for clonidine.

Since the introduction of nicotine gum in 1984, drug treatments of cigarette dependence have attracted much attention. The focus on pharmacological treatments is important. However, it raises several issues. The first is that the "medicalization" of cigarette smoking may have a negative effect on smoking treatment outcome. All addictions involve a complex interplay of psychological, sociological, and biological factors. It is naive to assume that the optimal treatment will include only one of these. Also, the concept of addiction implies disease to some and moral shortcomings to others. It is important to discourage smoking treatment patients from adopting the passive role that is associated with patients with acute diseases. The perception that smoking represents a moral defect may result in guilt that actually complicates the process of quitting and maintaining abstinence (Marlatt & Gordon, 1980). It must also be recalled that none of these treatments has consistently shown abstinence rates that are overwhelmingly higher than those of intensive behavioral treatments. Although behavioral treatments are more expensive of time, they are safe and have few negative side effects. All of the pharmacological treatments now available have some side effects, and, at least one, clonidine, requires skill and care on the part of the prescribing physician. Also, drug treatments involve less of the patient's time, but they are expensive. A physician must be involved. In some instances, it may be necessary to perform expensive medical tests before treatment begins.

VII. THOUGHTS ABOUT THE FUTURE OF SMOKING TREATMENT

We are on the verge of an explosion of pharmacological treatment techniques for nicotine dependence. To be sure, the plight of cigarette smokers has caught the eye of the pharmaceutical industry. There have been trials by pharmaceutical companies evaluating antidepressants for use in smoking treatment. Several companies are working on transdermal nicotine patches, which are thought to be a more convenient way of delivering nicotine than the resin of nicotine gum. However, behavioral treatments will continue to be useful for those who want to be treated without drugs or who cannot be treated with drugs for medical reasons. Clinical experience indicates that many smokers will fall into these categories. However, it would be unrealistic to expect that the development of treatment techniques that rely solely on behavioral strategies will be as rapid as those of pharmaceutical strategies in the next few years. However, there may be interesting exceptions to this prediction. For example, as the relationship between affect regulation and smoking becomes clearer, depression prevention techniques similar to those used in the cognitive-behavioral treatment of depression, may be developed and evaluated.

There is, and will continue to be, a need for research to determine the most effective behavioral treatment programs to use with pharmaceutical agents. It is possible that the best behavioral program will vary as a function of the pharmacological modality. For example, an important behavioral component to nicotine gum treatment is probably good instruction in how to use the gum so as to avoid adverse effects, and continued encouragement to use the gum. This is so because incorrect use of the gum can result in unpleasant side effects such as excessive salivation, heartburn, and nausea. One would not expect such a component to be so useful with a nicotine patch, however, where the mode of administration eliminates these gastrointestinal side effects. A related area for investigation will be adaptation of findings from the large literature on compliance with other drug treatments to pharmacological treatment of smoking.

Another area of interest is better determination of who benefits by which strategy. Currently, most researchers and clinicians believe that only heavy smokers benefit from nicotine gum use, even though it does not harm light smokers. Whether this will be so with other modalities is not known. Similarly, it is unclear which smokers benefit from intensive behavioral programs in addition to pharmacological programs, or if there are certain types of smokers who would benefit more from, or certain points in a smoker's "career" when, behavioral treatments are more useful than pharmacological ones.

The proportion of ex-smokers to current smokers is increasing (*Report of the Surgeon General*, U.S. PHS, 1988). It seems likely that the smokers remaining will be more physically or behaviorally dependent on cigarettes than those who have quit. The net results will be treatment subpopulations that require more intensive treatment techniques that are targeted at the barriers to quitting. Specific examples are smokers who experience troubling weight gains after quitting, or those who need alternative ways of regulating the dysphoric affect. Both behavioral and pharmacological treatments need to be developed that address these special needs.

REFERENCES

Abrams, D. B., & Wilson, G. T. (1979). Self-monitoring and reactivity in the modification of cigarette smoking. *Journal of Consulting and Clinical Psychology, 47*, 243-251.

Barbarin, O. A. (1978). Comparison of symbolic and overt aversion in the self-control of smoking. *Journal of Consulting and Clinical Psychology, 46*, 1569-1571.

Benfari, R. C., & Eaker, E. (1984). Cigarette smoking outcomes at four years of follow-up, psychosocial factors, and reaction to group interventions. *Journal of Clinical Psychology, 40*, 1089-1097.

Benowitz, N. L. (1987). The use of biological fluid samples in assessing tobacco smoke consumption. In J. Grabowski & C. S. Bell (Eds.), *Measurement in the analysis and treatment of smoking behavior* (pp. 6-25). Rockville, MD: National Institute on Drug Abuse.

Benowitz, N. L., Hall, S. M., Herning, R. I., Jacob, P., Jones, R. T., & Osman, A. L. (1983). Smokers of low-yield cigarettes do not consume less nicotine. *New England Journal of Medicine, 309*, 139-142.

Berecz, J. M. (1979). The reduction of cigarette smoking through self-administered wrist band aversion therapy. *Behavior Therapy, 10*, 669-675.

Best, J. A., Owen, L. E., & Trentadue, L. (1978). Comparison of satiation and rapid smoking in self-managed smoking cessation. *Addictive Behaviors, 3*, 71-78.

Bowers, T. G., Winett, R. A. & Fredericksen, L. W. (1987). Nicotine fading, behavioral contracting, and extended treatment effects on smoking cessation. *Addictive Behaviors, 12*, 181-184.

Brandon, T. H., Zelman, D. C., & Baker, T. B. (1987). Effects of maintenance session on smoking relapse: Delaying the inevitable? *Journal of Consulting and Clinical Psychology, 55*, 780-782.

Brantmark, B., Ohlin, P., & Westling, H. (1973). Nicotine-containing chewing gum as an anti-smoking aid. *Psychopharmacologia, 31*, 191-200.

British Thoracic Society. (1983). Comparing four methods of smoking withdrawal in patients with smoking-related diseases. *British Medical Journal, 286*, 595-597.

Brown, R. A., Lichtenstein, E., McIntyre, K. O., & Harrington-Kostur, J. (1984). Effects of nicotine fading and relapse prevention on smoking cessation. *Journal of Consulting and Clinical Psychology, 52,* 3087-3088.

Burse, R. L., Bynum, G. D., Pandolf, K. B., Goldman, R. F., Simms, E. A. H., & Danforth, E. R. (1982). Increased appetite and unchanged metabolism upon cessation of smoking with diet held constant. *The Physiologist, 18,* 157.

Carroll, M. E., & Meisch, R. A. (1984). Increased drug-reinforced behavior due to food deprivation. In T. Thompson, P. B. Dews, & J. E. Barrett (Eds.), *Advances in behavioral pharmacology* (pp. 47-88). New York: Academic Press.

Christen, A. G., McDonald, J. L., Olson, B. L., Drook, C. A., & Stookey, G. K. (1984). Efficacy of nicotine chewing gum in facilitating smoking cessation. *Journal of the American Dental Association, 108,* 594-597.

Coan, R. W. (1967). Research strategy in the investigation of personality correlates. In S. V. Zagona (Ed.), *Studies and issues in smoking behavior* (pp. 133-141). Tucson: University of Arizona Press.

Dallosso, H. M., & James, W. P. T. (1984). The role of smoking in the regulation of energy balance. *International Journal of Obesity, 8,* 365-375.

Danaher, B. G. (1977a). Rapid smoking and self-control in the modification of smoking behavior. *Journal of Consulting and Clinical Psychology, 45,* 1068-1075.

Danaher, B. G. (1977b). Research on rapid smoking: Interim summary and recommendations. *Addictive Behaviors, 2,* 151-166.

Danaher, B. G., Jeffery, R. W., Zimmerman, R., & Nelson, E. (1980). Aversive smoking using printed instructions and audiotape adjuncts. *Addictive Behaviors, 5,* 353-358.

Davis, J. R., & Glaros, A. G. (1986). Relapse prevention and smoking cessation. *Addictive Behaviors, 11,* 105-114.

DeWit, H., & Camic, P. M. (1986). Behavioral and pharmacological treatment of cigarette smoking: End of treatment comparisons. *Addictive Behaviors, 11,* 331-335.

Fagerstrom, K. O. (1978). Measuring degree of physical dependence to tobacco smoking with reference to individualization of treatment. *Addictive Behaviors, 3,* 235-241.

Fagerstrom, K. O. (1982). A comparison of psychological and pharmacological treatment in smoking cessation. *Journal of Behavioral Medicine, 5,* 343-351.

Fagerstrom, K. O. (1984). Effects of nicotine chewing gum and follow-up appointments in physician-based smoking cessation. *Preventive Medicine, 13,* 517-527.

Fagerstrom, K. O. (1987). Reducing the weight gain after stopping smoking. *Addictive Behaviors, 12,* 91-93.

Fee, W. M., & Stewart, M. J. (1982). A controlled trial of nicotine chewing gum in a smoking withdrawal clinic. *The Practitioner, 226,* 150-151.

Flaxman, J. (1978). Affect management and habit mechanism in the modification of smoking behavior. *Addictive Behaviors, 4,* 39-46.

Foxx, R. M., & Axelroth, E. (1983). Nicotine fading, self-monitoring, and cigarette fading to produce cigarette abstinence or controlled smoking. *Behaviour Research and Therapy, 21,* 17-27.

Foxx, R. M., & Brown, R. A. (1979). Nicotine fading and self-monitoring for cigarette abstinence or controlled smoking. *Journal of Applied Behavior Analysis, 12,* 111-125.

Gilman, A. G., Goodman, L. S., Rall, T. W., & Murad, F. (1985). *Goodman and Gilman's, the Pharmacological Basis of Therapeutics* (7th ed.) New York: Macmillan.

Ginsberg, D., Hall, S. M., & Rosinski, M. (1988). *Nicotine gum, psychological treatment, and partner support: An incremental study.* Poster session presented at the annual meeting of the Society of Behavioral Medicine, Boston.

Glasgow, R. E. (1978). Effects of self-control manual, rapid smoking, and the amount of therapist contact on smoking reduction. *Journal of Consulting and Clinical Psychology, 46,* 1439-1447.

Glassman, A. H., Jackson, W. K., Walsh, B. T., & Roose, S. P. (1984). Cigarette craving, smoking withdrawal, and clonidine. *Science, 226,* 864-866.

Glassman, A. H., Stetner, F., Walsh, T., et al. (1988). Heavy smokers, smoking cessation, and clonidine. *Journal of the American Medical Association, 259,* 2863-2866.

Glauser, S. C., Glauser, E. M., Reindenberg, M. M., Rusy, B. F., & Tallarida, R. J. (1970). Metabolic changes associated with the cessation of cigarette smoking. *Archives of Environmental Health, 20,* 337-381.

Gritz, E. R., Carr, C. R., & Marcus, A. C. (in press). Unaided smoking cessation: Great American Smokeout and New Year's Day Quitters. *Psychosocial Oncology.*

Grunberg, N. E. (1982). Effects of nicotine on cigarette smoking and food consumption and taste preferences. *Addictive Behaviors, 1,* 371-331.

Grunberg, N. E. (1985). Behavioral and biological factors in the relationship between tobacco use and body weight. In E. S. Katkin & S. B. Manuck (Eds.), *Advances in behavioral medicine* (Vol. 2). Greenwich, CT: JAI.

Grunberg, N. E., Bowen, D. J., Maycock, V. A., & Nespor, S. M. (1985). *The importance of sweet taste and caloric content in the effects of nicotine on specific food consumption.* Unpublished manuscript.

Guilford, J. S. (1966). *Factors related to successful abstinence from smoking: Final report.* Washington, DC: U.S. Public Health Service, Division of Chronic Diseases, Bureau of State Services.

Hall, R. G., Sachs, D. P. L., & Hall, S. M. (1979). Medical risk and therapeutic effectiveness of rapid smoking. *Behavior Therapy, 10,* 249-259.

Hall, R. G., Sachs, D. P. L., Hall, S. M., & Benowitz, N. L. (1984). Two-year efficacy and safety of rapid smoking therapy in patients with cardiac and pulmonary disease. *Journal of Consulting and Clinical Psychology, 52,* 574-581.

Hall, S. M. (1980). Self-management and therapeutic maintenance: Theory and research. In P. Karoly & J. Steffan (Eds.), *Improving the long-term effects of psychotherapy* (pp. 263-300). New York: Gardner.

Hall, S. M., Bachman, J., Henderson, J. B., Barstow, R., & Jones, R. T. (1983). Smoking cessation in patients with cardiopulmonary disease: An initial study. *Addictive Behaviors, 8,* 33-42.

Hall, S. M., Ginsberg, D., & Jones, R. T. (1986). Smoking cessation and weight gain. *Journal of Consulting and Clinical Psychology, 54,* 342-346.

Hall, S. M., & Hall R. G. (1987). Treatment of cigarette smoking. In J. A. Blumenthal & D. C. McKee (Eds.), *Applications in behavioral medicine and health psychology: A clinician's source book* (pp. 301-323). Sarasota: Professional Research Exchange.

Hall, S. M., Herning, R. I., Jones, R. T., Benowitz, N. L., & Jacob, P. (1984). Blood cotinine levels as indicators of smoking treatment outcome. *Clinical Pharmacology and Therapeutics, 35,* 810-814.

Hall, S. M., McGee, R., Tunstall, C. D., Duffy, J. S., & Benowitz, N. (1989). Changes in food intake and activity after quitting smoking. *Journal of Consulting and Clinical Psychology, 57,* 81-86.

Hall, S. M., Rugg, D., Tunstall, C. D., & Jones R. T. (1984). Preventing relapse to cigarette smoking by behavioral skill training. *Journal of Consulting and Clinical Psychology, 52,* 372-382.

Hall, S. M., Tunstall, C. D., Ginsberg, D., Benowitz, N. L., & Jones, R. T. (1987). Nicotine gum and behavioral treatment: A placebo-controlled trial. *Journal of Consulting and Clinical Psychology, 55,* 603-605.

Hall, S. M., Tunstall, C. D., Ginsberg, D., & Jones, R. T. (1985). Double-blind, placebo-controlled trial of nicotine gum and psychological treatment. *Pharmacology, Biochemistry & Behavior, 22,* 1079-1088.

Hall, S. M., Tunstall, C. D., Rugg, D., Jones, R. T., & Benowitz, N. (1985). Nicotine gum and behavioral treatment in smoking cessation. *Journal of Consulting and Clinical Psychology, 53*, 256-258.

Harris, D. E., & Lichtenstein, E. (1971). *Contribution of nonspecific social variables to a successful behavioral treatment of smoking.* Paper presented at the meeting of the Western Psychological Association, San Francisco.

Hatsukami, D. K., Hughes, J. R., & Pickens, R. W. (1985). Characterization of tobacco withdrawal: Physiological and subjective effects. In J. Grabowski & S. M. Hall (Eds.), *Pharmacological adjuncts in smoking cessation* (pp. 56-67). Rockville, MD: National Institute on Drug Abuse.

Hatsukami, D. K., Hughes, J. R., Pickens, R. W., & Svikis, D. (1984). Tobacco withdrawal symptoms: An experimental analysis. *Psychopharmacology, 84*, 231-236.

Henningfield, J. E., & Jasinski, D. R. (1988). Pharmacologic basis for nicotine replacement. In Pomerleau & Pomerleau (Eds.), *Nicotine replacement: A critical evaluation* (pp. 35-62). New York: Alan R. Liss.

Hjalmarson, A. I. M. (1984). Effect of nicotine chewing gum in smoking cessation: A randomized, placebo-controlled, double-blind study. *Journal of the American Medical Association, 252*, 2835-2838.

Hofstetter, A., Schutz, Y., Jequier, E., & Wahren, J. (1986). Increased 24-hour energy expenditure in cigarette smokers. *New England Journal of Medicine, 314*, 79-82.

Holmes, T. H., & Rahe, R. H. (1967). The social readjustment rating scale. *Journal of Psychosomatic Research, 11*, 213-218.

Hughes, J. R., Gust, S. W., & Pechacek, T. F. (1987). Prevalence of tobacco dependence and withdrawal. *American Journal of Psychiatry, 144*, 205-208.

Hymowitz, N., Lasser, N. L., & Safirstein, B. H. (1982). Effects of graduated external filters on smoking cessation. *Preventive Medicine, 11*, 85-95.

Jacobs, M. A. (1972). The addictive personality: Predictions of success in a smoking withdrawal program. *Psychosomatic Medicine, 34*, 30-38.

Jamrozik, K., Fowler, G., Vessey, M., & Wald, N. (1984). Placebo-controlled trial of nicotine chewing gum in general practice. *British Medical Journal, 289*, 794-797.

Jarvik, M. E., & Henningfield, J. E. (in press). Pharmacologic treatment of tobacco dependence. *Pharmacology, Biochemistry and Behavior.*

Jarvik, M. E., & Schneider, N. G. (1984). Degree of addiction and effectiveness of nicotine gum therapy for smoking. *American Journal of Psychiatry, 141*, 790-791.

Jarvis, M. J., Raw, M., Russell, M. A. H., & Feyerabend, C. (1982). Randomised controlled trial of nicotine chewing-gum. *British Medical Journal, 285*, 537-540.

Jasinski, D. R., & Henningfield, J. E. (1988). Conceptual basis of replacement therapies for chemical dependence. In Pomerleau & Pomerleau (Eds.), *Nicotine replacement: A critical evaluation* (pp. 13-34). New York: Alan R. Liss.

Karas, A., & Kane, J. M. (1980). Naloxone reduces cigarette smoking. *Life Sciences, 27*, 1541-1545.

Killen, J. D., Maccoby, N., & Taylor, C. B. (1984). Nicotine gum and self-regulation training in smoking relapse prevention. *Behavior Therapy, 15*, 234-248.

Knutson, A. L. (1952). Personal security as related to station in life. *Psychological Monographs, 66*, 336.

Kozlowski, L. T. (1979). Psychosocial influences on cigarette smoking. In N. A. Krasnegor (Ed.), *The behavioral aspects of smoking.* Washington, DC: Department of Health, Education and Welfare.

Lando, H. A., Kalb, E. A., & McGovern, P. G. (in press). Behavioral self-help materials as an adjunct to nicotine chewing gum. *Additive Behaviors.*

Lando, H. A., & McCullough, J. A. (1978). Clinical application of a broad-spectrum behavioral approach to chronic smokers. *Journal of Consulting and Clinical Psychology, 46,* 1583-1585.

Lando, H. A., & McGovern, P. G. (1982). Three year data on a behavioral treatment for smoking: A follow-up role. *Addictive Behaviors, 1,* 143-154.

Lando, H. A., & McGovern, P. G. (1985). Nicotine fading as a non-aversive alternative in a broad spectrum treatment for elementary smoking. *Addictive Behaviors, 10,* 153-161.

Leventhal, H., & Cleary, P. D. (1980). The smoking problem: A review of the research and theory in behavioral role modification. *Psychological Bulletin, 88,* 370-405.

Lichtenstein, E., Antonuccio, D. O., & Rainwater, G. (1977). *Unkicking the habit: The resumption of cigarette smoking.* Seattle, WA: Western Psychological Association.

Lichtenstein, E., & Glasgow, R. E. (1977). Rapid smoking: Side effects and safeguards. *Journal of Consulting and Clinical Psychology, 45,* 815-821.

Lichtenstein, E., Harris, D. E., Birchler, G. R., Wahl, J. M., & Schmahl, D. P. (1973). Comparison of rapid smoking, warm, smoky air, and attention placebo in the modification of smoking behavior. *Journal of Consulting and Clinical Psychology, 40,* 92-98.

Malcolm, R. E., Sillett, R. W., Turner, M., & Ball, K. P. (1980). The use of nicotine chewing gum as an aid to stopping smoking. *Psychopharmacology, 70,* 295-296.

Marlatt, G. A., & Gordon, J. R. (1980). Determinants of relapse: Implications of the maintenance of behavior change. In P. O. Davidson & S. M. Davidson (Eds.), *Behavioral medicine: Changing health lifestyles.* New York: Brunner/Mazel.

McArthur, C., Waldron, E., & Dickenson, J. (1958). The psychology of smoking. *Journal of Abnormal Psychology, 56,* 267-275.

McFall, R. M., & Hammen, C. L. (1971). Motivation, structure, & self-monitoring: Role of non-specific factors in smoking reduction. *Journal of Consulting and Clinical Psychology, 37,* 80-86.

Miller, L. C., Schilling, A. F., Logan, D. L., & Johnson, R. L. (1977). Potential hazards of rapid smoking as a technique for the modification of smoking behavior. *New England Journal of Medicine, 297,* 590-592.

Moss, R. A., Prue, D. M., Lomax, D., & Martin, J. E. (1982). Implications of self-monitoring for smoking treatment: Effects on adherence and session attendance. *Addictive Behaviors, 7,* 381-386.

Nicki, R. M., Remington, R. E., & McDonald, G. A. (1984). Self-efficacy, nicotine fading, self-monitoring, and cigarette smoking behavior. *Behavioral Research and Therapy, 22* (5), 477-485.

Norton, G. R., & Barske, B. (1977). The role of aversion in the rapid-smoking treatment procedure. *Addictive Behaviors, 2,* 21-25.

Ohlin, P., & Westling, H. (1972). Nicotine-containing chewing gum as a substitute for smoking. In R. G. Richardson (Ed.), *The Second World Conference on Smoking and Health* (pp. 171-174). London: Pitman.

Paxton, R. (1980). The effects of a deposit contract as a component in a behavioral program for stopping smoking. *Behaviour Research and Therapy, 18,* 45-50.

Pechacek, T. F., & McAlister, A. L. (1980). Strategies for the modification of smoking behavior: Treatment and prevention. *The Comprehensive Handbook of Behavioral Medicine, 3,* 257-298.

Pederson, L. L., & Lefcoe, N. M. (1976). A psychological and behavioral comparison of ex-smokers and smokers. *Journal of Chronic Disease, 29,* 431-434.

Pomerleau, O. F., Adkins, D., & Pertschuk, M. (1978). Prediction of outcome and recidivism in smoking cessation treatment. *Addictive Behaviors, 3,* 65-70.

Pomerleau, O. F., & Pomerleau, C. S. (1977). *Break the smoking habit: A behavioral program for giving up cigarettes.* Champaign, IL: Research Press.

Prue, D. M., Davis, C. J., Marden, J. E., & Moss, R. A. (1983). An investigation of a minimal contact brand fading program for smoking treatment. *Addictive Behaviors, 8,* 307-310.

Puska, P., Björkquist, S., & Koskela, K. (1979). Nicotine-containing chewing gum in smoking cessation: A double-blind trial with half-year follow-up. *Addictive Behaviors, 4,* 141-146.

Raw, M., Jarvis, M. J., Feyerabend, C., & Russell, M. A. H. (1980). Comparison of nicotine chewing gum and psychological treatment for dependent symptoms. *British Medical Journal, 281,* 481-482.

Raw, M., & Russell, M. A. H. (1980). Rapid smoking, cue exposure and support in the modification of smoking. *Behaviour Research and Therapy, 18,* 363-372.

Robinson, S., & York, D. A. (1986). The effect of cigarette smoking on the thermic response to feeding. *International Journal of Obesity, 10,* 407-417.

Rodin, J. (1987). Weight change following smoking cessation: The role of food intake and exercise. *Addictive Behaviors, 12,* 303-317.

Russell, M. A. H., Jarvis, M. J., Feyerabend, C., & Russell. (1983). *British Medical Journal, 286,* 683-684.

Russell, M. A. H., Raw, M., & Jarvis, M. J. (1980). Clinical use of nicotine chewing gum. *British Medical Journal, 280,* 1599-1602.

Russell, M. A. H., Merriman, R., Stapleton, J., & Taylor, W. (1983). Effect of nicotine chewing gum as an adjunct to general practitioners' advice against smoking. *British Medical Journal, 287,* 1782-1785.

Russell, M. A. H., Raw, M., Taylor, C., Feyerabend, C., & Saloojee, Y. (1978). Blood nicotine and carboxyhemoglobin levels after rapid-smoking aversion therapy. *Journal of Consulting and Clinical Psychology, 46,* 1423-1431.

Russell, M. A. H., Wilson, Feyerabend, C., & Cole. (1976). Effects of nicotine chewing gum on smoking behavior and as an aid to cigarette withdrawal. *British Medical Journal, 76*(2), 391-393.

Sachs, D. P. L., Hall, R. G., & Hall, S. M. (1978). Effects of rapid smoking: Physiologic evaluation of a smoking cessation therapy. *Annals of Internal Medicine, 88,* 639-641.

Schmahl, D. P., Lichtenstein, E., & Harris, D. E. (1972). Successful treatment of habitual smokers with warm, smoky air and rapid smoking. *Journal of Consulting and Clinical Psychology, 38,* 105-111.

Schneider, N. G., Jarvik, M. E., Forsythe, A. B., Read, L. L., Elliott, M. L., & Schweiger, A. (1983). Nicotine gum in smoking cessation: A placebo-controlled, double-blind trial. *Addictive Behaviors, 8,* 253-261.

Schwartz, J. L. (1987). *Review and evaluation of smoking control methods: The United States and Canada, 1978-1985.* Washington, DC: U.S. Department of Health and Human Services, Public Health Service, National Cancer Institute, Division of Cancer Prevention and Control. (NIH Publication No. 87-2940)

Schwartz, J. L., & Dubitsky, M. (1968). Requisites for success in smoking withdrawal. In E. F. Borgatta & R. R. Evans (Eds.), *Smoking, health and behavior* (pp. 321-247). Chicago: Aldine.

Shiffman, S. (1982). Relapse following smoking cessation: A situational analysis. *Journal of Consulting and Clinical Psychology, 50,* 71-86.

Stamford, B. A., Matter, S., Fell, R. D., Sady, S., Cresanta, M. K., & Papanek, P. (1984). Cigarette smoking, physical activity, and alcohol consumption: Relationship to blood lipids and lipoproteins in premenopausal females. *Metabolism: Clinical and Experimental, 33,* 585-590.

Stitzer, M. L., & Bigelow, G. E. (1982). Contingent reinforcement for reduced carbon monoxide levels in cigarette smokers. *Addictive Behaviors, 7,* 403-412.

Straits, R. C. (1967). Discontinuation of cigarette smoking: A multiple discriminant analysis. In S. V. Zagone (Ed.), *Studies and issues in smoking behavior* (pp. 79-81). Tucson: University of Arizona Press.

Tennant, F. S., Tarver, A. L., & Rawson, R. A. (1983). Clinical evaluation of mecamylamine for withdrawal from nicotine dependence. In L. S. Harris (Ed.), *Problems of drug dependence, 1983: NIDA Research Monograph 49.* Washington, DC: Government Printing Office.

Tiffany, S. T., Martin, E. M., & Baker, T. B. (1986). Treatment for cigarette smoking: An evaluation of the contributions of aversion and counseling procedures. *Behaviour Research and Therapy, 24,* 437-452.

Tompkins, S. S. (1966). Psychological model for smoking behavior. *American Journal of Public Health, 56,* (Supp.) 17-20.

Tonnesen, P., Fryd, V., Hansen, M., Helsted, J., Gunnersen, A. B., Forchammer, H., & Stockner, M. (1988). Effect of nicotine chewing gum in combination with group counseling on the cessation of smoking. *New England Journal of Medicine, 318*(1), 15-18.

Tori, C. D. (1978). A smoking satiation procedure with reduced medical risk. *Journal of Clinical Psychology, 34,* 574-577.

Tunstall, C. D., Ginsberg, D., & Hall, S. M. (1984). Quitting smoking. *International Journal of the Addictions, 20,* 1089-1112.

U.S. PHS [U.S. Department of Health and Human Services]. (1980). *The health consequences of smoking for women: A Report of the Surgeon General.* Rockville, MD: Office on Smoking and Health.

U.S. PHS [U.S. Department of Health and Human Services]. (1988). *The health consequences of smoking nicotine addiction: A Report of the Surgeon General.* Washington DC: Government Printing Office.

COGNITIVE-BEHAVIORAL APPROACHES TO PERSONALITY DISORDERS

BARBARA FLEMING
Case Western Reserve University
School of Medicine, Department of Psychiatry

JAMES L. PRETZER
Case Western Reserve University
School of Medicine, Department of Family Medicine

Personality disorders are among the most difficult and least understood problems faced by therapists, and the treatment of clients with these disorders is often complex, time-consuming, and frustrating. However, these disorders are relatively common, constituting up to 50% of all cases seen in some clinical centers (Turkat & Maisto, 1985). It has been asserted that particular personality disorders are a major source of negative outcome in psychotherapy (Mays & Franks, 1985) and that at least some personality disorders are not responsive to cognitive-behavioral interventions (Rush & Shaw, 1983). Despite the apparent importance of developing behavioral approaches to understanding and treating personality disorders, efforts in this direction have been slow to develop until recently.

I. BEHAVIOR THERAPY AND THE
CONCEPT OF "PERSONALITY DISORDER"

Behaviorists have had a long tradition of rejecting the concept of personality, let alone personality disorder. As Marshall and Barbaree (1984, pp. 406-407) write

> No more than 15 years ago, a behavioral perspective of the personality disorders would have seemed far-fetched both to the proponents and opponents of behavioral analysis. . . . [T]he behavioral approach at that time saw learning as situationally specific so that it was anathema to suggest that personality disorders controlled behavior in various settings.

In a well-known paper that has frequently been cited by behaviorists in challenging their non-behavioral colleagues, Mischel (1969) argued that there was little empirical basis for the view that personality traits have a significant influence on individuals' behavior across a range of situations. However, a number of well-designed studies have subsequently demonstrated that "personality" variables can indeed account for a significant amount of behavioral variance (Block, 1971, 1977; Epstein, 1979; Olweus, 1977) but that there are wide variations in both the extent to which individuals demonstrate behavioral consistency across situations and the domains in which individuals demonstrate behavioral consistency (Endler & Magnusson, 1976; Epstein, 1979).

It is not difficult to develop possible explanations for behavioral consistencies across situations within the framework of established behavioral concepts. For example, complex, intermittent reinforcement schedules can establish behaviors that are quite persistent despite later changes in contingencies; aversive conditioning can establish avoidance behaviors that generalize to new stimulus situations; and dysfunctional beliefs and assumptions can affect behavior across a range of relevant situations. As Mischel (1973, p. 255) later wrote, "No one suggests that the organism approaches every new situation with an empty head, nor is it questioned by anyone that different individuals differ markedly in how they deal with most stimulus conditions."

Another problem for the behaviorist is that the term *personality disor-*

der implies that the individual who is so diagnosed "has" a "personality" that is "disordered" and that his or her problems result from this disordered personality. However, personality disorders have been defined in DSM-III-R as "enduring patterns of perceiving, relating to, and thinking about the environment and oneself," which "are exhibited in a wide range of important social and personal contexts" and "are inflexible and maladaptive and cause either significant functional impairment or subjective distress" (APA, 1987, p. 335). While the term "personality disorder" currently has some problematic connotations, and it is understandable that many behaviorists see the choice of the term as an unfortunate one, this definition of personality disorder is actually quite compatible with behavioral perspectives. It seems clear that a substantial number of clients do manifest relatively stable behavior patterns that satisfy DSM-III-R criteria for personality disorder diagnoses. Because clinicians, including behavioral clinicians, are faced with the task of trying to help these individuals and, just like clinicians using other approaches, behavioral clinicians find them difficult to treat, personality disorders are a legitimate and important area for further research.

II. THE EFFECTIVENESS OF SYMPTOMATIC TREATMENT OF PERSONALITY DISORDERS

The problematic behaviors and symptoms characteristic of clients diagnosed as having personality disorders, such as impulsive behavior, poor social skills, and inappropriate expression of anger, are not unique to these individuals; and behavioral treatments for such problems have received considerable empirical support. One commonsense approach to the behavioral treatment of clients with personality disorders is simply to apply established behavioral interventions to one symptom after another. One example of this type of approach is that advocated by Stephens and Parks (1981). They discuss treating these clients symptom by symptom, without presenting any broader conceptualization of personality disorders and without discussion as to whether treatment of these symptoms in clients with personality disorders differs from the treatment of these symptoms in other clients. Stephens and Parks cite empirical evidence of the efficacy of behavioral interventions for the treatment of each of the 10 categories of maladaptive behavior that they see as characterizing the personality disorders. However, they note that the vast majority of the studies cited were conducted either with subjects *not* diagnosed as having personality disorders or with subjects having a variety of diagnoses, including some subjects with personality disorders. Obviously, the finding that a particular symptom or problematic behavior can be treated effectively in a heterogeneous sample of subjects does not necessarily imply that the intervention in question will be equally effective when applied with clients diagnosed as having personality disorders. Two outcome studies have examined the effectiveness of standard behavioral treatment for subjects diagnosed as having personality disorders as compared with subjects without personality disorders. In a study of the cognitive-behavioral treatment of social phobia, Turner (1987) found that patients without personality disorders improved markedly after a 15-week group treatment and maintained their gains at a one-year follow-up. However, patients with personality disorder diagnoses in addition to their social phobias showed little or no improvement either posttreatment or at the one-year follow-up. Turner (1987, p. 142) concludes

> In summary, the present pilot data suggest that what is an effective treatment for a social phobia is not necessarily an effective treatment for a social phobia mixed with a personality disorder. . . . If the results of this study can be cross-validated under more exacting conditions, then behavior therapists' long-standing opposition to the concept of personality disturbance will require rethinking. This would be a major change in behavioral psychotherapy theory and practice.

In a study of the effects of personality disorder on the treatment of agoraphobia, Mavissakalian and Hamman (1987) found that 75% of subjects rated as being low in personality disorder characteristics responded well to a time-limited behavioral and pharmacological treatment, while only 25% of the subjects rated as being high in personality disorder characteristics responded to this treatment. They also found that four of seven subjects who had met diagnostic criteria for a single personality disorder diagnosis before treatment no longer met criteria for a personality disorder diagnosis following treatment, while subjects who had been diagnosed as having more than one personality disorder tended to merit either the same diagnoses or different personality disorder diagnoses following treatment. In addition, Mavissakalian and Hamman found that all personality disorders were not equally responsive or resistant to treatment. Characteristics associated with borderline, dependent, and passive-aggressive personality disorders were most affected by treatment for agoraphobia, while characteristics associated with histrionic and avoidant personality disorders showed little change.

In both of these outcome studies, the majority of individuals with personality disorder diagnoses were not responsive to well-established behavioral treatments, suggesting that the effectiveness of behavioral interventions with standard samples cannot be assumed to generalize to samples of persons diagnosed as having personality disorders. However, despite these generally poor results, behavioral interventions were effective with at least some individuals with personality disorders. When behavioral interventions were effective, broad changes in many aspects of the person's life were achieved rather than the improvement being confined to specific problem behaviors.

III. APPROACHES TO CONCEPTUALIZING AND TREATING PERSONALITY DISORDERS

In recent years, a number of authors have worked to develop behavioral and cognitive-behavioral theories of personality disorders in the hope that coherent conceptualizations of these disorders would lead to more effective treatment strategies than result from a symptomatic approach to treatment. One theory that might appear to be cognitive-behavioral at first glance is Millon's "biosocial-learning theory," which has influenced much of the contemporary work on personality disorders, including the categories of DSM-III. In his comprehensive work on personality disorders, Millon (1981) emphasizes the role of "vicious circles" in which the cognitive, affective, and behavioral aspects of personality disorders perpetuate each other and result in the disorders being persistent and inflexible. His work is vividly descriptive, and many of his concepts can be translated into cognitive-behavioral terminology. However, Millon considers himself to be psychoanalytically oriented (Millon, 1987) and, while he frequently discusses the effects of social learning, his views of some of the personality disorders include psychodynamic concepts that are not compatible with a behavioral approach.

In a more purely behavioral approach, Turner and Hersen (1981) and Marshall and Barbaree (1984) conceptualize personality disorders as disorders of social behavior acquired in accord with operant conditioning and social learning principles. They argue that through complex, combined schedules of both direct and vicarious reinforcement and punishment, behavior patterns are established that generalize across situations and that can be quite persistent. This perspective asserts that personality disorders are acquired and maintained in the same ways as other interpersonal behavior and that persons with personality disorders differ from other persons primarily in terms of their learning history. It suggests that, in order to treat personality disorders effectively, it is necessary to help the client master the social skills needed for adaptive social behavior and to modify naturally occurring contingencies so that adaptive social behavior will be established and maintained.

Turner and Hersen (1981) cite a number of studies in support of their perspective on personality disorders. These studies show that contingency management can produce persistent behavioral improvement with institutionalized offenders and juvenile delinquents, that social skills training can be used effectively with individuals labeled passive-aggressive, aggressive, or explosive, and that a combined behavioral treatment can be effective with individuals diagnosed as having histrionic personality disorder. However, as with Stephens and Parks (1981), most of the subjects in the studies cited were not shown to meet DSM-III criteria for personality disorder diagnoses, and, therefore, it is difficult to determine if the interventions used in these studies provide an effective and sufficient treatment for individuals with personality disorders.

With the rise of cognitive-behavioral approaches in recent years, a number of concepts have emerged that may prove useful in understanding personality disorders. Many cognitive-behavioral theorists discuss both situation-specific cognitions, such as self-instructions or automatic thoughts, and cognitions that are believed to persist independent of specific situations, such as irrational beliefs, underlying assumptions, or schemas. The latter may have potential for playing an important role in a cognitive-behavioral conceptualization of personality disorders, because they are hypothesized to have important effects on cognition, emotion, and behavior across a range of relevant situations.

A number of authors have expanded established cognitive perspectives to apply directly to the personality disorders, including Padesky's (1986, 1988) adaptation of Beck's cognitive theory (Beck, 1976; Beck, Rush, Shaw, & Emery, 1979) and DiGiuseppe's (personal communication, 1988) work adapting Rational-Emotive Therapy to the treatment of personality disorders. Detailed cognitive-behavioral conceptualizations and treatment strategies for each of the personality disorders have been based on Beck's Cognitive Therapy (Beck & Freeman, in press; Fleming, 1983, 1985, 1988; Freeman, Pretzer, Fleming, & Simon, in press; Pretzer, 1983, 1985, 1988; Simon, 1983, 1985). These authors emphasize the interplay between cognition and interpersonal behavior, present rationales for choosing among possible intervention techniques, discuss ways to modify interventions to accommodate the characteristics of clients with different personality disorders, and suggest ways to resolve the interpersonal difficulties that commonly arise in therapy with clients with personality disorders.

Some cognitive-behavioral theorists argue that, in order to adequately account for the characteristics of individuals with personality disorders, it is necessary to modify existing cognitive theories. For example, Young (1987; Young & Swift, 1988) advocates adding an additional construct, which he terms "early maladaptive schemas," to Beck's cognitive model of psychopathology. Other theorists are developing cognitive perspectives on the personality disorders that are more independent of established cognitive-behavioral approaches. For example, Murray (1988) asserts that personality disorders can be understood in terms of a "core rubric" incorporating self-perception, worldview, and instructions for action. Each of the above views regarding the role of cognition in personality disorders suggests that the individual's dysfunctional beliefs, underlying assumptions, or early maladaptive schemas form the core of the disorder and thus should be the primary focus of intervention. These theorists have presented interesting conceptual papers and have discussed approaches to intervention that they have used in their own clinical practices. However, there is little empirical evidence that bears either on the adequacy of the conceptualizations they have developed or on the effectiveness of the treatment strategies they recommend.

Turkat and his colleagues (i.e., Turkat & Maisto, 1985) have developed the one empirically based cognitive-behavioral approach to the understanding and treatment of the various personality disorders. They use single-case experimental designs to test detailed formulations of individual clients' problems based on a thorough initial assessment. Specific hypotheses are then generated and tested using the most appropriate available measures. Then a treatment plan is developed on the basis of the case formulation, and, as this treatment plan is implemented, successful intervention is seen as validating the therapist's formulation of the case while unsuccessful interventions spur reevaluation of the formulation.

The results reported by Turkat and Maisto are summarized in Table 1. The case examples reported by these authors provide empirical evidence that behavioral interventions based on an individualized conceptualization can be effective, with both behavioral observation and established measures used to document changes at both posttest and follow-up in some of the cases. Careful reading of several of the cases shows that interventions based on an individualized conceptualization were effective when symptomatic treatment had not been effective, and, in addition, the results reported suggest that Turkat and Maisto's approach can provide a comprehensive treatment for clients with personality disorders rather than simply treating specific symptoms. However, the overall results shown in Table 1 make it clear that treatment was also ineffective with many personality disordered clients. The most common difficulties mentioned by the investigators were inability to develop a formulation-based treatment approach, subjects being unwilling to engage in treatment, and premature termination. While Turkat and his colleagues have presented individualized conceptualizations and strategies that were used with particular clients, they are cautious about generalizing these ideas to other individuals with the same diagnoses. Turkat's approach is quite promising, but this research program is in its initial phase with data published from only a limited sample.

Table 1 Personality Disorder Cases Reported by Turkat and Maisto (1985)

Personality Disorder	N	Percentage of a Sample	N with Outcome Reported	Reported Outcome	Type of Outcome Data
Antisocial	2	2.7	2	Ss not interested in treatment	
Avoidant	4	5.4	1	Gradual improvement over 2 years of treatment	Anecdotal
Borderline	1	1.4	1	Discontinued treatment prematurely	
Compulsive	6	8.1	5	Ss unwilling to engage in treatment	
Dependent	1	1.4	1	Decreased anxiety, avoidance, & depression; increased independence	Self-ratings on hierarchy items, 1-year follow-up
Histrionic	8	10.8	1	Unable to develop formulation & treatment plan	
Narcissistic	2	2.7	1	Improved mood, impulse control, & compliance but terminated prematurely	Self-report, observation
Paranoid	8	10.8	1	Improved social skills & tolerance of criticism; decreased defensiveness	Self-report, observation
Passive-Aggressive	1	1.4	1	Unable to develop formulation & treatment plan	
Schizoid	2	2.7	2	Unable to develop formulation & treatment plan	
Schizotypal	0	0			
Total	35	47.4			

a. The total sample consisted of 74 patients seen in a clinical psychology service housed in a diabetes research and training center.

IV. THEORY AND RESEARCH ON SPECIFIC PERSONALITY DISORDERS

Mavissakalian and Hamman's (1987) finding that some personality disorders were more strongly affected by a behavioral/pharmacological treatment for agoraphobia than others and the perspectives advocated by Turkat (Turkat & Maisto, 1985), and by Fleming, Pretzer, and their colleagues (Freeman, Pretzer, Fleming, & Simon, in press), suggest that it is important to develop conceptualizations and treatment approaches tailored to specific personality disorders. A comprehensive review of the literature on each of the personality disorders is beyond the scope of this chapter. The following sections highlight some of the major points raised in papers discussing the conceptualization and treatment of each of the major personality disorders.

A. Antisocial Personality Disorder

Antisocial personality disorder is distinguished from other personality disorders by the large volume of empirical research that has been conducted both on individuals with a history of antisocial behavior and on individuals diagnosed as "psychopaths" or "sociopaths" (Brantley & Sutker, 1984; Marshall & Barbaree, 1984; Sutker, Archer, & Kilpatrick, 1981). Much of the research that has been conducted is in areas that are not directly related to behavioral and cognitive-behavioral approaches to this disorder. The interested reader is referred to Brantley and Sutker (1984) for a review of the literature regarding the possible role of genetic and neurochemical factors, the hypothesized need for sociopaths to receive intense and variable stimulation in order to maintain positive affect, and the possible role of neurological abnormalities in this disorder.

A number of different investigators have presented conceptualizations of antisocial behavior or antisocial personality disorder based on social learning theory, and the models presented by Marshall and Barbaree (1984) and by Sutker, Archer, and Kilpatrick (1981) appear to represent a consensus view. It has been hypothesized that, as a result of excessively harsh but inconsistent discipline combined with a lack of reinforcement for prosocial behavior, the sociopath-to-be not only fails to acquire prosocial behavior but also may become desensitized to punishment, acquire oppositional behavior, and/or acquire strategies for avoiding punishment such as lying or expressing superficial repentance. In addition, these theorists suggest that environments in which consequences are administered inconsistently do not encourage development of skills such as the ability to anticipate the long-term consequences of one's actions, the ability to resist immediate temptations, or the ability to generalize previous experiences to novel situations. Finally, it is suggested that sociopaths have little or no experience with consistent, supportive, and affectionate relationships and thus fail to master the skills necessary for close relationships and fail to become conditioned to find interpersonal interaction and closeness reinforcing. Thus the view suggests that in addition to having acquired "bad" behavior and having failed to acquire "good" behavior, the sociopath fails to master some of the basic skills needed for effective prosocial behavior and close interpersonal relationships, being conditioned to experience interpersonal relationships as neutral or aversive rather than as reinforcing.

Much research relevant to social learning theory analyses of antisocial behavior and antisocial personality disorder has been conducted. Many studies, including both retrospective and longitudinal designs, have investigated the relationship between punishment and reinforcement received in childhood and later antisocial behavior, and have produced findings that are generally consistent with social learning theory analyses (see Marshall & Barbaree, 1984). In addition, a number of widely held beliefs about antisocial personality disorder have been challenged or modified by the results of empirical research. These include the view that sociopaths are unable to defer the gratification of emotions and impulses to action, and the belief that sociopaths lack the capacity to attend to social cues and be responsive to the interests of others (see Brantley & Sutker, 1984).

The conclusions reached by Brantley & Sutker (1984, p. 463) are noteworthy:

> Overall results suggest that sociopaths are characterized by highly effective, though perhaps maladaptive, resources for coping with threat of punishment and for obtaining self-determined goals even in the face of great obstacles. They may tend to maintain minimal levels of anxiety, and their failure to respond emotionally or autonomically to environmental cues that signal impending punishment very likely interferes with avoidance learning of the passive type. In addition, sociopaths' tendencies toward overresponsivity to exciting or stimulating situations render them more vulnerable to immediate reward or sensation-seeking activities (e.g., the hot pursuit of goals seen as important). In the excitement of their ventures and adventures, they are likely to overlook important environmental contingencies and to encounter punishment more frequently than normals. At the same time, they seem less disturbed by the possibility of continued negative consequences to their behaviors, although they are capable of articulating with accuracy the probability of sociolegal difficulties.

This view suggests that sociopaths actually have many strengths and capabilities that would work to their, and society's, benefit if only they could be induced to respond more adaptively to naturally occurring contingencies rather than being underresponsive to anticipation of negative contingencies and overresponsive to anticipation of positive contingencies. Sociopaths are generally considered untreatable, and until recently authorities have been uniformly pessimistic about the prospects for developing effective interventions (Brantley & Sutker, 1984). However, several recent studies have reported success in treating sociopaths. A number of authors have described residential treatment programs that are reported to have low recidivism rates and to improve many aspects of individual functioning (Carney, 1986; Matthews & Reid, 1986; Reid & Solomon, 1986). While these programs differ somewhat in both rationale and methods for treatment, they share an emphasis on establishing controlled environments where contingencies are clear, where positive contingencies for prosocial behavior are emphasized, and where cooperation and reliance on others are necessary and are reinforced.

Even more encouraging is a recent report demonstrating that short-term outpatient cognitive-behavioral therapy can be effective with at least some clients with antisocial personality disorder. In a study of the treatment of opiate addicts in a methadone maintainence program, Woody, McLellan, Luborsky, and O'Brien (1985) found that subjects who met DSM-III diagnostic criteria for both major depression and antisocial personality disorder responded well to short-term treatment with either Beck's Cognitive Therapy (Beck, Rush, Shaw, & Emery, 1979) or a supportive-expressive psychotherapy systematized by Luborsky (Luborsky, McLellan, Woody, O'Brien, & Auerbach, 1985). These subjects showed statistically significant improvement on 11 of 22 outcome variables used, including psychiatric symptoms, drug use, employment, and illegal activity. Subjects who met criteria for antisocial personality disorder but not major depression showed little response to treatment, improving on only 3 of 22 variables. This pattern of results was maintained at a seven-month follow-up. While subjects not diagnosed as having antisocial personality disorder responded to treatment better than the sociopaths did, sociopaths who were initially depressed did only slightly worse than the nonsociopaths while the nondepressed sociopaths did much worse. The finding that two quite dissimilar treatment approaches were both effective might suggest that the improvement was due to nonspecific treatment effects. However, the degree to which the therapist adhered to the relevant treatment manual was significantly correlated with the degree of improvement both across therapists and within each therapist's case load (Luborsky et al., 1985), providing evidence to the contrary.

B. Avoidant Personality Disorder

Although some authors have used the term *socially dysfunctional* as interchangeable with avoidant personality disorder, this disorder involves a great deal more than just a lack of social skills or simple social anxiety. In a recent study comparing subjects with avoidant personality disorder and subjects with a social phobia, Turner, Beidel, Dancu, and Keys (1986) found that the avoidant sample demonstrated less social skill and reported significantly more social avoidance and subjective distress, greater interpersonal sensitivity, and higher levels of anxiety, depression, and rumination than did social phobics.

Unfortunately, much of the existing literature on socially anxious individuals has not differentiated between subjects with avoidant personality disorder and other socially anxious subjects. For example, the review of the literature on avoidant personality disorder presented by Pilkonis (1984) provides a concise summary of studies regarding the treatment of social anxiety and interpersonal avoidance, but the studies cited utilized subjects ranging from shy undergraduates to psychotic inpatients, with few subjects clearly meeting diagnostic criteria for avoidant personality disorder. Obviously, the validity of generalizing the findings of such studies to individuals with avoidant personality disorder is open to question.

A number of authors have presented conceptualizations that are specific to avoidant personality disorder (Freeman et al., in press; Millon, 1981; Turkat & Maisto, 1985). The views presented by these authors are quite similar and seem to form a consensus view. Millon hypothesizes that avoidant personality disorder results from a lack of reinforcement for childhood attempts at interpersonal interaction combined with frequent experiences of rejection, ridicule, or humiliation, possibly aggravated by a constitutional tendency to withdraw in response to aversive stimulation. This is seen as resulting in the individual both learning to avoid interpersonal interaction and developing a conviction that he or she is unworthy, unattractive, and unlovable. The individual's subsequent avoidance of interpersonal interaction results in delayed acquisition of social skills due to inexperience, which increases the likelihood that any attempts at social interaction will go poorly and perpetuate the problem. The avoidant individual's social isolation is seen as being accompanied by self-derogatory thoughts, contributing to an anticipation of rejection or humiliation in interpersonal interaction and perpetuating the avoidance. Turkat and Maisto (1985) and Freeman et al. (in press) present similar models but emphasize somewhat different factors. Turkat and Maisto focus on the avoidant individual's excessive sensitivity to evaluation by others, while Freeman et al. emphasize the client's negative view of him- or herself, his or her strong negative expectations about interpersonal interactions, and his or her biased perceptions of interpersonal interactions.

These views of avoidant personality disorder suggest that, if either exposure-based treatments to reduce social anxiety or social skills training approaches are used alone, they are likely to be of limited effectiveness because they address only a few aspects of the disorder. As both Millon (1981) and Freeman et al. (in press) note, therapy itself is an interpersonal situation that the person with avoidant personality disorder is likely to find threatening and will tend to avoid. Thus it is important to handle the initial stages of therapy with delicacy to avoid premature termination. Millon suggests first working to increase the client's self-esteem, next using pharmacological or behavioral interventions to reduce the client's anxiety, then working to modify the client's negative expectations about social interactions and his or her negative beliefs about self, and finally working to improve the client's social skills and frequency of social interaction, preferably starting in a relatively benign situation such as group therapy. A similar treatment strategy is proposed by Freeman et al. (in press, chap. 12), and these authors provide a more detailed discussion of the implementation of such a strategy. Turkat and Maisto (1985) do not present a detailed treatment plan because the client they discuss was treated elsewhere for practical reasons, but these authors suggest focusing on reducing the individual's sensitivity to negative evaluation.

While the empirical evidence regarding avoidant personality disorder is quite limited, the evidence that is available supports the conceptualizations and treatment strategies presented above. In discussing the results of their comparison of socially phobic subjects with subjects with avoidant personality disorder, Turner, Beidel, Dancu, and Keys (1986) suggest that, while exposure-based interventions appear appropriate for social phobics, social skills training may be more effective with clients with avoidant personality disorder. Both short-term social skills training and social skills training combined with cognitive interventions have been demonstrated to be effective in increasing the frequency of social interaction and decreasing social anxiety in subjects with avoidant personality disorder (Stravynski, Marks, & Yule, 1982). Greenberg and Stravynski (1985) report that the avoidant client's fear of ridicule appears to contribute to premature termination in many cases and that it is necessary for social skills training to include strategies for responding to rejection and embarrassment as well as training in socially appropriate behavior. They suggest that interventions that modify relevant aspects of the client's cognitions might add substantially to the effectiveness of intervention but note that Stravynski, Marks, and Yule (1982) found that a combined social skills training and cognitive treatment was no more effective than social skills training alone. Although Stravynski et al. (1982) interpreted this finding as demonstrating the "lack of value" of cognitive interventions, it should be noted that all treatments were provided by a single therapist (who was also the principal investigator) and that only one of many possible cognitive interventions (disputation of irrational beliefs) was used.

C. Borderline Personality Disorder

Borderline personality disorder has received considerable attention in recent years, in part because it is a relatively common disorder that can be quite difficult to treat. Psychotherapy with individuals with borderline personality disorder is typically quite complicated, and there is a significant risk of negative psychotherapy outcome regardless of the treatment approach used (Mays, 1985). Straightforward application of behavioral techniques has been reported to be less effective with borderline clients than with others (Mays, 1985), and until quite recently it was believed that these clients could not be treated effectively with Cognitive Therapy (Rush & Shaw, 1983). However, a number of different cognitive-behavioral perspectives on this disorder have been presented in recent years.

Turner (1986) presents a "bio-social-learning" conceptualization of borderline personality disorder, which argues that maladaptive schemas and a biological predisposition toward low stress tolerance distort information processing. He advocates a multicomponent behavioral treatment approach in which a wide range of intervention strategies are applied systematically in the context of a firm, open, honest therapeutic alliance. Among the interventions he advocates are actively evoking emotions to increase the client's tolerance for affect, anxiety management training, social skills training, cognitive therapy, contingency management, and supportive psychotherapy. Turner states that cognitive-behavior therapy with this population must be seen as a long-term therapeutic process including a year or more of active intervention. He reports that, in his experience, traditional short-term behavior therapy is ineffective with borderline clients while the more long-term approach that he proposes has proven valuable in individual cases. However, no outcome data on his approach are available.

An approach to this disorder based on Beck's Cognitive Therapy has been presented by Pretzer (Freeman et al., in press; Pretzer, 1983). His view is based on the observation that the borderline individual typically holds three strong dysfunctional assumptions: that the world is a dangerous, malevolent place; that he or she is not capable of independently handling the demands of daily life; and that he or she is inherently unacceptable and will inevitably be rejected or abandoned by others. These assumptions are seen as presenting borderline individuals with an insoluble dilemma, because the second assumption blocks them from relying on their own coping skills to handle the dangers assumed to be inherent in daily life, while the third assumption blocks them from relying on others. It is theorized that, as a result, the borderline vacillates between attempts at self-reliance, attempts to assure support from significant others, and periods of crisis when this support seems to be at risk or unavailable. In addition, one particular cognitive distortion, dichotomous thinking, is hypothesized to intensify the individual's mood swings, play an important role in the erratic and extreme behavior for which this disorder is noted, and block the individual from finding an adaptive resolution to the dilemma that results from his or her dysfunctional beliefs. Pretzer argues that, to be effective, interventions must be used strategically, and he advocates systematically using a wide range of behavioral and cognitive-behavioral interventions. He suggests that it is often useful to focus initially on a fairly concrete problem that can be addressed behaviorally. This allows time to gradually work on the intricacies of the therapist-client relationship before addressing problems that require greater trust or self-disclosure on the part of the client. He emphasizes the importance of focusing particular attention on the therapist-client relationship in order to identify and modify dysfunctional interpersonal behavior, to provide experiences that contradict the client's dysfunctional beliefs, and to facilitate other interventions. Pretzer's approach is clinically based and has not been tested empirically.

Linehan (1987a, 1987b, 1987c) presents a third perspective on borderline personality disorder. She conceptualizes this disorder as being characterized by three bipolar behavior patterns, or "dialectics": (a) emotional vulnerability versus invalidation, (b) active passivity versus the apparently competent person, and (c) unrelenting crisis versus inhibited grieving. She hypothesizes that borderline personality disorder is a product of a biological defect in emotional regulation and a learning history that did not support adaptive expression of emotion. She proposes a treatment approach that she terms "Dialectical Behavior Therapy." This approach incorporates traditional behavioral interventions, including skill training (in emotion regulation, interpersonal effectiveness, distress tolerance, and self-management), collaborative problem solving, and contingency clarification and management. These are combined with an emphasis on what she calls "dialectical process" (i.e., communicating acceptance of the client, acknowledgment and validation of the client's strong emotions, a matter-of-fact attitude toward the client's dysfunctional behaviors, and persistently "reframing" the client's dysfunctional behavior as part of his or her learned problem-solving repertoire). Linehan and her colleagues (Linehan, Armstrong, Allmon, Suarez, & Miller, 1988; Linehan, Armstrong, Suarez, & Allmon, 1988) have recently completed an outcome study of Dialectical Behavior Therapy versus "treatment as usual" with a sample of chronically parasuicidal borderline subjects. They found that the patients in the Dialectical Behavior Therapy condition had a significantly lower dropout rate and significantly less self-injurious behavior but did not show significant overall improvement in depression or other symptomatology. While these results are modest, it is encouraging to find that one year of cognitive-behavioral treatment can produce lasting improvement with a sample of female subjects who not only met diagnostic criteria for borderline personality disorder but also were chronically parasuicidal, had histories of multiple psychiatric hospitalizations, and were unable to maintain employment due to their psychiatric symptoms.

One of the characteristics of borderline clients that is problematic to many clinicians is the high incidence of self-mutilation and recurrent suicide attempts. Leibenluft, Gardner, and Cowdry's (1987) presentation of borderline clients' perspectives on incidents of self-mutilation and Linehan's response to that paper (Linehan, 1987c) are particularly useful in offering insight into this behavior, particularly given the evidence that

Linehan's treatment approach can reduce the incidence of self-injurious acts.

D. Dependent Personality Disorder

The treatment of unassertive clients has been addressed in considerable detail in the behavioral literature (summarized in Millman, Huber, & Diggins, 1982); however, clients with a dependent personality disorder are much more than simply dependent or unassertive. Overholser, Kabakoff, and Norman (in press) point out that the criteria for dependent personality disorder contain many traits commonly found in depression, including lack of initiative, feelings of helplessness, and difficulty making decisions. Reich and Noyes (1987) found that 54% of their depressed subjects qualified for a diagnosis of dependent personality disorder as well, while Koenigsberg, Kaplan, Gilmore, and Cooper (1985) found that major depression and adjustment disorder were the Axis I diagnoses most frequently associated with dependent personality disorder. Anxiety disorders often co-occur with dependent personality disorder as well. In a study of panic disordered patients, Reich, Noyes, and Troughton (1987) found dependent personality disorder to be the most frequent Axis II diagnosis, especially in the subgroup with phobic avoidance, where roughly 40% of these subjects met criteria for dependent personality disorder.

Cognitive-behavioral conceptualizations of dependent personality disorder are fairly straightforward and the various authors discussing this disorder demonstrate substantial consensus. Fleming (Fleming, 1985; Freeman et al., in press, chap. 12) asserts that these patients see themselves as inherently inadequate and helpless and, therefore, unable to cope with the world on their own. As a result, the dependent individuals attempt to find someone who seems competent to handle life and who will protect them and take care of them. The dependent individual gives up his or her autonomy and subordinates his or her needs and desires in exchange for this caretaking. By relying on others to handle problems and make decisions, the individual has little opportunity to master the skills needed for coping with life independently. Also, these individuals often have a strongly dichotomous view of dependence versus independence and fear that any signs of competence may result in being abandoned before they are equipped to cope independently. Thus any steps toward developing new capabilities may be terrifying. Turkat (Turkat & Carlson, 1984; Turkat & Maisto, 1985) presents a similar view, conceptualizing this disorder as being based on a fear of independent decision making.

Overholser (1987) proposes a model for intervention with dependent personality disorder that is compatible with the interventions advocated by Fleming (Fleming, 1985; Freeman et al., in press, chap. 12) and Turkat (Turkat & Carlson, 1984; Turkat & Maisto, 1985). This approach includes training in problem-solving strategies adapted from the work of D'Zurilla and Goldfried (1971), use of the Socratic method to elicit the client's beliefs and assumptions, and the self-control strategies proposed by Rehm (1977), including self-monitoring, self-evaluation, and self-reinforcement. Group therapy is seen as being particularly valuable with these clients because modeling has been found to help increase independent behavior (Goldstein et al. 1973). Also, group therapy can be used to provide a client with many models of assertion, problem solving, and decision making as well as providing a supportive and "safe" environment for practicing these skills.

While Fleming, Overholzer, and Turkat all suggest that cognitive-behavioral interventions can be effective with dependent personality disorder, no outcome studies conducted on this population have yet been reported. Turkat and Carlson (1984) present an interesting case example of a 48-year-old woman reporting anxiety and avoidance behavior following the diagnosis of her daughter as diabetic. When a strictly symptomatic, behavioral treatment was used to decrease the client's anxiety and avoidance, the client's symptoms improved substantially, but they returned in full force when the frequency of therapy sessions was decreased. When the case was reconceptualized as anxiety about independent decision making and the treatment was revised to focus on gradual exposure to independent decision making, the treatment proved successful, with significant improvements on self-ratings of anxiety being maintained at an 11-month follow-up.

E. Histrionic Personality Disorder

This disorder has received only limited attention in the behavioral literature. Fleming (1983; Freeman et al., in press, chap. 9) hypothesizes that a history of being rewarded from an early age for enacting certain roles rather than for competence or ability results in the individual learning to focus attention on the playing of roles and "performing" for others rather than on developing his or her own capabilities. As a consequence, the individual comes to assume that "I am inadequate and unable to handle life on my own," and that, therefore, "it is necessary to be loved and approved of by everyone." Fleming asserts that, rather than adopting the more passive strategy characteristic of dependent personality disorder, the histrionic aggressively works to attract attention and obtain the approval of others. A similar view is presented by Turkat and Maisto (1985, p. 530), who conceptualize a histrionic client's problems in terms of "an excessive need for attention and a failure to use the appropriate social skills in order to achieve attention from others."

Interventions designed to decrease the client's excessive desire for attention and to help him or her to master more appropriate social skills are recommended by Fleming as well as Turkat and Maisto. Fleming notes that the histrionic client's impulsive, overly dramatic interpersonal style, and global, impressionistic thought style are contrary to the systematic, problem-focused approach generally used by cognitive-behavioral therapists. This can produce some difficulties in the early stages of therapy, but Fleming asserts that gradually helping the client take a systematic, problem-solving approach within therapy can, in itself, be quite therapeutic. The intervention approaches advocated by Fleming and by Turkat and Maisto have not yet been tested empirically.

In the one study of the effectiveness of behavioral interventions with histrionic clients that has been reported, Kass, Silvers, and Abrams (1972) describe an inpatient group treatment in which group members reinforced assertion and extinguished dysfunctional, overly emotional responses and assert that this approach was helpful to four out of five group members. Although these results are encouraging, this study suffers from several flaws. First, the diagnoses were based on unusual diagnostic criteria (not DSM), and no check on the reliability of diagnoses was included. Second, the report of improvement in four of five subjects was based solely on the authors' subjective evaluation. Finally, no follow-up data were collected to determine the extent to which the reported changes persisted.

F. Narcissistic Personality Disorder

Although this disorder, characterized by an exaggerated sense of self-importance and excessive egocentrism, has received a great deal of attention from psychodynamic theorists, it has received little attention from behavioral and cognitive-behavioral authors. Turkat (Carey, Flasher, Maisto, & Turkat, 1984; Turkat & Maisto, 1985) reports one case of this disorder that he and his colleagues conceptualized as resulting from a childhood history of having generally received immediate reinforcement on demand and having little training in, or reinforcement for, complying with rules, acting responsibly, and fulfilling obligations. They hypothesized that this learning history resulted in excessive demandingness and attention seeking; deficits in problem solving, frustration tolerance, and impulse control; and excessive reliance on immediate reinforcement from others. On the basis of this conceptualization, a treatment approach directed toward improving the client's ability to respond adaptively to delayed reinforcement schedules was implemented. Good initial results were reported with the client reporting improved mood, decreased impulsiveness, and increased compliance with her medical regimen. However, treatment was terminated prematurely when the client became involved with a wealthy, indulgent boyfriend who provided substantial immediate reinforcement. This conceptualization of narcissistic personality disorder is plausible, has clear implications for treatment, and provided a basis for a treatment approach that produced promising initial results. However, a note of caution is needed. Turkat and Maisto (1985) report that a different, although unreported, conceptualization was used with their second case of narcissistic personality disorder and state that there is insufficient data to justify generalizing this conceptualization or treatment approach to other narcissistic clients.

Freeman et al. (in press, chap. 10) share Turkat's view that the narcissistic individual has learned to pursue immediate reinforcement to the detriment of long-term self-interest due to his or her earlier learning history, but they emphasize cognitive factors. They suggest that the central dysfunctional belief underlying this disorder is a conviction that the individual is, or must be, a "special" person. This is seen as contributing to the individual's manifesting selective attention to evidence of his or her superiority, to his or her rejection of evidence that he or she may be "ordinary" and to a conviction that he or she deserves special treatment because of this presumed specialness. These cognitive factors are seen as having an important impact on interpersonal behavior by interfering with effective problem solving, resulting in the individual's making repeated attempts to demonstrate his or her specialness and obtain special treatment, and precipitating "temper tantrums" when special treatment is not forthcoming. This view suggests that modification of the client's conviction that he or she is, or must be, "special" would be an important goal of intervention. However, no effective way of doing so has been developed, and Freeman et al. settle for more modest treatment goals, focusing on interventions designed to increase the client's tolerance for frustration and to improve his or her ability to respond adaptively to the delayed consequences of his or her actions. They suggest that this approach can moderate the client's narcissism and result in substantial improvement, but that the narcissistic pattern is not likely to be eliminated. Such an approach has not yet been tested empirically.

G. Obsessive-Compulsive Personality Disorder

There is an extensive behavioral literature on the treatment of obsessions and compulsions, but obsessive-compulsive personality disorder, which despite the terminology does not necessarily involve obsessions or compulsions, has received little attention from behavioral and cognitive-behavioral investigators. Turkat has presented a clinically based conceptualization of this disorder (Turkat, 1986; Turkat & Maisto, 1985). His view is based on the hypothesis that early in life the individual learns, via modeling and shaping, to work hard, be productive, and take on many obligations, but that at the same time he or she receives little training in identifying, expressing, and dealing with emotions in interpersonal relationships. He suggests that this can result in the individual's excelling in academics and work but being less successful in dealing with his or her own emotions and the emotions of others. As a result, the individual is likely to tend to focus on achievement and to avoid dealing with complex emotions. Over time, he or she is likely to fall further and further behind in emotion-related interpersonal skills, including empathy. Turkat concludes that this eventually leads to a variety of problems, including a tendency toward anger at others (due to a lack of empathy and an inability to understand others) and depression (due to relationship problems and lack of ability to handle his or her own emotions adaptively). Turkat suggests that the ideal treatment approach for this disorder would include social skills training focusing on handling the emotional aspects of interpersonal relationships and efforts to reduce the client's commitment to behaving rationally at all times (Turkat, 1986). However, he reports that *none* of his sample of five clients with obsessive-compulsive personality disorder was willing to engage in such a treatment. Therefore, none was treated successfully (Turkat & Maisto, 1985).

Simon (1983; Freeman et al., in press, chap. 11) presents a very similar conceptualization of the disorder but reports greater success in treating obsessive-compulsive clients. This appears to be due to a significant difference in treatment strategy. Simon and her colleagues argue that one of the major issues in successfully treating clients with obsessive-compulsive personality disorder is to develop treatment goals toward which the client is willing to work, because obsessive-compulsive clients are generally not interested either in becoming more skilled at handling strong emotions or in becoming less obsessive-compulsive. She recommends the simple expedient of beginning with the problems that led the client to seek treatment and using a guided discovery approach to developing an understanding of the factors contributing to them. This quickly leads to identifying the client's difficulty dealing with emotion, his or her high standards and dedication to work, and so on as problems that need to be addressed, but does so in a way that makes the need for doing so very clear to the client and increases the probability of compliance. Simon (Freeman et al., in press, chap. 11) goes on to provide detailed treatment recommendations that include the type of training in relationship skills that Turkat suggests but that focuses more strongly on addressing the cognitions that contribute to the individual's dedication to work, perfectionism, and avoidance of mistakes. Turkat (1986) cautions, on theoretical grounds, that cognitive interventions based on Ellis's approach (i.e., Ellis & Harper, 1977) could be counter-productive due to Ellis's emphasis on training the client to think more rationally. Simon and her colleagues argue that for their approach, which is based on Beck's Cognitive Therapy (Beck, 1976; Beck, Rush, Shaw, & Emery, 1979) and focuses on modifying dysfunctional cognitions rather than on increasing rationality, can be used effectively with obsessive-compulsive clients as long as it is applied appropriately. Given the differences in the conclusions reached by these investigators, empirical data would be quite valuable. However, both perspectives are based on clinical observation and no empirical data have yet been reported.

H. Paranoid Personality Disorder

Cognitive-behavioral authors have presented a variety of views of paranoid personality disorder. Colby (1981; Colby, Faught, & Parkinson, 1979) has developed a computer simulation of paranoia (rather than paranoid personality disorder per se that is based on the traditional assumption that paranoia is actually a set of strategies directed toward minimizing or forestalling shame and humiliation. Cameron (1963, 1974) sees the disorder as resulting from parental mistreatment and a lack of consistent parental love, leading the child to expect sadistic treatment from others, to be vigilant for signs of danger, and to act quickly to defend him- or herself. Turkat's (Turkat, 1985, 1986, 1987; Turkat & Maisto, 1985) view is that early interactions with parents result in the individual's being quite concerned about the evaluations of others but also being constrained to conform to parental expectations which interfere with acceptance by peers. He suggests that the individual spends much time ruminating about the resulting social isolation and mistreatment by peers and eventually concludes that he or she is being persecuted because he or she is special and the others are jealous; this "rational" explanation reduces the individual's distress over the social isolation. Finally, Pretzer (Freeman et al., in press, chap. 7; Pretzer, 1985) asserts that the disorder is based on strongly held assumptions about the motivations of others, which lead the individual to expect deception, trickery, and harm in interpersonal interactions. This leads him or her to conclude that vigilance for signs of deception, trickery, and malicious intentions is necessary, as is guarded, defensive behavior. Such vigilance and guarded behavior are seen as perpetuating the disorder, because it results in many observations and experiences that seem to support the view that people cannot be trusted.

Unfortunately, despite the amount of theoretical attention this disorder has received, there has been little empirical research that might aid in choosing between the competing conceptualizations. In part this has been due to the difficulty of assembling samples of individuals with paranoid personality disorder. Turkat and his colleagues (Thompson-Pope & Turkat, in press; Turkat & Banks, 1987) are attempting to circumvent this difficulty by identifying appropriate subjects among undergraduates enrolled in introductory psychology courses. Their initial findings indicate that it is possible to identify a subgroup of "paranoid personality" subjects. These individuals are similar to those with paranoid personality disorder in being vigilant, keen observers who are quick to reach definite conclusions in ambiguous situations, and they are often quite perceptive. But they are also prone to suspect that others are being deceptive and to report paranoid thoughts and experiences. If further research shows that the findings of studies using "paranoid personality" subjects can validly be generalized to individuals with paranoid personality disorder, this will greatly facilitate research.

Some success has been reported in using operant principles to decrease the frequency of paranoid verbalizations (e.g., Brink, 1980), but these reports have used subjects with diagnoses other than paranoid personality disorder. The authors of the various cognitive-behavioral perspectives on paranoid personality disorder suggest a different approach. Colby, Turkat, and Pretzer agree that it is rarely productive to directly challenge the paranoid individual's suspicions of others. They suggest instead that it is best first to work to decrease the client's feelings of inadequacy and vulnerability and then to work to increase his or her skills at handling problematic interpersonal situations effectively. They argue that when the individual is confident in handling whatever interpersonal problems arise, his or her suspiciousness, vigilance, and guardedness subside. Pretzer goes on to recommend further interventions designed to modify the individual's assumptions about the motivations of others and to improve empathy skills, suggesting that substantial additional improvement can result from adding these interventions. Both Turkat (Turkat & Maisto, 1985) and Pretzer (Freeman et al., in press; Pretzer, 1988) report case examples in which this approach to intervention has produced a lasting decrease in paranoia and associated problems, but no outcome studies testing this treatment strategy have been reported.

I. Passive-Aggressive Personality Disorder

Cognitive-behavioral conceptualizations of this disorder are based on the hypothesis that individuals who are unwilling to acknowledge anger and express it directly may express it indirectly while denying that they are, in fact, angry (Burns & Epstein, 1983; Freeman et al., in press, chap. 13; Perry & Flannery, 1982). If such an individual is chronically angry (possibly due to a strongly held belief that he or she "deserves" to be treated in certain ways and due to vigilance for indications that others are not doing so), then a chronic and pervasive pattern of passive-aggressive behavior results.

The cognitive-behavioral authors who have discussed this disorder agree that an important goal of intervention is to reduce the client's reluctance to acknowledge and express anger and at the same time help him or her to master adaptive ways of handling anger through interventions, such as assertion training and social skills training. Freeman et al. argue that the most difficult part of intervention is to carefully muster the evidence needed to persuade the client that his or her problems are related to the indirect expression of anger. Once that has been accomplished, it is possible to use assertion training to improve the client's ability to handle anger adaptively while using cognitive restructuring techniques both to eliminate cognitions that interfere with the client's handling anger adaptively and to modify any cognitions that contribute to chronic anger or resentment. The authors discussing this disorder present case examples of successful interventions, but the effectiveness of these treatment approaches has not been examined empirically.

J. Schizoid Personality Disorder

This disorder, which differs from avoidant personality disorder in that the schizoid denies both interest in interpersonal relationships and distress over their absence, has received little attention from behavioral and cognitive authors. Millon (1981) suggests that schizoid personality disorder may develop when individuals who are temperamentally predisposed to limited responsiveness receive limited stimulation in early childhood, possibly due to their being relatively unrewarding to interact with. He suggests that this could result in retarded social and cognitive development and lack of attachment to parental figures as well as providing little incentive for the child to attend to social and emotional cues or to learn the skills needed to form emotionally close relationships. Once established, this pattern could easily persist, because the individual is not likely to seek out social interaction and his or her bland interpersonal style does not attract advances from others.

Freeman et al. (in press, chap. 7) present a cognitive-behavioral view that is quite compatible with Millon's developmental hypotheses. They assert that typical thoughts reported by schizoid clients include the following: "There are few reasons to be close to people"; "I am my own best friend"; "Stay calm, displays of emotion are unnecessary and embarrassing"; "What others say is of little interest or importance to me." The schizoid client's expressed belief that there is no point to social interaction, in combination with the subsequent low frequency of social interaction, is seen as being sufficient to explain the primary characteristics of the disorder.

This perspective on schizoid personality disorder suggests that a major goal of intervention with schizoid individuals is to establish or increase positive views of social interaction and personal closeness and to reduce positive views of social isolation. However, as Freeman et al. note, this need not be done primarily through verbal interventions. The therapist can use the therapist-client relationship as a prototype for other interpersonal relationships, in addition to working to increase the client's frequency of interpersonal interactions outside the session and to structure these interactions so that they will be more rewarding. Because schizoid clients typically show little attention to interpersonal cues, seem to have little understanding of interpersonal relationships, and may have quite poor social skills, very basic social skills training may be needed. As Freeman et al. (in press, chap. 7) write, "At times it is as though the therapist were explaining human interactions to a Martian, newly arrived on our planet and completely naive about humans."

Both Millon and Freeman, Pretzer, Fleming, and Simon suggest, on the basis of clinical experience, that schizoid personality disorder is difficult to modify, in part due to the client's limited motivation for change, and that gains are likely to be modest. Freeman et al. assert that with persistence it is possible to improve the client's social skills, increase his or her frequency of social interaction, and decrease his or her "strangeness." However, they report that schizoid clients typically continue to be relatively distant and passive in interpersonal relationships at the close of treatment, and that they seem to develop little capacity for warmth and intimacy.

K. Schizotypal Personality Disorder

The term *schizotypal* is applied to persons who manifest an inability to establish close interpersonal relationships in combination with an odd style of communication and certain forms of thought disorder, such as magical thinking and ideas of reference. Until the advent of DSM-III, schizotypal personality disorder was not distinguished from schizoid personality disorder, and this disorder has received little attention in the short time that it has been considered a distinct disorder. The symptoms characterizing this disorder resemble a mild form of schizophrenia and, it is not surprising, the idea that this disorder is genetically related to schizophrenia has been popular.

Millon (1981) suggests that schizotypal personality disorder can be viewed as an extreme form of either schizoid or avoidant personality disorder, resulting from a learning history that would predispose the individual to the development of one of the two interacting with biological vulnerabilities that impair development and functioning. He suggests that, in the subtype that he refers to as "schizoid-schizotypals," a relative insensitivity to social stimuli, deficient learning of social attachment behaviors, and learning of a disjointed, unfocused thought style result in an extremely passive, unresponsive interpersonal style. This disengaged interpersonal style is hypothesized to contribute to increasing social isolation, which perpetuates the lack of social skills and social attachments. He suggests that these individuals then become increasingly preoccupied with personal fantasy "unchecked by the logic and control of reciprocal social communication and activity" (Millon, 1981, p. 424) and eventually present the full schizotypal picture.

Millon (1981) refers to another subgroup as "schizotypal-avoidants," and suggests that they may be genetically predisposed to "muddled" thinking and thus may initially be fearful and easily overwhelmed by stimulation. He hypothesizes that, if this elicits deprecation and humiliation from parents, siblings, and peers, the resulting low self-esteem and avoidance of social interaction lead to deficiencies in social skills and continuing avoidance of social interaction. Withdrawal into personal thought and fantasy is seen as a consequence of this cycle. Then, when the individual's tendency toward "muddled" thinking is combined with the lack of corrective feedback from interpersonal interactions, the individual's functioning can easily deteriorate into a schizotypal rather than avoidant pattern.

These conceptualizations are plausible and are compatible with a cognitive-behavioral point of view. Freeman et al. (in press, chap. 7) adopt Millon's conceptualization. They report that it has not been possible to elaborate further on the cognitive aspects of the disorder because the extreme difficulty in relating to these clients combined with their bizarre thought processes greatly complicate the process of assessment.

Freeman et al. note that the view that schizotypal personality disorder can be viewed as an extreme form of schizoid personality disorder or avoidant personality disorder might suggest that the intervention approaches recommended for use with each might be useful with schizotypals. However, they argue that the preponderance of illogical, "magical" thinking requires a somewhat different approach, at least initially. They suggest working to improve social skills (including grooming, interpersonal skills, and reducing peculiar behavior) to reduce anxiety and to improve social problem solving. Over time, if the client becomes somewhat less peculiar and if interactions with the therapist provide "the logic and control of reciprocal social communication and activity" to which Millon refers, the intervention strategies suggested for use with schizoid and avoidant clients may be quite appropriate.

Freeman et al. (in press, chap. 7) report, on the basis of clinical experience, that the bizarre thinking of individuals with schizotypal personality disorder greatly complicates intervention and particularly interferes with the use of purely cognitive interventions. They suggest that, if the therapist is persistent and active, schizotypal clients can learn to behave in more socially appropriate ways. Also, their vocational functioning and ability to cope with day-to-day problems can improve substantially. However, they suggest that schizotypal clients are likely to remain somewhat withdrawn and eccentric.

V. PROPOSED GUIDELINES FOR THE
TREATMENT OF PERSONALITY DISORDERS

Despite the difficulties encountered in treating clients with personality disorders, many of the authors discussed above suggest that it is possible to develop effective treatments for them without radically modifying behavioral and cognitive-behavioral treatment approaches. DiGiuseppe (personal communication, 1988) suggests that no basic modifications in Rational-Emotive Therapy are needed but that the therapist must muster much more disconfirming evidence in order to challenge irrational beliefs effectively, must take a more active role in helping the client develop adaptive paradigms and rational beliefs, and must dispute irrational beliefs in many different life domains rather than expecting changes in beliefs to generalize spontaneously. Both Padesky (1986) and Young (1987) observe that a number of problems arise in the treatment of clients with personality disorders, including difficulty obtaining clear reports of thoughts and emotions, low tolerance for strong emotions, and poor compliance with homework assignments. While no consensus has emerged regarding how to best approach the treatment of personality disorders, a set of general guidelines for intervention based on the available literature have recently been proposed (Pretzer & Fleming, in press):

Interventions are most effective when based on an individualized conceptualization of the client's problems. Clients with personality disorders are complex, and the therapist is often faced with choosing among many possible targets for intervention and a variety of possible intervention techniques. Not only does this present a situation in which intervention can easily become confused and disorganized if the therapist does not have a clear treatment plan, but the interventions that seem appropriate after a superficial examination of the client can easily prove ineffective or counterproductive.

It is important for therapist and client to work collaboratively toward clearly identified shared goals. With clients as complex as those with personality disorders, clear, consistent goals for therapy are necessary to avoid skipping from problem to problem without making any lasting progress. However, it is important for these goals to be mutually agreed upon in order to minimize the noncompliance and power struggles that often impede treatment of clients with personality disorders. It can be difficult to develop shared goals for treatment because clients with personality disorders often present many vague complaints and, at the same time, may be unwilling to modify some of the behaviors that the therapist sees as particularly problematic. However, the time and effort spent developing mutually acceptable goals can be a good investment.

It is important to focus more than the usual amount of attention on the therapist-client relationship. Behavioral and cognitive-behavioral therapists are generally accustomed to being able to establish a fairly straight-forward therapeutic relationship at the outset of therapy and then pro-ceed without paying much attention to the interpersonal aspects of therapy. However, this is generally not the case when working with clients who have personality disorders, because the dysfunctional interpersonal behaviors that the clients manifest in relationships outside of therapy are likely to interfere with the therapist-client relationship as well. When the client's interpersonal difficulties are manifested in the therapist-client re-lationship, the therapist is provided with the opportunity to do in vivo observation and intervention (Freeman et al., in press; Linehan, 1987c; Mays, 1985; Padesky, 1986).

Consider beginning with interventions that do not require extensive self-disclosure. Many clients with personality disorders are quite uncom-fortable with self-disclosure due to a lack of trust in the therapist, dis-comfort with even mild levels of intimacy, fear of rejection, and the like. While it is sometimes necessary to begin treatment with interventions that require extensive discussion of the client's thoughts and feelings, at times it can be more useful to begin treatment by working on a problem that can be approached through behavioral interventions that do not re-quire extensive self-disclosure. This allows time for the client to gradu-ally become more comfortable with therapy and for the therapist to gradually address the client's discomfort with self-disclosure (Freeman et al., in press, chap. 8).

Interventions that increase the client's sense of self-efficacy often reduce the intensity of the client's symptomatology and facilitate other interven-tions. Bandura (1977) has written at length regarding the concept of self-efficacy (i.e., the individual's appraisal of his or her ability to meet the demands of a particular situation). Many individuals with personality disorders manifest extreme emotional and behavioral responses in part because they doubt their ability to cope effectively with particular prob-lem situations. If it is possible to increase the individual's confidence that he or she will be able to handle these problem situations if they arise, this often lowers the client's level of anxiety, moderates his or her sympto-matology, and makes it easier to implement other interventions (Free-man et al., in press, chap. 7; Pretzer, Beck, & Newman, in press).

Do not rely primarily on verbal interventions. The more severe a client's problems are, the more important it is to use behavioral interventions to accomplish cognitive as well as behavioral change (Freeman et al., in press, chap. 3). A gradual hierarchy of "behavioral experiments" not only provides an opportunity for desensitization to occur and for the client to master new skills, but also can be quite effective in challenging unrealistic beliefs and expectations.

Try to identify and address the client's fears before implementing changes. Clients with personality disorders often have strong but unexpressed fears about the changes they seek or are asked to make during the course of therapy, and attempts to induce the client to simply go ahead without addressing these fears are often unsuccessful (Mays, 1985). If the therapist makes a practice of discussing the client's expectations and concerns before each change is attempted, this is likely to reduce the client's level of anxiety regarding therapy and improve compliance.

Anticipate problems with compliance. Many factors contribute to a high rate of noncompliance among clients with personality disorders. However, rather than simply being an impediment to progress, episodes of noncompliance can provide an opportunity for effective intervention. When noncompliance is predictable, addressing the issues beforehand may not only improve compliance with that particular assignment but also prove helpful with other situations where similar issues arise. When noncompliance arises unexpectedly, it provides an opportunity to identify issues that are impeding progress in therapy so that they can be addressed.

Do not presume that the client exists in a reasonable environment. Some behaviors, such as assertion, are so generally adaptive that it is easy to assume they are always a good idea. However, clients with personality disorders are often the product of seriously atypical families and live in atypical environments. When implementing changes, it is important to assess the likely responses of significant others in the client's environment rather than presuming that they will respond in a reasonable way.

Attend to your own emotional reactions during the course of therapy. Interactions with clients with personality disorders can elicit emotional reactions from the therapist, ranging from empathic feelings of depression to strong anger, discouragement, fear, or attraction. It is important for the therapist to be aware of these responses so that they do not unduly influence or disrupt the therapist's work with the client and so that they can be used as a source of potentially useful data. Because emotional responses do not occur randomly, an unusually strong emotional response is likely to be a reaction to some aspect of the client's behavior. Because a therapist may respond emotionally to a pattern in the client's behavior long before it has been recognized intellectually, accurate interpretation of one's own responses can speed recognition of these patterns.

Be realistic regarding the length of therapy, goals for therapy, and standards for self-evaluation. Many therapists using behavioral and cognitive-behavioral approaches to therapy expect to accomplish results quickly and can easily become frustrated, pessimistic, or self-critical when therapy proceeds slowly, as it often does when working with clients with personality disorders. Clinical reports suggest that behavioral and cognitive-behavioral interventions can accomplish substantial, apparently lasting, changes in some clients with personality disorders, but more modest results are achieved in other cases and little is accomplished in others (Freeman et al., in press; Turkat & Maisto, 1985). When therapy proceeds slowly, it is important to neither give up prematurely nor perseverate with an unsuccessful treatment approach. When treatment is unsuccessful, it is important to remember that therapist competence is not the only factor influencing the outcome of therapy.

VI. CONCLUSIONS

In a recent review of the empirical literature on personality disorders, Turkat and Levin (1984) observed that only 25% of the studies they reviewed used DSM diagnostic criteria in diagnosing personality disorders and that only half of the studies incorporated a check on the reliability of diagnoses. Furthermore, these authors concluded that "in most of the personality disorder literature, there are so few data that conclusions cannot even be attempted" (p. 519). In a similar vein, Kellner (1986) concluded that there were too few adequately controlled studies of behavioral treatment approaches with subjects clearly diagnosed as having personality disorders to provide an empirical basis for recommending specific interventions for them. In the few years since these two reviews were conducted, the situation has not changed dramatically. Turkat's program of research, designed to develop an empirical base for a behavioral approach to conceptualizing and treating the personality disorders using single-case experimental designs (Turkat & Maisto, 1985), provides a promising methodology. However, the data reported thus far come from 35 subjects who have 10 different personality disorder diagnoses among them and who were selected on the basis of availability from among clients seen in a specialized medical setting. Clearly, data from a larger and more representative sample will be needed.

The findings reported by Mavissakalian and Hamman (1987) and the case examples presented by Turkat and Maisto (1985) and by Freeman et al. (in press) provide indications that behavioral and cognitive-behavioral interventions can be effective with at least some clients with personality disorders. However, the conceptualizations and interventions that have been proposed have not yet been tested empirically, and it is not at all clear which treatment strategies are most appropriate or how effective they can be.

Given the prevalence of personality disorders and the consensus that behavioral and cognitive-behavioral intervention are greatly complicated in clients with personality disorders, it is clearly important that these disorders be a continued focus of empirical research, theoretical innovation, and clinical experimentation. For the time being, treatment recommendations based on clinical observation and a limited empirical base are the best we can offer to clinicians, who must try to work with personality disorder clients today rather than waiting for empirically validated treatment protocols to be developed. Fortunately, our experience has been that, when cognitive-behavioral interventions are based on an individualized conceptualization of the client's problems and the interpersonal aspects of therapy receive sufficient attention, many clients with personality disorders can be treated quite effectively.

REFERENCES

American Psychiatric Association (APA). (1987). *Diagnostic and statistical manual of mental disorders* (3rd ed., rev.). Washington, DC: Author.

Bandura, A. (1977). *Social learning theory.* Englewood Cliffs, NJ: Prentice-Hall.

Beck, A. T. (1976). *Cognitive therapy and the emotional disorders.* New York: International Universities Press.

Beck. A. T., & Freeman, A. (in press). *Cognitive therapy of the personality disorders.* New York: Guilford.

Beck, A. T., Rush, A. J., Shaw, B. F., & Emery, G. (1979). *Cognitive therapy of depression.* New York: Guilford.

Block, J. (1971). *Lives through time.* Berkeley, CA: Bancroft.

Block, J. (1977). Advancing the psychology of personality: Paradigmatic shift or improving the quality of research. In D. Magnusson & N. S. Endler (Eds.), *Personality at the crossroads: Current issues in interactional psychology.* Hillsdale, NJ: Lawrence Erlbaum.

Brantley, P. J., & Sutker, P. B. (1984). Antisocial personality disorder. In H. E. Adams & P. B. Sutker (Eds.), *Comprehensive handbook of psychopathology.* New York: Plenum.

Brink, T. L. (1980). Geriatric paranoia: Case report illustrating behavioral management. *Journal of the American Geriatrics Society, 28,* 519-522.

Burns, D. D., & Epstein, N. (1983). Passive-aggressiveness: A cognitive-behavioral approach. In R. D. Parsons & R. J. Wicks (Eds.), *Passive-aggressiveness: Theory and practice* (pp. 72-97). New York: Brunner/Mazel.

Cameron, N. (1963). *Personality development and psychopathology: A dynamic approach* (2nd ed.). Boston: Houghton Mifflin.

Cameron, N. (1974). Paranoid conditions and paranoia. In S. Arieti & E. Brody (Eds.), *American handbook of psychiatry* (Vol. 3). New York: Basic Books.

Carey, M. P., Flasher, L. V., Maisto, S. A., & Turkat, I. D. (1984). The a priori approach to psychological assessment. *Professional Psychology: Research and Practice, 15,* 515-527.

Carney, F. L. (1986). Residential treatment programs for antisocial personality disorders. In W. H. Reid, D. Dorr, J. I. Walker, & J. W. Bonner III (Eds.), *Unmasking the psychopath: Antisocial personality disorder and related syndromes.* New York: Norton.

Colby, K. M. (1981). Modeling a paranoid mind. *The Behavioral and Brain Sciences, 4,* 515-560.

Colby, K. M., Faught, W. S., & Parkinson, R. C. (1979). Cognitive therapy of paranoid conditions: Heuristic suggestions based on a computer simulation model. *Cognitive Therapy and Research, 3,* 5-60.

DiGiuseppe, R. (1988). Personal communication.

D'Zurilla, T. J., & Goldfried, M. R. (1971). Problem solving and behavior modification. *Journal of Abnormal Psychology, 78,* 107-126.

Ellis, A., & Harper, R. A. (1977). *A new guide to rational living.* Hollywood, CA: Wilshire.

Endler, N. S., & Magnusson, D. (1976). Toward an interactional psychology of personality. *Psychological Bulletin, 83,* 956-974.

Epstein, S. (1979). The stability of behavior: I. On predicting most of the people much of the time. *Journal of Personality and Social Psychology, 37,* 1097-1126.

Fleming, B. (1983, August). *Cognitive therapy with histrionic patients: Resolving a conflict in styles.* Paper presented at the meeting of the American Psychological Association, Anaheim, CA.

Fleming, B. (1985, November). *Dependent personality disorder: Managing the transition from dependence to autonomy.* Paper presented at the meeting of the Association for the Advancement of Behavior Therapy, Houston.

Fleming B. (1988). CT with histrionic personality disorder: Resolving a conflict of styles. *International Cognitive Therapy Newsletter, 4,* 4, 8-9, 12.

Freeman, A., Pretzer, J. L., Fleming, B., & Simon, K. M. (in press). *Clinical applications of cognitive therapy.* New York: Plenum.

Goldstein, A. P., Martens, J., Hubben, J., Van Belle, H. A., Schaaf, W., Wirsma, H., & Goedhart, A. (1973). The use of modeling to increase independent behavior. *Behaviour Research and Therapy, 11,* 31-42.

Greenberg, D., & Stravynski, A. (1985). Patients who complain of social dysfunction: I. Clinical and demographic features. *Canadian Journal of Psychiatry, 30,* 206-211.

Kass, D. J., Silvers, F. M., & Abrams, G. M. (1972). Behavioral group treatment of hysteria. *Archives of General Psychiatry, 26,* 42-50.

Kellner, R. (1986). Personality disorders. *Psychotherapy and Psychosomatics, 46,* 58-66.

Koenigsberg, H. W., Kaplan, R. D., Gilmore, M. M., & Cooper, A. M. (1985). The relationship between syndrome and personality disorder in DSM-III: Experience with 2,462 patients. *American Journal of Psychiatry, 142,* 207-217

Leibenluft, E., Gardner, D. L., & Cowdry, R. W. (1987). The inner experience of the borderline self-mutilator. *Journal of Personality Disorders, 1,* 317-324.

Linehan, M. M. (1987a). Dialectical behavior therapy in groups: Treating borderline personality disorders and suicidal behavior. In C. M. Brody (Ed.), *Women in groups.* New York: Springer.

Linehan, M. M. (1987b). Dialectical Behavioral Therapy: A cognitive behavioral approach to parasuicide. *Journal of Personality Disorders, 1,* 328-333.

Linehan, M. M. (1987c). Commentaries on "The inner experience of the borderline self-mutilator": A cognitive behavioral approach. *Journal of Personality Disorders, 1,* 328-333.

Linehan, M. M., Armstrong, H. E., Allmon, D. J., Suarez, A., & Miller, M. L. (1988). *Comprehensive behavioral treatment for suicidal behaviors and borderline personality disorder. II: Treatment retention and one year follow-up of patient use of medical and psychological resources.* Unpublished manuscript, University of Washington, Seattle, Department of Psychology.

Linehan, M. M., Armstrong, H. E., Suarez, A., & Allmon, D. J. (1988). *Comprehensive behavioral treatment for suicidal behaviors and borderline personality disorder: I. Outcome.* Unpublished manuscript, University of Washington, Seattle, Department of Psychology.

Luborsky, L., McLellan, A. T., Woody, G. E., O'Brien, C. P., & Auerbach, A. (1985). Therapist success and its determinants. *Archives of General Psychiatry, 42,* 602-611.

Marshall, W. L., & Barbaree, H. E. (1984). Disorders of personality, impulse, and adjustment. In S. M. Turner & M. Hersen (Eds.), *Adult psychopathology and diagnosis.* New York: John Wiley.

Matthews, W. M., & Reid, W. H. (1986). A wilderness experience treatment program for offenders. In W. H. Reid, D. Dorr, J. I. Walker, & J. W. Bonner III (Eds.), *Unmasking the psychopath: Antisocial personality disorder and related syndromes.* New York: Norton.

Mavissakalian, M., & Hamman, M. S. (1987). DSM-III personality disorder in agoraphobia: II. Changes with treatment. *Comprehensive Psychiatry, 28,* 356-361.

Mays, D. T. (1985). Behavior therapy with borderline personality disorders; One clinician's perspective. In D. T. Mays & C. M. Franks (Eds.), *Negative outcome in psychotherapy and what to do about it.* New York: Springer.

Mays, D. T., & Franks, C. M. (1985). Negative outcome: What to do about it. In D. T. Mays & C. M. Franks (Eds.), *Negative outcome in psychotherapy and what to do about it.* New York: Springer.

Millman, H. L., Huber, J. T., & Diggins, D. R. (1982). *Therapies for adults.* San Francisco: Jossey-Bass.

Millon, T. (1981). *Disorders of personality: DSM-III: Axis II.* New York: John Wiley.

Millon, T. (1987). On the genesis and prevalence of the borderline personality disorder: A social learning thesis. *Journal of Personality Disorders, 1,* 354-372.

Mischel, W. (1969). *Personality and assessment.* New York: John Wiley.

Mischel, W. (1973). Toward a cognitive social learning reconceptualization of personality. *Psychological Review, 80,* 252-283.

Murray, E. J. (1988). Personality disorders: A cognitive view. *Journal of Personality Disorders, 2,* 37-43.

Olweus, D. (1977). A critical analysis of the "modern" interactionist position. In D. Magnusson & N. S. Endler (Eds.), *Personality at the crossroads: Current issues in interactional psychology.* Hillsdale, NJ: Lawrence Erlbaum.

Overholser, J. C. (1987). Facilitating autonomy in passive-dependent persons: An integrative model. *Journal of Contemporary Psychotherapy, 17,* 250-269.

Overholser, J. C., Kabakoff, R., & Norman, W. H. (in press). Personality characteristics in depressed and dependent psychiatric inpatients. *Journal of Personality Assessment.*

Padesky, C. A. (1986, September). *Personality disorders: Cognitive therapy into the 90's.* Paper presented at the Second International Conference on Cognitive Psychotherapy, Umeå, Sweden.

Padesky, C. A. (1988). Schema-focused CT: Comments and questions. *International Cognitive Therapy Newsletter, 4,* 5, 7.

Perry, J. C., & Flannery, R. B. (1982). Passive-aggressive personality disorder: Treatment implications of a clinical typology. *Journal of Nervous and Mental Disease, 170,* 164-173.

Pilkonis, P. A. (1984). Avoidant and schizoid personality disorders. In H. E. Adams & P. B. Sutker (Eds.), *Comprehensive handbook of psychopathology,* New York: Plenum.

Pretzer, J. L. (1983, August). *Borderline personality disorder: Too complex for cognitive-behavioral approaches?* Paper presented at the meeting of the American Psychological Association, Anaheim, CA. (ERIC Document Reproduction Service No. ED 243 007)

Pretzer, J. L. (1985, November). *Paranoid personality disorder: A cognitive view.* Paper presented at the meeting of the Association for Advancement of Behavior Therapy, Houston.

Pretzer, J. L. (1988). Paranoid personality disorder: A cognitive view. *International Cognitive Therapy Newsletter, 4,* 4, 10-12.

Pretzer, J. L., Beck, A. T., & Newman, C. F. (in press). Stress and stress management: A cognitive view. *Journal of Cognitive Psychotherapy: An International Quarterly.*

Pretzer, J. L., & Fleming, B. (in press). Cognitive-behavioral treatment of personality disorders. *The Behavior Therapist.*

Rehm, L. (1977). A self-control model of depression. *Behavior Therapy, 8,* 787-804.

Reich, J., & Noyes, R. (1987). A comparison of DSM-III personality disorders in acutely ill panic and depressed patients. *Journal of Anxiety Disorders, 1,* 123-131.

Reich, J., Noyes, R., & Troughton, E. (1987). Dependent personality disorder associated with phobic avoidance in patients with panic disorder. *American Journal of Psychiatry, 44,* 323-326.

Reid, W. H., & Solomon, G. F. (1986). Community-based offender programs. In W. H. Reid, D. Dorr, J. I. Walker, & J. W. Bonner III (Eds.), *Unmasking the psychopath: Antisocial personality disorder and related syndromes.* New York: Norton.

Rush, A. J., & Shaw, B. F. (1983). Failures in treating depression by cognitive therapy. In E. B. Foa & P. G. M. Emmelkamp (Eds.), *Failures in behavior therapy.* New York: John Wiley.

Simon, K. M. (1983, August). *Cognitive therapy with compulsive patients: Replacing rigidity with structure.* Paper presented at the meeting of the American Psychological Association, Anaheim, CA.

Simon, K. M. (1985, November). *Cognitive therapy of the passive-aggressive personality.* Paper presented at the meeting of the Association for the Advancement of Behavior Therapy, Houston.

Stephens, J. H., & Parks, S. L. (1981). Behavior therapy of personality disorders. In J. R. Lion (Ed.), *Personality disorders: Diagnosis and management* (2nd ed.). Baltimore: Williams & Wilkins.

Stravynski, A., Marks, I., & Yule, W. (1982). Social skills problems in neurotic outpatients: Social skills training with and without cognitive modification. *Archives of General Psychiatry, 39,* 1378-1385.

Sutker, P. B., Archer, R. A., & Kilpatrick, D. G. (1981). Sociopathy and antisocial behavior: Theory and treatment. In S. M. Turner, K. S. Calhoun, & H. E. Adams (Eds.), *Handbook of clinical behavior therapy.* New York: John Wiley.

Thompson-Pope, S. K., & Turkat, I. D. (in press). Reactions to ambiguous stimuli among paranoid personalities. *Journal of Psychopathology & Behavioral Assessment.*

Turkat, I. D. (1985). The case of Mr. P. In I. D. Turkat (Ed.), *Behavioral case formulation.* New York: Plenum.

Turkat, I. D. (1986). The behavioral interview. In A. R. Ciminero, K. S. Calhoun, & H. E. Adams (Eds.), *Handbook of behavioral assessment* (2nd ed.). New York: John Wiley.

Turkat, I. D. (1987). Invited case transcript: The initial clinical hypothesis. *Journal of Behavioral Therapy & Experimental Psychiatry, 18,* 349-356.

Turkat, I. D., & Banks, D. S. (1987). Paranoid personality and its disorder. *Journal of Psychopathology and Behavioral Assessment, 9,* 295-304.

Turkat, I. D., & Carlson, C. R. (1984). Data-based versus symptomatic formulation of treatment: The case of a dependent personality. *Journal of Behavior Therapy and Experimental Psychiatry, 15,* 153-160.

Turkat, I. D., & Levin, R. A. (1984). Formulation of personality disorders. In H. E. Adams & P. B. Sutker (Eds.), *Comprehensive handbook of psychopathology.* New York: Plenum.

Turkat, I. D., & Maisto, S. A. (1985). Personality disorders: Application of the experimental method to the formulation and modification of personality disorders. In D. H. Barlow (Eds.), *Clinical handbook of psychological disorders: A step by step treatment manual.* New York: Guilford.

Turner, R. M. (1986, March). *The bio-social-learning approach to the assessment and treatment of borderline personality disorder.* Paper presented at the Carrier Foundation Behavioral Medicine Update Symposium, Belle Meade, NJ.

Turner, R. M. (1987). The effects of personality disorder diagnosis on the outcome of social anxiety symptom reduction. *Journal of Personality Disorders, 1,* 136-143.

Turner, S. M., Beidel, D. C., Dancu, C. V., & Keys, D. J. (1986). Psychopathology of social phobia and comparison to avoidant personality disorders. *Journal of Abnormal Psychology, 95,* 398-394.

Turner, S. M., & Hersen, M. (1981). Disorders of social behavior: A behavioral approach to personality disorders. In S. M. Turner, K. S. Calhoun, & H. E. Adams (Eds.), *Handbook of clinical behavior therapy.* New York: John Wiley.

Woody, G. E., McLellan, A. T., Luborsky, L., & O'Brien, C. P. (1985). Sociopathy and psychotherapy outcome. *Archives of General Psychiatry, 42,* 1081-1086.

Young, J. (1987). *Schema-focused cognitive therapy for personality disorders.* Unpublished manuscript.

Young, J., & Swift, W. (1988). Schema-focused cognitive therapy for personality disorders: Part I. *International Cognitive Therapy Newsletter, 4,* 5, 13-14.

BEHAVIORAL TREATMENT OF INSOMNIA

JAMIE K. LILIE
University of Illinois at Chicago

RUSSELL P. ROSENBERG
St. Mary's Medical Center and
University of Tennessee

I. INTRODUCTION

Clearly, insomnia can have a serious impact upon one's ability to perform at work and maintain healthy social relationships, and it can be the source of or contribute to a variety of psychological disturbances (Kales & Kales, 1984). Several studies (Belloc, 1973; Hammond, 1964; Wiley & Camacho, 1980; Wingard & Berkman, 1983) have indicated that the length and quality of sleep is related to general health and longevity. Given the potential impact insomnia can have on health and well-being, it is not surprising that there has been a proliferation of research in the areas of assessment and treatment for this sleep disorder in the past 10 years. The purpose of this chapter is to review the variety of behavioral techniques that have been developed for the treatment of the insomnias and to critically evaluate the methods and findings of research in this area. Since publication of the review by Bootzin and Nicassio (1978), the field of sleep disorders has rapidly expanded. We will examine the current literature with a focus on assessing the progress made since that review. In 1979, the Association of Sleep Disorders Centers (ASDC) published the first *Diagnostic Classification Manual,* which attempted to delineate major categories of sleep-wake disorders. Disorders of initiating and maintaining sleep (DIMS) became the new name for the category, which includes various types of insomnia.

A.   Definition of Insomnia

Literally, *insomnia* means "inability to sleep." In fact, there have been very few cases reported of individuals who never sleep, and these have usually been due to some form of brain insult or injury (Lugaresi, 1985). More often, *insomnia* refers to difficulty initiating sleep, maintaining sleep, or both. Insomnia is a complex problem, and it is now widely recognized that there can be multiple causes for sleep disruption, including conditions such as sleep apnea, delayed sleep phase, nocturnal myoclonus, gastroesophageal reflex, and drug reactions (Hauri, 1982; Kales & Kales, 1984; Mendelson, 1988). However, clinicians are more likely to treat insomnia that is the result of anxiety, depression, conditioned arousal, stress, and sleep-wake-cycle disturbances. Behavioral, cognitive, and psychological factors are important components to consider when evaluating the causes of and developing treatments for insomnia.

Bootzin and Nicassio (1978) noted that a common theme underlying definitions of insomnia is that it involves a chronic inability to obtain adequate sleep. This statement is sufficiently broad to permit classification of several types of insomnia, yet it captures the essential commonalties, which are (a) persistence of the complaint (i.e., more than a transient poor night of sleep) and (b) the subjective element as noted by the word *adequate.* The latter also highlights the fact that individuals vary in their need for sleep. While normative data (Williams, Karacan, & Hursch, 1974) suggest that taking longer than 30 minutes to fall asleep is "abnormal," a significant subjective component must be considered. Some individuals may take longer than 30 minutes to fall asleep but do not view this as problematic or disturbing. However, some individuals who take less than 30 minutes to initiate sleep complain of insomnia. A further distinction between primary and secondary insomnias has been noted. The former are thought to be abnormalities of sleep that are unrelated to other disorders. The latter, of course, are thought to be related to other medical and/or psychiatric conditions. It appears that the primary versus secondary distinction is of historical importance but is not necessarily useful in formulating an effective treatment plan. For example, Spielman, Caruso, and Glovinsky (1987) noted that factors that perpetuate insomnia may be operating long after the specific precipitants have subsided. Likewise, many areas of behavior therapy have shown that the learning of new responses or the modification of existing ones does not depend on the way in which they were acquired. Another way of distinguishing among types of insomnias is by the temporal pattern of the symptoms. Thus groups of patients have been subdivided into those with primarily sleep onset insomnia (prolonged latency to fall sleep), sleep maintenance insomnia, and early morning awakening (also called terminal insomnia).

Early insomnia research focused on individuals with chronic sleep difficulties. Two additional dimensions of insomnia have been examined extensively. Transient or short-term insomnia can usually be associated with an identified stress, illness, or shift in the sleep-wake pattern. A period of insomnia lasting one month or less is considered to fall into this category. Persistent, unremitting insomnia is considered to be chronic and has been the focus of the majority of studies utilizing behavioral treatments. Intermittent insomnia involves periodic difficulties with sleep for which the cause(s) may be psychological or medical.

B. Epidemiology

Despite advances in pharmacological and behavioral treatments, insomnia remains a common problem for both children and adults. Ware (1979) estimated that in the United States about 75 million people feel their sleep is inadequate. Several large-scale surveys of sleep problems both here and in Britain have found that about 30% to 35% of adults report at least occasional difficulties with falling asleep or staying asleep (Bixler, Kales, Soldatos, Kales, & Healy, 1979; Karacan et al., 1976; McGhie & Russell, 1982). Furthermore, these studies have consistently found that females report more sleep complaints than males and that the incidence of sleep complaints increases with age.

Children also experience difficulty initiating and maintaining sleep. Ferber (1987) reports that 15% to 35% of children have trouble sleeping. While there are substantial developmental factors involved in the evolution of a sleep-wake pattern, behavioral factors such as feeding patterns, cosleeping, and parental responsiveness play an important role in the development or maintenance of insomnia.

To summarize, the most consistent findings among the epidemiological studies of insomnia are as follows: (a) Approximately 33% of the adult population experience occasional insomnia; (b) 10% to 15% of the population consider that they have a serious problem with sleeping and about 5% of the population consider themselves insomniacs; (c) insomnia occurs slightly more often in females; (d) the complaint of insomnia is positively correlated with age; (e) the most frequently occurring pattern of insomnia is sleep maintenance insomnia followed by sleep onset insomnia, with early morning awakening occurring least often; (f) only 33% of those labeling themselves insomniacs seek professional help, with the vast majority of those seeking help discussing the problem with their family doctor; (g) of those individuals who discuss the problem with a physician, 57% receive a course of medication, 25% are treated nonpharmacologically, and 17.6% go untreated.

Another important consideration in the diagnosis and treatment of insomnia is the relative frequency of each diagnostic subgroup. Coleman et al. (1982) surveyed the prevalence of sleep disorders by ASDC category at a number of sleep centers across the country. They found that, in descending order of frequency, the following insomnia diagnoses were made: DIMS associated with psychiatric disorders (most often depression and anxiety disorders), psychophysiological DIMS (also known as conditioned insomnia), DIMS associated with use of drugs and alcohol, and DIMS associated with medical causes (most often central sleep apnea or nocturnal myoclonus). It is noteworthy that specific medical causes of insomnia (apnea and myoclonus) increase with age as does the complaint of poor sleep in general (Ancoli-Israel, Kripke, Mason, & Messin, 1981). DIMS associated with alcohol and drug use is a common and multifaceted category. Treatment of drug-dependent insomnia is also very difficult, because initially the patient uses alcohol or sedative-hypnotics as an expedient to sleep; but as tolerance develops, sleep deteriorates. Furthermore, most drugs are deleterious to sleep. Stimulants obviously disturb sleep, but many people are unaware of the stimulant properties of such drugs as caffeine and nicotine. It is now well established that sedative-hypnotics lose effectiveness after two to three weeks of continuous use (Kay, Blackburn, Buckingham, & Karacan, 1976). Their use should, therefore, be time limited. A further complication of long-term drug use is the rebound insomnia seen in the withdrawal phase. Such drug withdrawal effect may frighten the patient and convince him that he cannot sleep without drugs. The cycle of drug-dependent insomnia is thus perpetuated (Kales, Scharf, & Kales, 1978). Alcohol is often used as a soporific. However, it offers limited benefits. The acute effect is to shorten sleep latency, but as the alcohol metabolizes, intermediate awakenings are increased. In addition, alcohol significantly alters sleep architecture such that a patient is robbed of better quality sleep (Gross & Hastey, 1975; Johnson, Burdick, & Smith, 1970). Sleep architecture has even been shown to remain abnormal after several months of abstinence in chronic alcoholics (Williams & Rundell, 1981).

C. Diagnostic Categories

In 1979, the ASDC published the first diagnostic classification system of sleep and arousal disorders. Table 1 presents the categories of insomnia as defined by this organization (ASDC, 1979). Note that there are several inconsistencies in how the categories were defined. Some follow the primary versus secondary distinction. Others appear to be exclusively symptom based and descriptive (e.g., childhood onset DIMS). Furthermore, another category, "subjective DIMS without objective findings," also known as pseudoinsomnia or subjective insomnia, has proven controversial as it purports to define a disorder on the basis of a discrepancy between patient self-reported sleep (subjective) and electroencephalogram (EEG)-defined sleep measures (objective). For a discussion of the inadequacy of this particular diagnostic label, see Trinder (1988). The shortcomings of the current nosology probably reflect, in part, the atheoretical position from which it arose. A revision of the diagnostic classification system is currently being prepared.

Although the nosology of sleep-wake disorders provides an exhaustive list of causes of insomnia, in practice, one most often treats only the four most prevalent diagnostic groups noted above. The other types of insomnia are rare and/or self-limiting. Therefore, most behavioral treatment efforts have been focused on interventions for conditioned insomnia, drug-dependent insomnia, and insomnia associated with psychiatric conditions. Of course, treatment of underlying medical conditions causing insomnia is also important. Finally, as in the case of many other disorders, we have come to recognize the heterogeneity of insomnia (in terms of both etiology and symptomatology) and increasingly attempt to tailor specific treatments to the diagnostic subgroups.

D. Assessment

Assessment of insomnia involves careful evaluation of the full 24-hour sleep-wake cycle. The complex multidimensional nature of insomnia demands a comprehensive multimethod approach utilizing self-report measures, observer data, mechanical device data, and, when indicated or available, all-night polysomnography. Early insomnia treatment outcome studies (Bootzin, 1972; Borkovec & Fowles, 1973; Haynes, Price, & Simons, 1975; Lacks & Rotert, 1986; Woolfolk, Carr-Kaffashan, McNulty, & Lehrer, 1976) relied heavily upon self-report measures (e.g., sleep diaries). However, this approach alone is quite limited and is now considered insufficient for evaluating the severity of insomnia complaints as well as the effectiveness of a particular treatment. Additionally, behavior therapists and researchers need to be aware of and understand a variety of medical factors that may play a role in a disorder of initiating

Table 1 DIMS: Disorders of Initiating and Maintaining Sleep (insomnias)

1. Psychophysiological
   a. transient and situational
   b. persistent
2. Associated with psychiatric disorders
   a. symptom and personality disorders
   b. affective disorders
   c. other functional psychoses
3. Associated with use of drugs and alcohol
   a. tolerance to or withdrawal from CNS depressants
   b. sustained use of CNS stimulants
   c. sustained use of or withdrawal from other drugs
   d. chronic alcoholism
4. Associated with sleep-induced respiratory impairment
   a. sleep apnea DIMS syndrome
   b. alveolar hypoventilation DIMS syndrome
5. Associated with nocturnal myoclonus and restless legs
   a. sleep-related nocturnal myoclonus DIMS syndrome
   b. restless legs DIMS syndrome
6. Associated with other medical, toxic, and environmental conditions
7. Childhood-onset DIMS
8. Associated with other DIMS conditions
   a. repeated REM sleep interruptions
   b. atypical polysomnographic features
   c. not otherwise specified
9. No DIMS abnormality
   a. short sleeper
   b. subjective DIMS compliants without objective findings
   c. not otherwise specified

and maintaining sleep. Medical factors should be given careful consideration before patients or subjects enter into behavioral treatment for insomnia.

The most comprehensive assessment of insomnia should include information gathered from three domains: self-report measures of sleep pattern, standardized measures of waking function (symptoms and personality or trait measure), and electrophysiological data obtained from polysomnography. When all three sets of data are compared, then a specific diagnosis can be made, an individualized treatment package designed, and a number of target variables examined for treatment efficacy.

1. BEHAVIORAL AND SELF-REPORT MEASURES

As noted previously by Bootzin & Nicassio (1978), global self-reports of sleep symptoms tend to be most subject to demand characteristics and least sensitive to treatment differences. They are seldom used except as an adjunct to more detailed and objective measures, such as sleep logs or diaries. These are varied in type, but essentially ask the patient to systematically record time spent in bed each night and to estimate total sleep obtained, latency to fall asleep, number of awakenings, and so on. Another form of sleep log requires a patient to keep a record of all sleep obtained per 24-hour period. This type is especially helpful in documenting a circadian rhythm disturbance (see the Appendix for examples of each). Lacks, Bertelson, Gans, and Kunkel (1983) noted that, although insomniacs usually overestimate sleep latency and underestimate total sleep time, their self-reports are consistent and thus provide a reliable and valid relative measure of insomnia. Sleep logs have also been shown to have high test-retest reliability and to correlate well with both EEG-defined measures of sleep and bed-partner reports (Bootzin & Engle-Friedman, 1981; Coates et al. 1982; Frankel, Coursey, Buchbinder, & Snyder, 1976; Lichstein, Nickel, Hoelscher, & Kelley, 1982). In short, the sleep log or diary has become the standard self-report measure of severity and type of insomnia, and its widespread use has permitted across-study comparisons.

In recent years, four specific parameters of sleep appear to be used most often for assessing insomnia. They are as follows:

(1) Sleep onset latency (SOL) is simply the length of time it takes for an individual to initiate sleep.
(2) Wake after sleep onset (WASO) is the amount of time an individual is awake after sleep onset and prior to final awakening. This measure is useful for evaluating the extent of a sleep maintenance problem.
(3) Sleep efficiency (SE) is the ratio of total sleep time to total time in bed.
(4) Total sleep time (TST) is the sum of the time spent in sleep throughout a sleep period and is usually measured in minutes.

While these parameters of sleep are often the focus of insomnia treatment outcome studies, a number of other specialized measures have been developed and can be useful assessment tools. These include the Pre-Sleep Arousal Scale, developed by Nicassio, Mendlowitz, Fussell, and Petras (1985) to assess the impact of cognitive and somatic tension or arousal on sleep; the Insomnia Symptom Questionnaire (Spielman, Saskin, & Thorpy, 1987); the Sleep Hygiene and Practice Scale, developed by Patricia Lacks and her colleagues at Washington University in St. Louis; and the Self-Efficacy Scale (Lacks, 1987).

The Self-Efficacy Scale consists of nine questions regarding sleep behaviors and how confident the individual is that he or she can accomplish them. Each item is rated on a scale of 1 (not confident) to 5 (very confident). Thus total scores range from 9 to 45. It is suggested that this measure be administered at baseline and again at the end of treatment. As of yet, no normative data are available. However, Cook and Lacks (1984) found that for 28 sleep onset insomniacs who had received a course of stimulus control treatment, the average perceived self-efficacy increased approximately 10 points.

The most stringent test of validity is demonstrated in research that utilized all-night polysomnography. It appears that the correlation between sleep onset latency and polysomnography ranges from .62 to .99, with the higher values occurring when more conservative criteria for sleep onset are used. For other sleep parameters the correlations are less encouraging.

More recently, attention has also been focused on how the insomniac feels during the day. The most frequent measures of interest are daytime sleepiness (as measured by the Daytime Sleepiness Scale; see the Appendix) or by laboratory measurement of sleep tendency throughout the day (Multiple Sleep Latency Test, or MSLT). It is of interest that insomniacs differ from normals in the subjective appreciation of daytime sleepiness (Schneider-Helmert, 1987), but patients with insomnia are objectively more alert than normal controls on the MSLT (Stepanski, Zorick, Roehrs, Young, & Roth, 1988).

Finally, a number of standardized measures of mood and psychological functioning are used in studies of patients with insomnia. The single most widely used personality inventory is the MMPI. It has by now been well established that patients with insomnia differ from normal sleepers and from patients with other types of sleep disorders in their typical MMPI profile (Hauri & Fisher, 1986; Kales, Caldwell, Preston, Healey, & Kales, 1976; Lilie & Kravitz, 1983; Monroe, 1967; Piccione, Tallarigo, Zorick, Wittig, & Roth, 1981). Noting the fact that many insomniacs present with symptoms of depression, anxiety, and hysteria (Scales 2, 7, and 3, respectively), other self-report scales that elaborate these symptoms have been employed. These include the Beck Depression Inventory (Beck, 1967), the State-Trait Anxiety Inventory (Spielberger, Gorsuch, & Lushene, 1970), and the Profile of Mood States (Pillard, Atkinson, & Fisher, 1967).

2. SLEEP LABORATORY

Sleep laboratory measurements are essential in diagnosing and treating disorders of excessive somnolence such as sleep apnea and narcolepsy (Guilleminault, 1982; Mitler, 1982). Increasingly, the information garnered from polysomnography is also thought to be necessary to evaluate the insomnias. For example, Reynolds, Jacobs, Kupfer, Levin, and Ehrenpreis (1987) demonstrated that polysomnography added to, refuted, or failed to support the initial clinical impression in nearly 50% of a sample of consecutive cases referred for insomnia.

(a) Polysomnography. Polysomnography permits continuous collec-

tion of physiological data during a subject's customary sleep hours (usual recording time duration of seven to eight hours) in a standardized way. The minimum number of channels needed for staging of human sleep is four. This minimum montage consists of EEG (usually C3/A1 or C4/A2 and occipital placement), electro-oculogram (EOG), and submental electromyogram (EMG). Depending upon the subject's presenting complaint, age, and general health, the following ancillary channels may be selected:

(1) nasal-oral air flow
(2) respiratory effort
(3) oxygen saturation
(4) muscle activity in limbs or masseter
(5) EKG
(6) skin temperature
(7) blood pressure
(8) additional EEG leads

Because of the existence of a "first-night effect" and even of a "reverse first-night effect," many sleep laboratories perform multiple consecutive nights of recording (see Agnew, Webb, & Williams, 1966; Mosko, Dickel, & Ashurst, 1988; Webb & Campbell, 1979). Particularly for research studies, the first night of data is often discarded or averaged into subsequent nights of recording. This is not always the case, however, for clinical diagnoses in which one laboratory night is usual. The scoring of human sleep is standardized (Rechtschaffen & Kales, 1968). Although polysomnography provides a wealth of information about the sleeping brain, it does not tell the whole story about human sleep disorders. For example, it has long been known that the sleep of patients with insomnia is not like that of good sleepers. Early studies suggested that insomniacs consistently overestimated their sleep latency and underestimated their total sleep time (Carskadon et al., 1976; Monroe, 1967). Patients with a complaint of insomnia were also shown to have more night-to-night variability in their sleep (Dement & Guilleminault, 1973). Finally, insomniacs were seen to be distinguishable from controls on various symptom and personality measures (e.g., anxiety, depression, neuroticism; Kales, Caldwell, Preston, Healey, & Kales, 1976; Monroe, 1967).

Recently, polysomnography technology has shown that many insomniacs do indeed have heightened awareness, increased vigilance, and ability to process information during stages of EEG-defined sleep (Mendelson, James, Garnett, Sack, & Rosenthal, 1986). Of further importance has been the work of Bootzin and his colleagues on the experimental differentiation of subjective insomniacs (SI) from psychophysiological (conditioned) insomniacs (PI) (Dorsey & Bootzin, 1987; Dorsey, Bootzin, &

Rosenberg, 1988; Engle-Friedman, Baker, & Bootzin, 1985). Findings from these studies have indicated that (a) SIs overestimate the amount of time it takes them to fall asleep; also, they have difficulty distinguishing between being awake and nonrapid eye movement (NREM) sleep; (b) SIs have higher Eysenck neuroticism scores than PIs or noncomplaining sleepers; and (c) PI appears to be affected by increased presleep cognitive activity, while SI is more related to the phenomenology of sleep. Hence, we have seen the need to reexamine the continuum of conscience experience from waking to sleep and to acknowledge important individual differences in perception of sleep. We have also come full circle in taking the patient's self-report seriously and for what it is. Subjective awareness of having slept is no less "real" than EEG-defined sleep. Both are important.

(b) Ambulatory monitoring. Another category of measurement is that of ambulatory home monitoring. Such measures provide many advantages, including low cost relative to sleep laboratory nights, physiological data as compared with purely paper-and-pencil home measurements of sleep, and high external validity. For example, Sewitch and Kupfer (1985a, 1985b) compared the Oxford-Medilog 9000 and the Telediagnostic System with standard laboratory polysomnography on 24 normal sleepers. They found that both ambulatory systems reliably reflected the sleep parameters obtained in the laboratory. This form of assessment is particularly applicable in cases of sleep-wake-cycle disturbance. A case in point is a patient with sleep onset insomnia who actually proves to have a circadian rhythm disturbance (Phase Delay Sleep Syndrome). In this syndrome, the individual's biological propensity to fall asleep is later than the desired clock time as determined by social or occupational demands. In such cases, behavioral and physiological variables are monitored. For example, two types of behavioral measures may be obtained. First, self-report measures of sleep-wake patterns are obtained (sleep logs). Second, automatic recordings of body movements (actography) from which sleep and wakefulness are inferred are collected. The sleep-wake cycle is further elucidated by examining a physiological measurement such as core body temperature. Recording is accomplished via ambulatory monitoring with use of a rectal probe. All of the measures mentioned above are able to generate long series of data on the patient's sleep-wake cycle. This is necessary for assessing and treating circadian rhythm disturbances.

II. TREATMENT

A. Relaxation Therapies, Biofeedback, and Meditation

Historically, patients with insomnia were thought to be hyperaroused physically and mentally. Also, good and poor sleepers were thought to be reliably distinguishable on those dimensions. From these assumptions, techniques for reducing somatic and cognitive arousal were developed. Coates and Thoresen (1981) provided a thorough review of the various treatments for insomnia. Their overview of treatment modalities suggests the following individualized treatment plans: When somatized tension is high, apply somatic relaxation techniques such as progressive muscle relaxation (Jacobson, 1938) or EMG (usually frontalis muscle) biofeedback. Hauri (1981) demonstrated that some insomniacs who are muscularly relaxed will not benefit from such procedures. He hypothesized that these patients have a weakness in their sleep system that may respond to other forms of treatment. With the growth of cognitive-behavior therapy, we have seen the application of cognitively mediated relaxation responses to the problem of insomnia (e.g., Mitchell, 1979; Morin & Azrin, 1987). Chief among these has been autogenic training in which patients use self-suggestions to generate feelings of heaviness and warmth in their extremities (Schultz & Luthe, 1959). The proposed mechanisms of action include a reduction in skeletal muscle tone and a lowering of sympathetic tone. Meditation is another cognitive treatment for insomnia. Although a variety of meditative relaxation procedures are known, Woolfolk, Carr-Kaffashan, McNulty, and Lehrer (1976) found that simply focusing on the sensations of respiration while repeating a mantra of "in" and "out" in concert with inhalation and exhalation produced significant improvement in the sleep of a group of adult insomniacs. Training in thought stopping or imaging may also be helpful to those patients with intrusive or ruminative thoughts at bedtime (Nicassio & Jahn, 1980). These insomniacs require active coping skills to overcome their negative expectations at bedtime.

B. Sleep Hygiene

Recent multimodal treatments for insomnia have included an educational component referred to as sleep hygiene. These are sets of rules and basic information about intrapersonal and environmental variables that affect sleep (Kirmil-Gray, Eagleston, Thoresen, & Zarcone, 1985; Lacks, 1987; Spielman, Caruso, & Glovinsky, 1987). Hauri (1981) outlined eleven classic rules of sleep hygiene. These include the following:

(1) Sleep as much as needed to feel refreshed and healthy during the following day, but no more. Curtailing the time in bed seems to solidify sleep; excessively long times in bed seem related to fragmented and shallow sleep.
(2) A regular arousal time in the morning strengthens circadian cycling and, finally, leads to regular times of sleep onset.
(3) A steady daily amount of exercise probably deepens sleep; occasional exercise does not necessarily improve sleep the following night.

(4) Occasional loud noises (e.g., aircraft flyovers) disturb sleep even in people who are not awakened by noises and who cannot remember them in the morning. Sound-attenuated bedrooms may help those who must sleep close to noise.

(5) Although excessively warm rooms disturb sleep, there is no evidence that an excessively cold room solidifies sleep.

(6) Hunger may disturb sleep; a light snack may help sleep.

(7) An occasional sleeping pill may be of some benefit, but their chronic use is ineffective in most insomniacs.

(8) Caffeine in the evening disturbs sleep, even in those who feel it does not.

(9) Alcohol helps tense people fall asleep more easily, but the ensuing sleep is then fragmented.

(10) People who feel angry and frustrated because they cannot sleep should not try harder and harder to fall asleep but should turn on the light and do something different.

(11) The chronic use of tobacco disturbs sleep.

Although many people know which substances and conditions interfere with sleep, not all of them practice good sleep hygiene on a consistent basis. Establishing knowledge and practice of these principles is a necessary but seldom sufficient condition for alleviation of the complaint of insomnia. Thus sleep hygiene awareness forms the background for application of other behavioral treatments. Lacks and Rotert (1986) compared awareness and practice of sleep hygiene among SOIs, SMIs, and good sleepers. They found that poor sleepers had more knowledge of sleep hygiene than good sleepers but practiced it less often. SOIs had poorer sleep hygiene habits than SMIs.

Thus far, only one study has attempted to determine whether sleep hygiene alone is sufficient treatment for insomnia. Schoicket, Bartelson, and Lacks (1988) compared the effectiveness of stimulus control, meditation, and sleep hygiene for sleep maintenance insomnia. They recruited 65 subjects with sleep maintenance insomnia of at least six months' duration. All subjects were asked to monitor their compliance to treatment.

All three treatment groups achieved significant improvement. However, there were no statistical differences between the groups at the end of treatment or at follow-up. There were differences in the rates of compliance for the groups. Subjects in the hygiene and meditation groups complied more than those in the stimulus control group. All treatments combined resulted in a 31% decrease in wake after sleep onset, a 20% decrease in number of arousals, and a 21% decrease in the duration of arousals.

The results of this study suggest that improvement of sleep hygiene can result in decreases in the subjective complaint of sleep maintenance insomnia. The efficacy of sleep hygiene for sleep onset insomnia has not been empirically determined. Additionally, it is clear that sleep hygiene instructions will not be effective for improving the sleep of everyone who complains of insomnia. Studies that establish effectiveness of sleep hygiene in those with poor preexisting sleep hygiene are needed.

C. Stimulus Control

Stimulus control instructions as a treatment for insomnia have been developed, refined, and tested extensively by Bootzin and his colleagues as well as others (Bootzin, 1972, 1973, 1976, 1977; Haynes, Price, & Simons, 1975; Turner & Ascher, 1979a). This technique is derived from an operant analysis of sleep and insomnia in which falling asleep is an instrumental response and sleep itself is reinforcing. An emphasis is placed on the discriminatory cues present in the sleeping environment and in the individual's presleep activities. Bootzin and Nicassio (1978) noted that the goals of stimulus control treatment for insomnia are to improve the patient's sleep-wake rhythm, to strengthen the bed as a cue for sleep, and to weaken the bed as a cue for other activities that may interfere with sleep (e.g., eating, reading, watching TV, worrying). The following is an outline of stimulus control instructions:

(1) Lie down intending to go to sleep only when you are sleepy.
(2) Do not read, watch TV, eat, or worry in bed. Sexual activity is the only exception to this rule.
(3) If you find yourself unable to fall asleep after 10 minutes, get up immediately and go do something else and return to bed when sleepy.
(4) If you still cannot fall asleep, repeat Step 3. Do this as often as necessary throughout the night.
(5) Set your alarm and get up at the same time every morning irrespective of how much sleep you got during the night.
(6) Do not nap during the day.

Several experiments have demonstrated the efficacy of stimulus control procedures in reducing sleep onset latency (Haynes, Price, & Simons, 1975; Turner & Ascher, 1979b; Zwart & Lisman, 1979). Furthermore, it has been shown to work as well as or better than a number of alternative behavioral treatments. For example, Turner and Ascher (1979b) compared three behavioral treatments for insomnia: stimulus control, progressive relaxation, and paradoxical intention. They found that all three therapies significantly reduced subjective sleep complaints in contrast to placebo and waiting list controls. No appreciable differences were observed among the three treatments.

In another comparative study of behavioral treatments, Lacks, Bertelson, Gans, and Kunkel (1983) found that stimulus control was more effective than progressive relaxation and paradoxical intention across three levels of severity of sleep onset insomnia. Of interest was the fact that stimulus control produced substantial clinically meaningful changes in percentage of subjects who improved, in degree of improvement in sleep onset latency, and in number of nights in which insomnia was experienced.

Zwart and Lisman (1979) developed a treatment called countercontrol. This treatment is similar to the stimulus control treatment with the exception of leaving the bed. Patients or subjects are asked to engage in the nonstimulating activity in bed whenever they are unable to initiate or reinitiate sleep. Individuals are also instructed to spend 30 minutes per day engaging in nonsleep activities while in bed. Their initial study found stimulus control and countercontrol to be equally effective.

Davies, Lacks, Storandt, and Bertelson (1986) administered countercontrol treatment to 34 sleep maintenance insomniacs ranging in age from 35 to 78. They closely modeled the Zwart and Lisman (1979) procedures. If subjects were unable to fall asleep within 10 minutes of waking up, they were to sit up in bed and engage in a nonstimulating activity such as reading, watching TV, or listening to the radio. To preclude explanation of treatment effects, participants were instructed to engage in noncognitive activities in bed 30 minutes every day. The results indicated that countercontrol is indeed useful for treatment of sleep maintenance insomnia. After four weeks of treatment, countercontrol therapy reduced the sleep complaints for the total group by about 30%, with gradual improvement continuing through the four-week follow-up period. The number of nocturnal arousals decreased by 20% with the reported nights of insomnia being reduced an average of one night per subject. Sleep onset, while not a target of this study, was also reduced.

D. Paradoxical Intention

Turner and DiTomasso (1980) suggest that sleep problems are maintained by the individual's attempt to control the sleeping process. These attempts presumably result in arousal of the sympathetic nervous system, making sleep very difficult to initiate. Fears about sleep deprivation and its cumulative effects on health generate an increased demand to sleep, leading to performance anxiety. Quite often, patients report that they try hard to sleep, not realizing that they are creating a cycle in which increased tension and arousal result in sleep onset difficulties.

The effects of performance anxiety on the ability to initiate sleep have been tested experimentally. Shaffer, Dickel, Marik, and Slak (1985) asked a group of good sleepers to fall asleep as quickly as possible with a cash prize for the shortest sleep latency. The average baseline time for sleep onset was 11.6 minutes. On the night of the experimentally induced performance anxiety, these same subjects took an average of 21.9 minutes to initiate sleep.

Paradoxical intention is a cognitive technique that has been shown to have some usefulness in treating sleep onset insomnia (Ascher & Turner, 1979). A defining characteristic of paradoxical intention is to make explicit the paradox of weakening a behavior by asking clients to strengthen or augment that behavior. Such a suggestion is especially appropriate for clients with severe sleep onset insomnia marked by trying too hard to fall asleep. The paradoxical treatment involves instructing the client to lie in bed in a darkened room and keep his eyes open (or remain awake) for as long as possible. The client is thereby placed in a "win-win" situation in which he successfully completes the task or he falls asleep. Either way, a new coping strategy for sleep has been learned. Despite the intuitive appeal of paradoxical intention for sleep onset insomnia, there is modest empirical support for the efficacy of this technique. It has been studied less than progressive relaxation and stimulus control, and results have been inconsistent across studies (see the review by Borkovec, 1982; Lichstein & Fischer, 1985). Thus far, there has been a relative absence of studies that isolate crucial mechanisms of effect. Polysomnography studies should be utilized in future studies to verify outcome.

E. Sleep Restriction

Sleep restriction is one of the most promising new behavioral treatments of insomnia. First described by Spielman, Saskin, and Thorpy (1987), the treatment consists of markedly restricting time in bed (TIB) available for sleep followed by extension of TIB contingent upon improved sleep efficiency. Sleep efficiency is defined as the ratio of total sleep time (TST) to TIB. Healthy young adult sleepers typically have very high sleep efficiency (e.g., above 95%), while insomniacs often spend excessive waking time in bed (Williams, Karacan, & Hursch, 1974; Spielman, Saskin, & Thorpy, 1983). The method involves first collecting baseline sleep logs for two weeks. An individualized sleep-wake schedule is then prescribed as follows: Average subjective TST is set equal to initial TIB. For example, if a patient is spending eight hours in bed but only sleeping for an average for five hours, then TIB equals five hours. Morning rise time is set in accordance with the patient's needs. Therefore, if the patient in the example above needs to get up at 6:00 a.m., his initial bedtime would be 1:00 a.m. This schedule is followed until the patient demonstrates a mean sleep efficiency of 90% or better over five consecutive days. Once this criterion is met, the patient "earns" additional TIB by setting retiring time earlier in 15-minute increments. With each TIB increment, the same 90% sleep efficiency criterion must be met. Spielman, Saskin, and Thorpy (1987) found that, at the end of eight weeks of treatment, patients reported significant improvement in TST, sleep latency, sleep efficiency, and subjective assessment of their insomnia. Moreover, improvement remained significant at a mean of 36 weeks posttreatment for a subset of patients (66% of the original sample) who participated in the follow-up study. Another study, comparing sleep restriction therapy with relaxation training in geriatric insomniacs, found only a modest improvement in sleep efficiency (Bliwise, Friedman, and Yesavage, 1988). These authors granted that the effectiveness of the sleep restriction therapy may have been limited by the short treatment time (four weeks versus eight weeks).

F. Chronotherapy

Some patients who present a complaint of sleep onset insomnia prove to have a circadian rhythm disorder (Weitzman et al., 1981). Delayed Sleep Phase Syndrome occurs when sleep itself is normal in length and architecture but is misplaced in the 24-hour clock at a time later than desired by the patient. For example, a person who must get up at 6:00 a.m. and requires eight hours of sleep to feel adequately rested would need to fall asleep about 10:00 p.m. If this person's sleep cycle were delayed, then he might be unable to fall asleep until 2:00 a.m. In this case, sleep length would either be severely curtailed (i.e., wake up at 6:00 a.m. and obtain four hours of sleep) or sleep length would be preserved but the person would "oversleep" his morning appointments (i.e., wake up at 10:00 a.m. with a total sleep time of eight hours). A recommended treatment for this disorder is chronotherapy (Czeisler et al., 1981). The field of chronobiology has shown us that all humans have a free-running sleep-wake period of slightly greater than 24 hours (Weitzman et al., 1979; Wever, 1979). This fact explains why it is easier for us to extend our day by delaying bedtime rather than shortening our day by advancing the sleep cycle. Chronotherapy is a behavioral treatment that employs progressive delaying of sleep onset and offset time to reset the circadian clock to an earlier time (see the Appendix). Most often used is a one- or two-hour delaying interval. Patients are instructed to go to bed later each night by the prescribed interval. It is a time-consuming and arduous procedure, but it is effective in resetting the circadian clock for earlier times. Chronotherapy has to be repeated periodically to sustain improvement and patients must adhere to a strict sleep-wake schedule between treatments.

III. OVERVIEW AND FUTURE TRENDS

To date, a critical review of the treatments mentioned above indicates that we are far from understanding the causes of insomnia and we have only begun to explore effective interventions. It is clear that the complaint of insomnia is prevalent, persistent, and troublesome in the adult population. Insomnia may be the end result of perturbations in a variety of systems—environmental, physiological, psychological, and behavioral. Many studies in the past that have shown modest success in treating insomnia have a number of shortcomings. First, analog studies in which young adults with mild sleep disturbances have been treated may not generalize to clinical populations. The most relevant studies will focus on adults with severe, chronic sleep onset and maintenance insomnia. Generalizability must also be addressed by noting the increased incidence of insomnia with age and the gender ratio in favor of women. Few studies have examined the efficacy of behavioral techniques for such special populations. Second, even the most effective and reliable behavioral treatments (stimulus control and sleep restriction) are rigorous for the patient. Therefore, compliance is a problem that merits further attention. Detailed reports of subject selection, dropout rates, and strategies for enhancing compliance are needed in future research. Third, to date, most studies have reported a limited number of dependent variables (usually sleep latency and TST). These have been chosen more for expediency and cost-effectiveness than for validity and heuristic value. Carskadon et al. (1976) found that these two variables have less relevance to the clinical syndrome of insomnia than was previously thought. Also, Bonnet (1985) found that disturbances in sleep continuity lead to rapid decline in waking mood and performance even without large cumulative sleep loss. Periodic disturbance of nocturnal sleep is common in severe sleep-maintenance insomnia. Further research is needed into the waking consequences of insomnia. Fourth, there have been common methodological flaws, including reliance on self-report sleep logs or diaries without convergent information from polysomnography or other automated physiological recordings. When polysomnography was employed, there was usually a failure to complete multinight recordings so that internight variability and first-night effects could be controlled.

There is a pressing need to increase diagnostic precision because the insomnias represent a heterogeneous group of disorders. Further, treatments must then be tailored to the individual. Often, sequential application of behavioral techniques is necessary to successfully treat the patient with insomnia. Newer, multimodal therapies for insomnia have been described by Lacks (1987) and Kirmil-Gray, Eagleston, Thoresen, and Zarcone (1985). These treatments usually encompass an initial phase of supervised drug withdrawal from hypnotics, education about sleep hygiene, and application of specific behavioral techniques, such as relaxation training, cognitive therapy, stimulus control, and so on. Such innovative procedures appear to hold the most promise for alleviating the variety of sleep-wake symptoms experienced by patients with insomnia.

APPENDIX

SLEEP LOG (TWO WEEKS)

NAME: _____

Day & Date	Pre-Sleep Mood Use all scale from 10 = very good 1 = very upset	Medications taken	Notes – Important events of the day	Bedtime (what time you turned out the lights to fall asleep)	Approx. length of time to fall asleep	Number of awaken-ings during the night	Morning time of awakening	Total time asleep	Post-Sleep mood in the morning 10 = very good 1 = very upset

NOTES:

Appendix Figure 1. Nighttime sleep log.

PLEASE RECORD SLEEP TIMES AS SOON AS YOU WAKE UP   DON'T FORGET NAPS

PLEASE PLACE A LINE IN EACH HALF-HOUR PERIOD DURING WHICH YOU SLEPT

Appendix Figure 2. 24-hour sleep log.

DAYTIME SLEEPINESS SCALE

Please rate your degree of sleepiness for each hour as
indicated today.   Place a vertical mark on the line which
best describes how you feel at that time.

Name: _____
Date: _____

                          very sleepy   very alert

7:00 a.m.   _____

8:00 a.m.   _____

9:00 a.m.   _____

10:00 a.m.   _____

11:00 a.m.   _____

Noon   _____

1:00 p.m.   _____

2:00 p.m.   _____

3:00 p.m.   _____

4:00 p.m.   _____

Appendix Figure 3. Daytime sleepiness scale.

CHRONOTHERAPY SCHEDULE

Name: _____

Sleep Period	Time in Bed*	Hours of Sleep	Date
1	12 M - 8 a.m.	_____	_____
2	3 a.m.-11 a.m.	_____	_____
3	6 a.m.- 2 p.m.	_____	_____
4	9 a.m.- 5 p.m.	_____	_____
5	12 N - 8 p.m.	_____	_____
6	3 p.m.-11 p.m.	_____	_____
7	6 p.m.- 2 a.m.	_____	_____
8	9 p.m.- 5 a.m.	_____	_____

*You must stay in bed and rest during these hours even if not asleep. You are not to nap during other hours.

Appendix Figure 4. Chronotherapy schedule.

REFERENCES

Agnew, H. W., Webb, W. B., & Williams, R. L. (1966). The first night effect: An EEG study of sleep. *Psychophysiology, 2,* 263-266.
Ancoli-Israel, S., Kripke, D. F., Mason, W., & Messin, S. (1981). Sleep apnea and nocturnal myoclonus in a senior population. *Sleep, 4,* 349-358.
Ascher, L. M., & Turner, R. M. (1979). Paradoxical intention and insomnia: An experimental investigation. *Behaviour Research and Therapy, 17,* 408-411.
Association of Sleep Disorders Centers (ASDC). (1979). Diagnostic classification of sleep and arousal disorders (1st ed.). *Sleep, 2,* 1-137.
Beck, A. T. (1967). *Depression: Clinical, experimental, and theoretical aspects.* New York: Harper & Row.
Belloc, N. B. (1973). Relationship of health practices and mortality. *Preventive Medicine, 2,* 67-81.
Bixler, E. O., Kales, A., Soldatos, C. R., Kales, J. D., & Healy, S. (1979). Prevalence of sleep disorders in the Los Angeles metropolitan area. *American Journal of Psychiatry, 136,* 1257-1262.
Bliwise, D. L., Friedman, L., & Yesavage, J. A. (1988). A pilot study comparing sleep restriction therapy and relaxation training in geriatric insomniacs. *Sleep Research, 17,* 148.

Bonnet, M. H. (1985). Effect of sleep disruption on sleep, performance, and mood. *Sleep, 8,* 11-19.

Bootzin, R. R. (1972). A stimulus control treatment for insomnia. *Proceedings of the 80th Annual Convention of the American Psychological Association, 7,* 395-396.

Bootzin, R. R. (1973). *A stimulus control treatment of insomnia.* Presented at "The Treatment of Sleep Disorders." P. Hauri, chair, symposium presented at the American Psychological Association Convention, Montreal.

Bootzin, R. R. (1976). Self-help techniques for controlling insomnia. In C. M. Franks (Ed.), *Behavior therapy: Techniques, principles and patient aids.* New York: Biomonitoring Applications, Inc.

Bootzin, R. R. (1977). Effects of self-control procedures for insomnia. In R. B. Stuart (Ed.), *Behavioral self-management: Strategies and outcomes.* New York: Brunner/Mazel.

Bootzin, R. R., & Engle-Friedman, M. (1981). The assessment of insomnia. *Behavioral Assessment, 3,* 107-126.

Bootzin, R. R., & Nicassio, P. M. (1978). Behavioral treatments for insomnia. In M. Hersen, R. Eisler, & P. Miller (Eds.), *Progress in behavior modification* (Vol. 6, pp. 1-45). New York: Academic Press.

Borkovec, T. D. (1982). Insomnia. *Journal of Consulting and Clinical Psychology, 50,* 880-895.

Borkovec, T. D., & Fowles, D. C. (1973). Controlled investigation of the effects of progressive and hypnotic relaxation on insomnia. *Journal of Abnormal Psychology, 82,* 153-158.

Carskadon, M. A., Dement, W.C., Mitler, M. M., Guilleminault, C., Zarcone, V. P., & Spiegel, R. (1976). Self-reports vs. sleep laboratory findings in 122 drug-free subjects with complaints of chronic insomnia. *American Journal of Psychiatry, 133,* 1382-1388.

Coates, T. J., Killen, J. D., George, J., Silverman, S., Marchini, E., & Thoresen, C. E. (1982). Estimating sleep parameters: A multitrait-multimethod analysis. *Journal of Consulting and Clinical Psychology, 50,* 345-352.

Coates, T. J., & Thoresen, C. E. (1981). Treating sleep disorders: Few answers, some suggestions, and many questions. In S. M. Turner, K. S. Calhoun, & H. E. Adams (Eds.), *Handbook of clinical behavior therapy* (pp. 240-289). New York: John Wiley.

Coleman, R. M., Roffwarg, H. P., Kennedy, J. F., Guilleminault, C., Cinque, J., Cohn, M. A., Karacan, I., Kupfer, D. J., Lemmi, H., Miles, L. E., Orr, W. C., Phillips, E. R., Roth, T., Sassin, J. F., Schmidt, H. S., Weitzman, E. D., & Dement, W. C. (1982). Sleep-wake disorders based on a polysomnographic diagnosis: A national cooperative study. *Journal of the American Medical Association, 247,* 997-1003.

Cook, M. A., & Lacks, P. (1984). *The effectiveness of booster sessions in the treatment of sleep onset insomnia.* Paper presented at the annual meeting of the Association for the Advancement of Behavioral Therapy, Philadelphia.

Czeisler, C. A., Richardson, G. S., Coleman, R. M., Zimmerman, J. C., Moore-Ede, M. C., Dement, W. C., & Weitzman, E. D. (1981). Chronotherapy: Resetting the circadian clocks of patients with delayed sleep phase insomnia. *Sleep, 4,* 1-21.

Davies, R., Lacks, T., Storandt, M., & Bertelson, A. D. (1986). Countercontrol treatment of sleep maintenance insomnia in relation to age. *Psychology and Aging, 1,* 233-238.

Dement, W. C., & Guilleminault, C. (1973). Sleep disorders: The state of the art. *Hospital Practice, 8,* 57-71.

Dorsey, C., & Bootzin, R. R. (1987). Subjective and psychophysiologic insomnia: Multiple sleep latency test, sleep tendency, and personality. *Sleep Research, 16,* 328.

Dorsey, C., Bootzin, R. R., & Rosenberg, R. S. (1988). Perception of depth of sleep in insomnia. *Sleep Research, 17,* 169.

Engle-Friedman, M., Baker, E. A., & Bootzin, R. R. (1985). Reports of wakefulness during EEG identified stages of sleep. *Sleep Research, 14,* 152.

Ferber, R. (1987). The sleepless child. In C. Guilleminault (Ed.), *Sleep and its disorders in children.* New York: Raven.

Frankel, B. L., Coursey, R. D., Buchbinder, R., & Snyder, F. (1976). Recorded and reported sleep in chronic primary insomnias. *Archives of General Psychiatry, 33*, 615-623.

Gross, M. M., & Hastey, J. M. (1975). The relation between baseline slow wave sleep and the slow wave sleep response to alcohol in alcoholics. In M. M. Gross (Ed.), *Alcohol intoxication and withdrawal: Experimental studies II.* New York: Plenum.

Guilleminault, C. (1982). Sleep and breathing. In C. Guilleminault (Ed.), *Sleeping and waking disorders: Indications and techniques* (pp. 155-182). Reading, MA: Addison-Wesley.

Hammond, E. C. (1964). Some preliminary findings on physical complaints from a prospective study of 1,064,004 men and women. *American Journal of Public Health, 54*, 11-23.

Hauri, P. (1981). Treating psychophysiologic insomnia with biofeedback. *Archives of General Psychiatry, 38*, 752-758.

Hauri, P. (1982). *The sleep disorders.* Kalamazoo, MI: Upjohn.

Hauri, P., & Fisher, J. (1986). Persistent psychophysiologic (learned) insomnia. *Sleep, 9*, 38-53.

Haynes, S. N., Price, M. G., & Simons, J. B. (1975). Stimulus control treatment of insomnia. *Journal of Behavior Therapy and Experimental Psychiatry, 6*, 279-282.

Jacobson, E. (1938). *Progressive relaxation.* Chicago: University of Chicago Press.

Johnson, L. C., Burdick, J. A., & Smith, J. (1970). Sleep during alcohol intake and withdrawal in the chronic alcoholic. *Archives of General Psychiatry, 22*, 406-418.

Kales, A., Caldwell, A. B., Preston, T. A., Healey, S., & Kales, J. D. (1976). Personality patterns in insomnia. *Archives of General Psychiatry, 33*, 1128-1134.

Kales, A., & Kales, J. D. (1984). *Evaluation and treatment of insomnia.* New York: Oxford University Press.

Kales, A., Scharf, M. D., & Kales, J. D. (1978). Rebound insomnia: A new clinical syndrome. *Science,, 201*, 1039-1041.

Karacan, I., Thornby, J. I., Anch, M., Holzer, C. P., Wacheit, G. J., Schwab, J. J., & Williams, R. L. (1976). Prevalence of sleep disturbances in a primarily urban Florida county. *Social Science and Medicine, 10*, 239-244.

Kay, D. C., Blackburn, A. B., Buckingham, J. A., & Karacan, I. (1976). Human pharmacology of sleep. In R. L. Williams & I. Karacan (Eds.), *Pharmacology of sleep.* New York: John Wiley.

Kirmil-Gray, K., Eagleston, J. R., Thoresen, C. E., & Zarcone, V. P. (1985). Brief consultation and stress management treatments for drug-dependent insomnia: Effects on sleep quality, self-efficacy, and daytime stress. *Journal of Behavioral Medicine, 8*, 79-99.

Lacks, P. (1987). *Behavioral treatment of persistent insomnia.* New York: Pergamon.

Lacks, P., Bertelson, A. D., Gans, L., & Kunkel, J. (1983). The effectiveness of three behavioral treatments for different degrees of sleep onset insomnia. *Behavior Therapy, 14*, 593-605.

Lacks, P., & Rotert, M. (1986). Knowledge and practice of sleep hygiene techniques in insomniacs and good sleepers. *Behaviour Research and Therapy, 24*, 365-368.

Lichstein, K. L., & Fischer, S. M. (1985). Insomnia. In M. Hersen & A. S. Bellack (Eds.), *Handbook of clinical behavior therapy with adults* (pp. 319-352). New York: Plenum.

Lichstein, K. L., Nickel, R., Hoelscher, T. J., & Kelley, J. E. (1982). Clinical validation of a sleep assessment device. *Behaviour Research and Therapy, 20*, 292-297.

Lilie, J. K., & Kravitz, H. M. (1983). A survey of alcohol use in sleep disorder patients. *Sleep Research, 12*, 260.

Lugaresi, E. (1985). Fatal familial insomnia: A new thalamic disease. *Sleep Research, 14*, 189.

McGhie, A., & Russell, S. M. (1962). The subjective assessment of normal sleep patterns. *Journal of Mental Science, 108*, 642-654.

Mendelson, W. B. (1988). *Human sleep: Research and clinical care.* New York: Plenum.

Mendelson, W. B., James, S. P., Garnett, D., Sack, D. A., & Rosenthal, N. E. (1986). A psychophysiological study of insomnia. *Psychiatry Research, 19,* 267-284.

Mitchell, K. R. (1979). Behavioral treatment of presleep tension and intrusive cognitions in patients with severe predormital insomnia. *Journal of Behavioral Medicine, 2,* 57-69.

Mitler, M. D. (1982). The multiple sleep latency test as an evaluation for excessive somnolence. In C. Guilleminault (Ed.), *Sleeping and waking disorders: Indications and techniques* (pp. 145-153). Reading, MA: Addison-Wesley.

Monroe, L. J. (1967). Psychological and physiological differences between good and poor sleepers. *Journal of Abnormal Psychology, 72,* 255-264.

Morin, C. M., & Azrin, N. H. (1987). Stimulus control and imagery training in treating sleep-maintenance insomnia. *Journal of Consulting and Clinical Psychology, 55,* 260-262.

Mosko, S. S., Dickel, M. J., & Ashurst, J. (1988). Night-to-night variability in sleep apnea and sleep-related periodic leg movements in the elderly. *Sleep, 11,* 340-348.

Nicassio, P., & Jahn, M. (1980). *Evaluation of a cognitive behavior therapy package as a treatment for insomnia.* Paper presented at the Academy of Psychosomatic Medicine, Miami.

Nicassio, P. M., Mendlowitz D. R., Fussell, J. J., & Petras, L. (1985). The phenomenology of the pre-sleep state: The development of the pre-sleep arousal scale. *Journal of Behaviour Therapy and Research, 23,* 263-271.

Piccione, P., Tallarigo, R., Zorick, F., Wittig, R., & Roth, T. (1981). Personality differences between insomniac and non-insomniac psychiatry outpatients. *Journal of Clinical Psychiatry, 42,* 261-263.

Pillard, R. C., Atkinson, K. W., & Fisher, S. (1967). The effect of different preparations on film-induced anxiety. *Psychological Record, 17,* 35-41.

Rechtschaffen, A., & Kales, A. (Eds.). (1968). *A manual of standardized terminology, techniques and scoring system for sleep stages of human subjects.* Washington, DC: National Institutes of Health.

Reynolds, C. F., Jacobs, E. A., Kupfer, D. J., Levin, P. A., & Ehrenpreis, A. B. (1987). Is polysomnography useful in the evaluation of chronic insomnia? *Sleep Research, 16,* 416.

Schneider-Helmert, D. (1987). Twenty-four-hour sleep-wake function and personality patterns in chronic insomniacs and healthy controls. *Sleep, 10,* 452-462.

Schoiket, S. L., Bertelson, A. D., & Lacks, P. (1988). Is sleep hygiene a sufficient treatment for sleep maintenance insomnia? *Behavior Therapy, 19,* 183-190.

Schultz, J. H., & Luthe, W. (1959). *Autogenic training.* New York: Grune & Stratton.

Sewitch, D. E., & Kupfer, D. J. (1985a). A comparison of the Telediagnostic and Medilog systems for recording normal sleep in the home environment. *Psychophysiology, 22,* 718-726.

Sewitch, D. E., & Kupfer, D. J. (1985b). Polysomnographic telemetry using Telediagnostic and Oxford Medilog 9000 systems. *Sleep, 8,* 288-293.

Shaffer, J. I., Dickel, M. J., Marik, N., & Slak, S. (1985). The effect of excessive motivation to fall asleep on sleep onset. *Sleep Research, 14,* 102.

Speilberger, C. D., Gorsuch, R. L., & Lushene, R. E. (1970). *State-Trait Anxiety Inventory manual.* Palo Alto, CA: Consulting Psychologists Press.

Speilman, A. J., Caruso, L. S., & Glovinsky, P. B. (1987). A behavioral perspective on insomnia treatment. *Psychiatric Clinics of North America, 10,* 541-553.

Speilman, A. J., Saskin, P., & Thorpy, M. J. (1983). Sleep restriction: A new treatment of insomnia. *Sleep Research, 12,* 286.

Spielman, A. J., Saskin, P., & Thorpy, M. J. (1987). Treatment of chronic insomnia by restriction of time in bed. *Sleep, 10,* 45-56.

Stepanski, E., Zorick, F., Roehrs, T., Young, D., & Roth, T. (1988). Daytime alertness in patients with chronic insomnia compared with asymptomatic control subjects. *Sleep, 11,* 54-60.

Trinder, J. (1988). Subjective insomnia without objective findings: A pseudo diagnostic classification? *Psychological Bulletin, 103,* 87-94.

Turner, R. M., & Ascher, L. M. (1979a). A within-subject analysis of stimulus control therapy with severe sleep-onset insomnia. *Behaviour Research and Therapy, 17,* 107-112.

Turner, R. M., & Ascher, L. M. (1979b). Controlled comparison of progressive relation, stimulus control, and paradoxical intention therapies for insomnia. *Journal of Consulting and Clinical Psychology, 47,* 500-508.

Turner, R. M., & DiTomasso, R. A. (1980). The behavioral treatment of insomnia: A review and methodologic analysis of the evidence. *International Journal of Mental Health, 9,* 129-148.

Ware, J. C. (1979). The symptom of insomnia: Causes and cures. *Psychiatric Annals, 9,* 27-49.

Webb, W. B., & Campbell, S. S. (1979). The first night effect revisited with age as a variable. *Waking and Sleeping, 3,* 319-324.

Weitzman, E. D., Czeisler, C. A., Coleman, R. M., Dement, W. C., Richardson, G. S., & Pollak, C. P. (1979). Delayed sleep phase syndrome: A biological rhythm sleep disorder. *Sleep Research, 8,* 221.

Weitzman, E. D., Czeisler, C. A., Coleman, R. M., Spielman, A. J., Zimmerman, J. C., & Dement, W. (1981). Delayed sleep phase syndrome: A chronobiological disorder with sleep-onset insomnia. *Archives of General Psychiatry, 38,* 737-746.

Wever, R. (1979). *The circadian system of man.* New York: Springer-Verlag.

Wiley, J. A., & Camacho, T. C. (1980). Lifestyle and future health: Evidence from the Alameda County study. *Preventive Medicine, 9,* 1-21.

Williams, H. L., & Rundell, O. H. (1981). Altered sleep physiology in chronic alcoholics: Reversal with abstinence. *Alcoholism: Clinical and Experimental Research, 5,* 318-325.

Williams, R. L., Karacan, I., & Hursch, C. J. (1974). *EEG of human sleep: Clinical applications.* New York: John Wiley.

Wingard, D. L., & Berkman, L. F. (1983). Mortality risk associated with sleeping patterns among adults. *Sleep, 6,* 102-107.

Woolfolk, R. L., Carr-Kaffashan, L. McNulty, T. F., & Lehrer, P. M. (1976). Meditation training as a treatment for insomnia. *Behavior Therapy, 7,* 359-365.

Zwart, C. A., & Lisman, S. A. (1979). Analysis of stimulus control treatment of sleep-onset insomnia. *Journal of Consulting and Clinical Psychology, 47,* 113-118.

BEHAVIORAL ASSESSMENT AND
TREATMENT OF
PARENT-ADOLESCENT CONFLICT

ARTHUR L. ROBIN
THOMAS KOEPKE
Children's Hospital of Michigan and
Wayne State University School of Medicine

I. Introduction 178
II. Theoretical Model 180
III. Assessment 183
    A. Clinical Interview 185
    B. Self-Report Inventories 187
    C. Direct Observation 190
    D. Integrating Assessment Data for Functional Analysis 192
IV. Intervention 192
    A. Problem-Solving Training 193
    B. Communication Training 195
    C. Cognitive Restructuring 197
        1. Reframing 197
        2. Formal Cognitive Restructuring 198
    D. Structural/Functional Interventions 199
        1. Weak Parental Coalition/Hierarchy Reversal 200
        2. Overinvolved Mother and Disengaged Father 200
V. Treatment Outcomes 202
    A. Problem-Solving Communication Training (PSCT) 202
    B. Functional Family Therapy (FFT) 204
    C. Relationship Enhancement (RE) 206
    D. Summary of Outcome Research 207
VI. Future Directions 207
    References 209

I. INTRODUCTION

Over the past decade behaviorally oriented clinicians have become increasingly interested in the assessment and treatment of adolescent behavior disorders (Feindler & Ecton, 1986; Karoly & Steffan, 1984; Stein & Davis, 1982). Conflict between parents and adolescents is a developmental phenomenon experienced, to varying degrees, by all families and is a common feature associated with a variety of externalizing behavior disorders, particularly attention-deficit hyperactivity disorders, oppositional defiant disorders, and conduct disorders. *Conflict* is defined here as predominantly verbal disagreements or arguments between parents and adolescents about a variety of issues, such as chores, curfew, dating, school, and choice of friends.

A number of treatment programs have been developed that address parent-adolescent conflict (Alexander & Parsons, 1982; Guerney, Coufal, & Vogelsong, 1981; Robin & Foster, 1984, 1989; Stuart, 1971). These treatment programs have grown out of an integrationist tradition that blends social learning, cognitive, and family systems approaches (Epstein, Schlesinger, & Dryden, 1988; Foster & Hoier, 1982); they share a common emphasis on behavioral exchange, problem-solving and communication skills, cognitive distortions, and the family as a self-maintaining, hierarchically ordered system. The populations that have been treated have included juvenile offenders, clinic-referred and self-referred families with independence-related conflicts, adolescents with attention-deficit hyperactivity disorders and school difficulties, and mild to moderately disturbed parent-adolescent dyads seeking an educationally oriented enrichment program. Treatment outcome investigations have also spurred the development and validation of new assessment tools and theoretical constructs (Foster & Robin, 1988).

There has also been a major parallel growth of research concerning normal adolescent development within a family context (Grotevant & Cooper, 1983; Montemayor & Adams, 1985; Youniss & Smollar, 1985). Developmental psychologists have challenged traditional thinking concerning the role of adolescent autonomy in parent-adolescent conflict (Montemayor, 1986) and provided exciting data documenting relationships, such as that between intrafamily power and adolescent pubertal status (Steinberg, 1981; Steinberg & Hill, 1978). Unfortunately, there has been very little cross-fertilization between adolescent developmental psychologists and behaviorally oriented clinicians studying parent-adolescent conflict.

The purpose of this chapter is to review behavioral approaches to the assessment and treatment of parent-adolescent conflict. Included is a discussion of an integrative behavioral family systems account of such conflict. The major assessment measures and treatment methods are reviewed, along with the data evaluating them. Because an exhaustive account of research on parent-adolescent conflict would go beyond the limitations of a single chapter, we have been selective, including major approaches and controlled outcome studies and excluding case studies and less effective approaches that are of mainly historical interest. Finally, suggestions for directions of future research will be offered.

II. THEORETICAL MODEL

Parent-adolescent conflict needs to be understood within a developmental context that recognizes that adolescence is a period of exponential physiological, cognitive, behavioral, and emotional change. To become a competent, healthy adult, the adolescent must master four developmental tasks: (a) becoming autonomous from parents, (b) developing an identity and value system, (c) establishing effective peer relationships, and (d) preparing for a career/vocation (Conger, 1977). Many early theorists and clinicians believed that parent-adolescent relations were inevitably characterized by storm and stress, with frequent bitter conflicts concerning autonomy. However, more recent empirical studies of normal parent-adolescent relations have refuted this hypothesis, suggesting instead that the majority of parents and adolescents do not argue excessively, have relatively harmonious relations, and feel close to each other (Montemayor, 1983, 1986).

In-depth recent analyses of the relationships between intraindividual adolescent development and family transformations have begun to uncover intriguing bidirectional findings. On one hand, adolescent characteristics mold family relations. For example, in a longitudinal study, Steinberg (1981) found that, for boys, parent-adolescent conflict was closely associated with changes in physical maturity. From the onset of puberty until its apex, mother-son conflict escalated, but during later puberty, such conflict decreased, with mothers deferring to adolescents. By contrast, in the father-adolescent dyad, there was a steady, linear increase in parental dominance and adolescent deference over the entire course of puberty.

On the other hand, family factors may mold intraindividual adolescent development. For example, Cooper, Grotevant, and Condon (1983) found that the degree of individuality or connectedness in family communication was predictive of the adolescent's abilities to develop a strong identity and take another's perspective or role. Other investigators have examined the interdependence between family interaction and ego strength (Powers, Hauser, Schwartz, Noam, & Jacobson, 1983) or empathy (Reiss, Oliveri, & Curd, 1983). To date, these studies have been conducted with nonclinical populations; it will be important to replicate and extend such findings to a variety of clinically distressed populations and to demonstrate more clearly the linkage between cognitive-mediational and family-interactional variables (Laursen & Collins, 1988).

Given the emerging evidence concerning the interdependence of individual and familial factors and the nonconflictual nature of the modal parent-adolescent relationship, serious questions arise about the conditions under which clinically significant conflict will develop. Robin and Foster (1984, 1989) have outlined a behavioral family systems model that postulates that the developmental changes of adolescence interrupt previously stable homeostatic interaction patterns in the family, and the manner in which the family attempts to reestablish new interaction patterns determines the degree of conflict. Three factors in the families' responses to the developmental changes of adolescence are thought to be central to the resulting increase in conflict: (a) deficits in problem-solving communication skills, (b) cognitive distortions, and (c) dysfunctional family structure.

In order to resolve specific disputes, parents and adolescents need to be proficient at the following steps of interpersonal problem solving (D'Zurilla, 1988; Robin, Koepke, & Nayar, 1986): (a) problem sensing—recognizing the existence of a problem; (b) problem definition—clearly specifying the nature of the problem in nonaccusatory terms; (c) solution listing—generating a variety of creative alternatives for resolving the problem; (d) decision making—evaluating the positive and negative consequences of implementing each solution and negotiating a mutually acceptable solution; (e) implementation planning—specifying the details necessary for carrying out the solution; and (f) verification—evaluating whether the implemented solution had the predicted outcomes. Inability to engage in one or more of these skills will promote conflict because disputes will remain unresolved.

Negative communication impedes effective problem solving because parents and adolescents may become so angered by the way they are talking to each other that they do not listen to what the other is saying (Robin, Koepke, & Nayar, 1986). Common examples of negative communication include accusations, lectures, poor eye contact, slouching posture, defensive remarks, name-calling, ridiculing, and so on. Excessive displays of negative communication from one member evoke reciprocally negative responses from the others, sidetracking families into endless, unproductive cycles of mutual accusations and defensiveness (Alexander, 1973; Robin & Weiss, 1980).

Cognitive distortions complement skill deficits in aggravating conflict, because extreme, absolutistic thought processes evoke excessively negative affect and strong negative affect impedes rational resolution of disagreements. Cognitive therapists have outlined the manner in which an individual may respond to environmental events with unrealistically negative self-evaluations, resulting in depressions or anxious affect (DeRubeis & Beck, 1988; Dryden & Ellis, 1988). Parents and adolescents may respond to relationship events with unrealistically negative cognitions directed toward each other, resulting in angry or hostile affect (Epstein, Schlesinger, & Dryden, 1988; Robin & Foster, 1989). Parents often adhere to the following unreasonable belief themes: (a) ruination—if adolescents are given too much freedom, they will ruin their lives; (b) obedience—it is catastrophic if teenagers do not always obey their parents; (c) perfectionism—teenagers should instinctively know how to behave flawlessly; (d) malicious intent—teenagers misbehave purposely to hurt their parents; and (e) self-blame—parents are at fault for their adolescents' problems. Adolescents, in turn, often adhere to similar beliefs: (a) ruination—parental rules will ruin prospects for having fun; (b) unfairness—parental restrictions are intrinsically unfair; (c) autonomy—adolescents should be granted as much freedom as they desire.

Difficulties in family structure also contribute to parent-adolescent conflict (Aponte & Van Deusen, 1981). All families are hierarchically ordered, with parents theoretically in charge of children. As the children make the transition through adolescence to adulthood, it is assumed that parents are to give their adolescents more control and power, upgrading their position in the family dominance hierarchy. Several types of hierarchical disturbances are postulated to aggravate parent-adolescent conflict. Most of these disturbances are variations on patterns of *alignment* or side-taking. In the case of coalitions, two people consistently take sides against the third. If a mother and son consistently take sides against a father, the parents will be unable to work well as a team, discipline will be diluted, and the son's problem behavior may go unchecked; such a structure problem is called a *cross-generational coalition.* In the case of *triangulation,* two people pull a third in opposite directions, and the third vacillates between siding with each of the others. In a stepfamily, for example, when the son misbehaves, and his stepfather issues a punishment, the son may complain to his natural mother that her new husband is unfair and cruel; sometimes, she will side with her husband and sometimes with her natural son; the mother is triangulated or caught in the middle. Conflict will persist as the adolescent attempts to triangulate his mother to avoid following rules, accepting responsibilities, and accepting the logical consequences of his or her behavior. If an adolescent gains too much emotional or instrumental power and control over his or her parents, there is a *hierarchy reversal* problem (e.g., the child is higher in the dominance hierarchy than the parent). Such a problem can be the cumulative result of years of "spoiling" a child or may be a situational response to parental disagreement over rules and discipline.

Conflictual interactions between parents and adolescents occur within the context of the family's attempt to regulate its relationship. Effective assessment and intervention require an understanding of the functions of interpersonal behavior within a family system. Problem behaviors must be "chunked" into clinically meaningful units or repetitive sequences of interpersonal interaction, which help explain the payoffs or functions of each person's behavior within the interaction. Within a functional family therapy model, Alexander (Alexander & Parsons, 1982; Morris, Alexander, & Waldron, 1988) has classified the interpersonal payoffs in terms of two primary functions: closeness (intimacy, merging) and distance (independence, autonomy). *Closeness* refers to interpersonal behaviors that tend to increase intimacy, psychological intensity, physical and emotional contact, and interpersonal interaction between parents and adolescents, while *distancing* refers to behaviors that tend to decrease intimacy and dependence as well as physical/emotional contact. Alexander and associates analyze a conflictual interaction with regard to the degree of closeness or separation produced by each person's behavior, particularly the extent to which family members are striving to achieve incompatible functions (e.g., adolescents distancing from parents while parents try to maintain closeness with their adolescents).

Robin and Foster (1984, 1989) classify interpersonal payoffs in terms of social learning functions, such as reinforcement, punishment, reciprocity, and coercion. They analyze conflictual interactions with regard to whether parents and adolescents are reciprocating positive or negative behavior, engaging in mutual reinforcement or punishment, or displaying the coercive patterns that Patterson (1982) has delineated in his performance theory of aggressive behavior in preadolescents.

Problem-solving communication skills, cognitive distortions, and structural patterns of alignment and hierarchy represent the atoms or molecules that fuse together to produce sequences of interactions serving interpersonal functions regulating parent-adolescent relationships. Difficulties in one or more of these dimensions is postulated to promote conflict when families with developing adolescents attempt to achieve interpersonal functions. Thus a comprehensive account of parent-adolescent conflict requires both a molecular analysis of individual behavior, thought, and affect as well as a molar analysis of the regulatory nature of sequences of interaction.

Robin and Foster (1989) extensively reviewed research supporting this theoretical model. Although there have been many studies supporting the molecular analysis of problem-solving communication skills and cognitive distortions, only recently have researchers begun to examine the molar, self-regulatory patterns of structure and function (Kinsley & Bry, 1988).

III. ASSESSMENT

A comprehensive assessment represents the first phase of a behavioral family systems approach to parent-adolescent conflict. The assessment phase has as its goals the collection of information, the establishment of rapport, and the formulation of a therapeutic contract. Three general methods are utilized: clinical interviews, self-report inventories, and direct observation. There are many different ways to structure the assessment phase, with little empirical basis to date for the selection of a particular sequence. Robin and Foster's (1989) assessment sequence will be presented as one illustrative approach.

Robin and Foster (1989) divide assessment into three parts. First, the therapist interviews the parents and adolescents together, obtaining a description of the presenting problems, the issues of dispute, problem-solving skills, and communication patterns. Afterward, a history of the onset and development of the presenting problems is taken, culminating in a summary of what was learned during the session. The initial phase terminates with the assignment of self-report measures as homework and the administration of a standardized audiotaped or videotaped interaction task (described below). Second, the therapist interviews the adolescent individually for 30 minutes and the parents as a couple for 30 minutes. The therapist deepens his rapport with the adolescent by empathetically listening to the teen's concerns, establishing the teen's goals for parental change, dispelling myths about therapy and family conflict (e.g., people who seek therapy are crazy) and conveying that the adolescent's viewpoint will be taken seriously. In addition, the therapist can assess peer relations, suicidal risk, substance abuse, depression, and other forms of individual adolescent pathology. A developmental history is taken in the interview with the parents, blending naturally in an assessment of adolescent behavior disorders, such as attention-deficit hyperactivity disorder, depression, substance abuse, and so on. The developmental history also provides the opportunity to discuss the history of the parents' marriage, families of origin, and personal growth and development in a relatively nonthreatening manner. When cognitive ability or educational testing is appropriate, this would be conducted during this second phase of assessment. Third, the therapist integrates all of the information collected from the family and individual interviews, self-report measures, and direct observations into a comprehensive formulation of the skill deficits, cognitive distortions, individual psychopathological patterns, and circular, interlocking contingency patterns within the family. The therapist meets with the parents and adolescent together and gives them feedback concerning the formulation of the problem, the results of the self-report inventories, and the directions that therapy might take. Mutual goals for change are established, and a therapeutic contract is formulated that outlines a time-limited framework for therapy, session attendance and scheduling policies, homework responsibility, fees, and so on.

A. Clinical Interview

The interview remains the primary assessment technique used with parents and adolescents. Helpful interviewing techniques include making all family members feel comfortable by greeting each individually, selectively responding to characteristics of each family member (e.g., noticing and commenting about the adolescent's sports shirt with the emblem of a local professional basketball team), and rephrasing or "reframing" remarks made by one family member to another. With reframing, the therapist provides an alternative, more positive meaning or explanation for a behavior, which minimizes blaming and helps the family view the problems in interactional rather than individualistic terms. For example, an adolescent female has just been hospitalized for the ingestion of several aspirin. The adolescent explained to the clinician that she no longer wants to die, but felt no one cared about her. Furthermore, she was very upset by her parents' frequent marital arguments and felt that her life was hopeless. During a predischarge family session, the therapist reframed the adolescent's suicidal gesture as a "cry for help for the family and an attempt to reunite the parents" rather than a sign of individual psychopathology. Reframing was used in this instance to show the family the positive intent of the suicide gesture and to shape a family interactional perspective on the problem. The effectiveness of relabeling in reducing blaming cognitions is currently under investigation (Alexander, Waldron, Barton, & Mas, in press).

A combination of content- and process-oriented questions are helpful as the interviewer tries to pinpoint sequences of problems, interactions, and cognitions (Robin & Foster, 1989). The following is an example of a content-focused question: "What do you and your parents argue about?" Process-focused questions address the style in which the family interacts, as when the interviewer asks: "If you wanted to get your teenager to change his/her behavior, how would you go about it?" Cognitions may be assessed in the interview by asking family members to reconstruct their thoughts and feelings during a recent episode of problem interactions, stopping the session when the therapist notices a shift of mood and probing their associated thoughts and feelings, or asking family members to comment on the extent to which common belief themes or inaccurate cognitive processes apply to their family (Epstein, Schlesinger, & Dryden, 1988).

There have been surprisingly few investigations of the psychometric characteristics of the family interview, given its importance as a clinical assessment tool (Foster & Robin, 1988). Research on individual interviews with children and adolescents has suggested that the client may be inconsistent in providing information and the therapist may be inconsistent in evaluating information (Edelbrock, Costello, Dulcan, Kalas, &

Conover, 1985; Herjanic & Reich, 1982). Furthermore, therapists' identification of problem areas and controlling variables may be remarkably unreliable (Felton & Nelson, 1984; Hay, Hay, Angle, & Nelson, 1979). The generalizability of behavior displayed during the interview and information supplied by the interviewees was assessed with marital couples comparing interview-based reports with later direct observations and standardized questionnaires (Haynes, Jensen, Wise, & Sherman, 1981). Interview-based data correlated more highly with questionnaires and observations when the spouses were interviewed separately rather than conjointly, suggesting that the presence of the spouse elicits greater conformity in verbal reports.

Two recent investigations examined the reliability, criterion-related validity, and construct validity of the family interview (Koepke, 1986; Webb, 1987). In these studies families were administered structured, one-hour interviews assessing problem-solving communication skills, cognitive distortions, structural problems, and specific issues of dispute (e.g., school and sibling conflict). Trained coders reviewed videotapes of the interviews and completed seven-point Likert ratings of the relevant dimensions. These ratings were correlated with scores from standardized self-report measures, particularly the Parent Adolescent Relationship Questionnaire (Robin, Koepke, & Moye, 1989). Using a sample of 50 clinic-referred families with acting-out adolescents, Koepke (1986) found moderate correlations between interview ratings and standardized self-report inventories for dimensions such as global distress, communication, problem solving, cohesion, and triangulation but few significant correlations for dimensions such as cognitive distortions and coalitions. Reliability between the two coders was acceptable (.65 to .87.)

Webb (1987) employed a similar structured parent-adolescent interview for the purpose of identifying the structural differences between recently blended (remarried) and nonblended (intact) parent-teen triads, comparing interview ratings with the Parent Adolescent Relationship Questionnaire. Five constructs were examined across interviews and self-report measures: global distress, cohesion, coalitions, triangulation, and hierarchy reversal. Two sources of data were collected from the interviews: (1) family members' responses to direct questions concerning the five constructs and (2) trained observers' ratings of the constructs based upon a review of videotapes of the interviews. There were moderately high correlations between both interview-based measures and the self-report inventory for global distress (.46 to .65), cohesion (.34 to .55), and triangulation (.41 to .46), but not for coalitions and hierarchy reversal. In Webb's (1987) study, interrater reliability was also high, averaging .86. In addition, Webb was able to demonstrate the criterion-related validity of the behavioral assessment interview, in that the blended families displayed more global distress and less cohesion than the intact families on the observers' interview-based ratings.

Although these recent investigations are promising beginnings in validating the family interview for assessing parent-adolescent conflict, much remains to be done. Previous research on interviewing techniques has produced mixed results, indicating that clients respond with varying reliability to interview questions. Interrater reliability can be adequately established on specific structured research interviews that are time limited and narrowly focused; however, the clinical interview may be used session after session and week after week. Family members are often reticent to reveal significant information about their own pathology in early assessment or treatment interviews, and even if such interviews meet ideal psychometric criteria, they may be limited in scope. Investigators need to evaluate experienced clinicians' ratings of families in the early, middle, and late stages of therapy to help clarify this issue.

B. Self-Report Inventories

Self-report inventories and rating scales provide a comprehensive and relatively inexpensive, face-valid method to collect useful information. Correctly developed, self-report instruments may provide data concerning parent-adolescent functioning, which may be compared to a normative data base indicating the clinical relevance of problem behaviors and providing a baseline against which treatment effects may easily be measured. It is important to realize, however, that responses to questionnaires do not necessarily mirror behavior at home, and that an appropriate psychometric framework is necessary to develop reliable and valid inventories (Foster, 1987; Skinner, 1987). Table 1 lists commonly available self-report inventories, several of which will be reviewed below.

The *Issues Checklist* (Prinz, Foster, Kent, & O'Leary, 1979; Robin & Foster, 1988b) assesses parent-adolescent reports of the frequency and intensity of specific disputes regarding 44 common issues. Family members recall whether issues, such as chores, telephone calls, homework, or dating, have been discussed during the past few weeks. They rate the frequency and anger intensity (on a 5-point scale) of the discussions, yielding three scores: (1) the number of issues discussed, (2) the mean anger intensity level of the discussions, and (3) a weighted average of frequency and anger intensity. Psychometric studies of the Issues Checklist have found that it discriminates distressed from nondistressed families, is sensitive to changes produced by family-based treatment programs, correlates moderately with other self-report and observational measures of family interaction, but varies greatly in test-retest reliability (Robin & Foster, 1988a, 1989). The relationship of self-reported specific disputes to actual disputes is unclear.

Table 1   Self-Report and Observational Measures

Self-Report Measures:	
Conflict Behavior Questionnaire	Robin & Foster (1988a)
Decision Making Questionnaire	Prinz, Foster, Kent, & O'Leary (1979)
Family Adaptability and Cohesion Scales	Olson (1986)
Family Beliefs Inventory	Vincent-Roehling & Robin (1986)
Family Assessment Device	Epstein, Baldwin, & Bishop (1983)
Family Environment Scale	Moos & Moos (1981)
Issues Checklist	Robin & Foster (1988b)
Parent Adolescent Relationship Questionnaire	Robin, Koepke, & Moye (1989)
Parental Control Questionnaire	Prinz, Foster, Kent, & O'Leary (1979)
Observational Coding Systems:	
Defensive and Supportive Communication Code	Alexander (1973)
Community Members' Rating Scale	Robin & Canter (1984)
Family Alliance Coding System	Gilbert, Christensen, & Margolin (1984)
Family Interaction Scales	Riskin & Faunce (1970a, 1970b)
Interaction Behavior Code	Prinz & Kent (1978)
Parent Adolescent Interaction Coding System	Robin (1988b)
Structural Interaction Coding System	Webb (1987)

The *Conflict Behavior Questionnaire* (CBQ) (Prinz, Foster, Kent, & O'Leary, 1979; Robin & Foster, 1988a) consists of 75 dichotomous (true-false) items assessing communication-conflict behavior, yielding scores for each family member's appraisal of the other's behavior and an appraisal of the dyadic interaction. The CBQ has proven to be a sensitive discriminator of distressed versus nondistressed parents and adolescents, to be sensitive to changes produced by behavioral and nonbehavioral family treatment programs, to be correlated with direct observations of parent-adolescent communication behavior, and to demonstrate excellent internal consistency (Robin & Foster, 1988a, 1989). A short-form CBQ, consisting of 20 items, has been constructed that maintains the psychometric characteristics of the long form while taking approximately five minutes to complete.

A commonly used inventory is the *Family Environment Scale* (FES), a 90-item, true-false measure developed by Moos and Moos (1981) to measure the social-environmental characteristics of families. Focusing on the interpersonal, sociological, and environmental aspects of family functioning, the FES includes 10 scales: cohesion, expressiveness, conflict, independence, achievement orientation, intellectual-cultural orientation, active-recreational orientation, moral-religious emphasis, organization, and control. A review of the FES validation research suggests that it has high test-retest reliability, adequate internal consistency, but mixed evidence of concurrent and construct validity (Anderson, 1984; Forman & Hagan, 1983). Two studies (Oliveri & Reiss, 1984; Russell, 1980) found that FES cohesion did not correlate well with other measures of the same construct, but Moos and Moos (1981) report that several of the scales are good discriminators of families in crisis and are sensitive to therapeutic outcomes.

Olson and his colleagues (Olson, 1986; Olson, Bell, & Portner, 1982) have developed the *Family Adaptability and Cohesion Evaluation Scales* (FACES) based upon their circumplex model of family functioning, which reduces the major constructs in family functioning to orthogonal dimensions: cohesion and adaptability. Now in its third revision, FACES III consists of 20 five-point Likert items. Family members respond twice, first indicating how they currently perceive the family, and, second, indicating how they ideally would like the family to be. Scores are obtained for current and ideal cohesion and adaptability as well as for the discrepancy between the two. FACES III has been found to have internal consistency of .76 and .63 for cohesion and adaptability (Joanning & Kuehl, 1986) and to have good concurrent and construct validity with delinquent and nondelinquent families (Rodnick, Henggeler, & Hanson, 1986), with distressed adolescents receiving therapy (Dickerson & Coyne, 1987), with chemically dependent families, and with families with sex offenders (Olson, 1986). Difficulties found with the earlier versions of FACES (Alexander, Johnson, & Carter, 1984) appear to have been corrected with the current version. However, the instrument may be more useful in research than practice because Olson's circumplex model of family functioning taps molar concepts, which do not necessarily provide specific targets for assessment and intervention in individual clinical cases.

A clinician who wishes to gain a multidimensional picture of family skill deficits, distorted cognitions, and difficulties in family structure might employ the *Parent Adolescent Relationship Questionnaire* (PARQ) (Koepke, 1986; Robin, Koepke, & Moye, 1989; Robin, Koepke, & Nayar, 1986). The PARQ consists of 250-300 true-false items in parallel forms for parents and adolescents, including 16 scales that have been factor analyzed into three broad dimensions: (a) skill deficits/overt conflict—global distress, communication, problem solving, warmth/hostility, cohesion, school conflict, sibling conflict, and conventionalization; (b) cognitive distortions—ruination, obedience, perfectionism, self-blame, and malicious intent (adolescents—ruination, unfairness, autonomy, approval, perfectionism); and (c) family structure—coalitions, triangulation, and somatic concerns. The PARQ has been shown to discriminate between clinic and nonclinic families (Robin, Koepke, & Moye, 1989), to correlate with other self-report inventories (Koepke, Hull, & Robin, 1989; Webb, Young, & Robin, 1988), to have construct validity in correlations with family interviews and direct observations (Koepke, 1986), and to have internal consistency above .80 (Robin, Koepke, & Moye, 1989). Profiles depicting an individual family's scores compared with normative data from over 300 families can be plotted for clinical interpretation and decision making.

The measures reviewed here and listed in Table 1 assess many aspects of conflict, communication, cognitions, and family structure. Although they vary in psychometric characteristics, many meet the minimum standards necessary to provide useful information concerning parent-adolescent interaction. None of these measures will replace the family interview as a basic assessment tool, and in many cases the relationship between perceived and actual family interaction is unclear. Nonetheless, such self-report inventories often corroborate interview-based perceptions.

C. Direct Observation

Given the complexity of parent-adolescent interactions, incorporation of observational methods in assessment cannot be overemphasized. Because of the practical difficulties of obtaining naturalistic in-home observation samples with highly mobile adolescents and their parents, most parent-adolescent observation has relied upon 10- to 30-minute interaction samples audio- or videotaped in a clinic or laboratory analog setting. The family is usually given a structured task to complete, such as resolving a conflictual issue or planning a family activity. Later, the interaction sample is coded with one of a variety of specific coding systems (Grotevant & Carlson, 1987; Foster & Robin, 1988; Markman & Notarius, 1987), several of which are listed in Table 1.

Despite its greater objectivity than self-report, such direct observation is less than perfect for a number of reasons. The extent to which the observed behavior can be generalized to the natural family environment is questionable, and it depends upon the interaction setting and task, subject reactivity, and the psychometric characteristics of the observation code (Foster, 1987; Foster & Robin, 1988; Jacob, Tennenbaum, & Krahn, 1987). While empirical investigations of these factors are far from complete, current evidence suggests that clinicians can maximize the chances of generalization by utilizing highly salient, structured tasks, such as having a family resolve an intensely conflictual dispute and coding the interactions with a system carefully selected to yield adequate reliability and validity (Jacob, Tennenbaum, & Krahn, 1987).

The observational codes developed for use with parents and adolescents most commonly assess problem solving, communication, and, to a lesser extent, family structure. Most have been evaluated primarily by their developers, with few attempts at cross-laboratory replication. They vary widely in degree of molecularity, ranging from microanalytic codes that sequentially classify every utterance or behavior into one or more categories, to molar codes that involve global-inferential ratings of an entire interaction on Likert-type rating scales. Microanalytic techniques require extended periods of observer training and are, therefore, practical primarily in research settings, where exact frequency counts and fine-grained analyses of sequences of interaction are needed; molar techniques are easier to use but provide only an overall impression of the quality of interaction (Foster & Robin, 1988).

An example of a molecular code is Robin's *Parent Adolescent Interaction Coding System* (PAICS) (Robin, 1988b; Robin & Fox, 1979). With the PAICS, parent-adolescent verbal behavior during structured discussions is classified into 15 mutually exclusive categories on the basis of homogeneity of content. Derived from the Marital Interaction Coding System (Weiss & Summers, 1973), the PAICS includes categories for agree/assent, appraisal, consequential statements, facilitation, humor, problem solution, specification of the problem, command, complaint, defensive behavior, interruptions, put-down, no response, problem description, and talk. Summary scores can be obtained for positive, negative, and neutral behavior. Psychometric studies of several versions of the PAICS have indicated that percentage agreement reliability on individual discussions averages 64%-76% (Robin, 1981; Robin & Weiss, 1980), while individual category reliability ranges from 0%-100%. The validity of the PAICS has been demonstrated in studies showing that its categories discriminate between distressed and nondistressed dyads (Robin & Weiss, 1980) and eating-disordered and non-eating-disordered adolescents and their families (Humphrey, Apple, & Kirschenbaum, 1986); are sensitive to changes produced by family treatment (Robin, 1981), correlate highly with clinician's global ratings of communication and problem solving (Robin & Canter, 1984); and correlate moderately with self-report measures (Robin & Foster, 1989). Most recently, a shorter, six-category version of the PAICS has been validated (Adams, 1987) and is being used in an outcome study (Barkley, 1987).

By contrast, with the *Interaction Behavior Coding System* (IBCS) (Prinz & Kent, 1978; Foster, Prinz, & O'Leary, 1983), multiple coders review an entire interaction and rate the presence/absence of 33 discrete problem-solving communication behaviors (e.g., "negative exaggeration," "making suggestions") as well as four Likert scales. Composite scores are computed for positive and negative behavior, averaged across all of the coders. Because the coders provide global impressions rather than frequency counts of parent-adolescent behaviors, the system does not permit sequential analysis of behavior; however, coders can be trained within 2-3 hours, in contrast to 56-60 hours with the PAICS. The reliability of the IBCS has been found to be .83 to .97 in three investigations (Foster, Prinz, & O'Leary, 1983; Prinz & Kent, 1978; Robin & Koepke, 1985). The IBCS has also been shown to discriminate between distressed and nondistressed parent-adolescent dyads (Prinz & Kent, 1978; Robin & Koepke, 1985), to be sensitive to treatment effects (Foster, Prinz, & O'Leary, 1983; Stern, 1984), and to correlate .51 to .82 with the PAICS (Robin & Koepke, 1985).

Recently, several investigators have attempted to develop codes of family structure. Gilbert, Christensen, and Margolin (1984) coded family alliances using a system similar to the PAICS in orientation but with a weighting system that permitted derivation of alliance scores. Beavers and Voeller (1973) relied upon five-point Likert ratings of overt power, parental coalitions, and closeness to assess structure. Webb, Young, and Robin (1988) developed a Structural Interaction Rating System consisting of global-inferential ratings based upon the model of the IBCS to assess coalitions, triangulation, cohesion, and hierarchy reversal. It remains for future research to establish more definitively the psychometric characteristics of these new codes.

D. Integrating Assessment Data for Functional Analysis

Assessment data from interview, self-report inventories, and direct observation can be integrated to help depict the functions and patterns of communication and conflictual behavior for family members. The therapist must describe the antecedents and consequences of problem behaviors and then hypothesize important determinants and maintaining conditions for the behaviors under consideration. Decisions must be made about the degree of molarity or molecularity necessary to punctuate the interaction in a clinically meaningful manner. At the present time, there are no empirically based guidelines or studies of the process of depicting functions of interactive behavior, although many clinically based suggestions have been made (Alexander & Parsons, 1982; Arrington, Sullaway, & Christensen, 1988; Foster, 1987; Robin & Foster, 1989). Clearly, functional analysis is an area of parent-adolescent assessment in dire need of further investigation.

IV. INTERVENTION

Multidimensional problems require multidimensional solutions; parent-adolescent conflict is no exception. Interventions have been

aimed at teaching effective problem-solving communication skills, identifying and modifying distorted cognitions, and addressing difficulties in
the family structure along with the functions of adolescent misbehavior
within the family system. Robin and Foster's (1984, 1989) problem-
solving communication training, Guerney's (1977) relationship enhancement, and Alexander and Parsons's (1982) functional family therapy are
the three major interventions that have been developed and researched
for ameliorating parent-adolescent conflict. These interventions share a
common emphasis upon treating parents and adolescents together, setting short-term time-limited therapeutic contracts of 5 to 15 sessions, and
employing a high degree of structure within a psychoeducational context.

Families differ in the extent to which their problems reflect skill deficits, cognitive distortions, structural difficulties, or more than one of
these areas. Thus therapists need to be prepared to intervene in as many
areas as are indicated by their thorough behavioral assessments. In this
chapter, intervention "modules" for skill training, cognitions, and family
structure will be outlined, and then the outcome research conducted by
Robin, Guerney, and Alexander with their blends of these modules will
be reviewed.

A. Problem-Solving Training

Problem-solving training is a comprehensive cognitive-behavioral intervention for facilitating social competence by teaching individuals to
find effective means of coping with common problems encountered in
daily life (D'Zurilla, 1988). It has been applied extensively with both
adults and children within individual, marital, group, and family therapy
contexts (D'Zurilla, 1986). In the case of parent-adolescent conflict, the
goals of problem solving are to help the family identify and resolve current conflicts and to teach the family generalized skills that will enable
them to deal more effectively and independently with future conflicts. In
addition, problem-solving training sets the stage for families to "negotiate" the conflicts that arise during adolescence by encouraging a
democratic—as opposed to the extremes of either an autocratic or a
permissive—framework for decision making concerning rules and regulations. Research in child development has concluded that adolescents
individuate more responsibly from their parents if parents gradually permit increased freedom and decision making using democratic approaches
rather than resorting to authoritarian or permissive approaches (Conger,
1977). The mutuality of a problem-solving training format is ideally
suited to accomplishing this developmental task of adolescence.

Parents and adolescents are taught to follow five steps of problem solving to resolve specific disputes: (a) define the problem; (b) generate alternative solutions; (c) evaluate the solutions and decide upon a mutually

acceptable alternative; (d) plan the details of solution implementation; and (e) verify the outcome of the solution implementation. They define the problem by making a succinct, specific statement pinpointing the others' behaviors that are upsetting and why. Adequate problem definition statements name actions, words, or situations rather than accusing or demeaning persons. As each person defines his or her problem, the others are asked to paraphrase the speaker's definition to verify that they accurately received the intended message. The speaker is asked to acknowledge the accuracy of the paraphrase or correct any inaccuracies. The therapist notes that there may be several different problem definitions and that such discrepant perceptions are normal when conflicts exist.

During the generation of the alternatives phase, the therapist asks the family members to take turns brainstorming creative ideas to solve the problem. Unusual ideas are welcomed and premature evaluations of ideas are interrupted. If a family is unable to go beyond its initial positions, the therapist may suggest ideas, often extreme or outlandish in an attempt to lighten the atmosphere and stimulate creativity. Brainstorming is designed to teach parents and teenagers to think flexibly. One member usually writes down the solutions for later review.

When the family has generated eight to ten ideas and the therapist judges that they have gone beyond their initial positions, the evaluation phase is begun. The therapist asks each person to project the positive and negative consequences of each idea for solving the problem, culminating in a rating of "plus" or "minus." The therapist guides members to explore each other's perspectives in an attempt to broaden their horizons. The ratings are recorded in writing. Afterward, the family looks for a consensus upon one or more ideas (rated "plus" by all). If there is a consensus, the problem is tentatively "solved." The family plans the details for implementing the solution by deciding who will do what, when, where, and so on and what consequences will be administered for compliance or noncompliance. The final agreement may be written in the form of a behavioral contract.

If the family fails to reach a mutually acceptable solution, then the therapist introduces special techniques for resolving the impasse (Robin, 1982). The solution on which the family came closest to consensus serves as the basis for brainstorming a variety of possible compromises, followed by evaluation of the compromises in an attempt to narrow the differences between family members. Alternatively, the conflict may be fractionated into smaller elements, and an attempt could be made to reach agreement upon one element, even if the entire conflict cannot be resolved.

After family members have implemented the solution for one week, they report the outcome to the therapist and verify whether the solution worked. If the solution was effective, the therapist praises the family members and guides them to problem-solve a new issue. Otherwise, the therapist reframes the unsuccessful implementation as a breakdown in problem solving rather than an accusatory-defensive interchange and guides the family to renegotiate the problem, carefully assessing at what stage the breakdown occurred.

Over successive sessions, the family problem-solves increasingly intense issues, with the therapist employing modeling, instructions, behavior rehearsal, and feedback to teach effective problem-solving skills. To promote generalization, the therapist assigns as homework additional problem-solving discussions to be conducted during regular family meetings and audiotaped for later review.

B.   Communication Training

Communication training is designed to identify and correct difficulties in the way parents and adolescents talk to each other. Table 2 lists common negative communication habits and their positive counterparts. Modeling, instructions, behavior rehearsal, and feedback are used to conduct communication training. There are several variations on the communication training theme.

Robin and Foster (1989) conduct communication training in conjunction with problem-solving training. After the family has participated in several problem-solving discussions, the therapist introduces communication training in a didactic discussion, reviewing Table 2 with them. Family members are asked to report recent examples of accusations, defensive comments, and the like. The therapist models reflective listening, assertive expression of feeling, and appropriate posture and eye contact, and so on. Then, the therapist targets one or two specific negative communication skills and announces that, whenever the targeted behaviors occur, he or she will interrupt the conversation, give feedback, and ask members to restate their point in a more constructive manner. The family then proceeds to another task, such as a problem-solving discussion. The therapist corrects negative communication as often as needed. Over successive sessions the therapist targets additional behaviors, persisting at interrupting as often as necessary.

Homework is assigned for practice of individual communication skills. For example, parents might be asked to practice short, nonaccusatory expressions of feelings while teenagers might be asked to practice nondefensive responses to criticism. One member might be asked to monitor communication between two others and prompt correction of negative patterns.

By contrast, Guerney and his colleagues (Guerney, Coufal & Vogelsong, 1981; Ginsberg, 1981; Guerney, 1977) make the basic communication skills of openness and empathy the cornerstone of their Par-

Table 2 Negative and Positive Communication Skills

Negative Habits	Positive Habits
Accusing, blaming.	Using I-statements.
Putting down, shaming.	Criticizing the behavior, not the person.
Interrupting.	Gesturing when you need to talk or waiting patiently.
Lecturing, preaching.	Making brief, clear statements.
Talking sarcastically.	Talking in neutral tone.
Failing to make eye contact.	Looking when you talk.
Mind-reading.	Reflecting, paraphrasing.
Getting off topic.	Talking about one thing at a time.
Commanding, ordering.	Asking nicely but assertively.
Dredging up the past.	You can't change the past; so stick to the present.
Hogging the conversation.	Taking turns; talking briefly.
Intellectualizing.	Speaking in simple language.
Not listening.	Using reflective listening.

ent Adolescent Relationship Development Program (PARD), the adolescent variation of Relationship Enhancement (RE). Problem solving is reconceptualized as "democratic communication" and taught within the context of improving the ability to take turns, hear out the other person, respect divergent views, and compromise and understand the other person. There is a more direct focus on routinely teaching positive communication than correcting negative communication.

Groups of two or three parent-adolescent dyads meet with a therapist for ten 90-minute PARD sessions, during which time they are taught to use the roles of listener (empathy) and speaker (openness). When listening, a family member holds his or her own feelings in abeyance and reflects the speaker's messages in a Rogerian manner. When speaking, a family member directly communicates affect and opinions, criticizing behaviors but not persons, and accepting responsibility for his or her own actions. The therapist teaches the dyads to alternate the roles of speaker and listener in an attempt to resolve the major issues creating turmoil in their relationship. Homework is assigned for practice of communication exercises, and excerpts are audiotaped for the therapist for further review and feedback.

The therapist, using either Robin and Foster's or Guerney's approach, may augment standard training techniques with either role-reversal or doubling. In role-reversal, the parent role-plays the adolescent and the adolescent role-plays the parent. In doubling, one parent-adolescent dyad "doubles" for another by repeating in a simulated role-play the first dyad's interchange but attempting to improve upon their use of positive listening and speaking skills. Both role-reversal and doubling are designed to deepen family members' ability to take each other's perspectives and increase their flexibility in resolving conflicts.

C. Cognitive Restructuring

Cognitive restructuring techniques teach parents and adolescents to modify distorted cognitive sets, unrealistic expectations, incorrect labels, inappropriate attributions, and unreasonable beliefs. These cognitive variables mediate strong negative affectual responses (e.g., anger, guilt, and fear), which block families from adjusting their interactions to accommodate the developmental changes of an individuating adolescent.

Cognitive distortions vary in intensity and pervasiveness. At a simplistic level, a family member may occasionally make an inaccurate attribution about a specific behavior, as when a father misinterprets an attention-deficit-disordered adolescent's forgetting to turn the lights off as a malicious attempt to waste his hard-earned money. Unrealistic expectations represent a more pervasive, intense form of cognitive distortions. Specific issues between parents and adolescents reliably activate unrealistic relationship expectations, coloring affectual reactions and jeopardizing attempts at conflict resolution. Each time an adolescent daughter comes home late, for example, her father may think that her friends will corrupt her to drink alcohol, have sexual relations, and take drugs. His ruinous thoughts may set the stage for an angry overreaction on his part. Some parents and adolescents at the extreme degree of rigidity and cognitive distortion enter therapy with distorted "family paradigms." They may have misconceptions about their relationships and the adolescent's problem behaviors, viewing the adolescent as "crazy" or "mentally ill." They may expect flawless conduct and superior academic achievement, and they actively resist family involvement in treatment because of underlying fears that they will be blamed by the therapist or that their own weaknesses will be exposed and ridiculed.

A continuum of cognitive restructuring techniques has been developed for use depending upon the degree and pervasiveness of the distortion. Reattributional/reframing techniques can speedily correct occasional misattributions, while a more formal set of cognitive restructuring techniques have proven useful with the more pervasive unrealistic expectations and distorted paradigms.

1. REFRAMING

Reframing refers to providing a family member with a benign alternative explanation for an initially negative attribution or cognition (Minuchin & Fishman, 1981). Unfair parental restrictions can be reinterpreted as concern for an adolescent's welfare; forgetful behavior in an attention-deficit-disordered adolescent can be reframed as a manifestation of a biologically based tendency toward inattentiveness; adolescent rebellion can be reframed as an unskilled attempt at individuation. The absolute veracity of the reframe is less important than its salience to the situation and family. Reframing is one example of a general set of reattributional techniques that involve changing the labels that family members attach to their behavior (Valins & Nisbett, 1976).

2. FORMAL COGNITIVE RESTRUCTURING

Robin and Foster (1989) have outlined a six-step model of cognitive restructuring for correcting unrealistic expectations and beliefs: (1) Provide a rationale linking thoughts, feelings, and negative interaction. The therapist explains how absolutistic thinking induces angry affect and elicits negative communication, reviewing unreasonable belief themes with the family and asking them to report recent exchanges that illustrate these themes in action in their family. (2) Identify the unreasonable belief. The therapist stops an interchange when a family member clearly expresses a distorted belief (as when a mother asserts that failure to complete the chores means her son will grow up to be an irresponsible adult) or when resistance to problem solving suggests the possibility of an underlying cognitive distortion (as when a father rigidly refuses to compromise concerning his daughter's curfew, claiming she isn't "mature enough" to stay out later). The therapist clearly articulates the hypothesized belief, asking the family member for verification and exploring the impact of the belief upon their interactions. (3) Challenge the unreasonable belief. The therapist provides a logical challenge to the premises underlying the belief, often exaggerating it to absurd proportions in a gentle but persuasive manner, or finding counterinstances that contradict the belief. (4) Suggest an alternative belief. The therapist models suggestions for more flexible cognitions and asks the family to brainstorm a number of alternative cognitions. Emphasis is placed upon toning down extremist phrases, such as "should" or "always" to "it would be nice if" or "as often as possible." (5) Design an experiment to disconfirm the unreasonable belief. The therapist arranges an experiment designed to help the parents and adolescent convince themselves of the veracity of the flexible beliefs rather than relying upon logical persuasion alone to refute their distorted cognitions. The mother who infers adult irresponsibility from adolescent failure to complete chores might be instructed to survey five "model adults" as to whether they ever failed to complete their chores as adolescents; her "discovery" that they sometimes left their chores incomplete is likely to lead her to reconsider the reasonableness of her ruinous cognitions. These experiments typically involve "normative surveys," the use of reference materials, or trial runs of anxiety-provoking solutions with built-in safeguards. Readers interested in additional discussion of cognitive change techniques should consult Epstein, Schlesinger, and Dryden (1988).

D. Structural/Functional Interventions

Structural/functional interventions are designed to address the circular sequences of interpersonal interaction that subsume the functions of adolescent problem behavior. Assuming that each person's behavior has a "payoff," which, taken together, maintain family homeostasis, the therapist must design an intervention that alters the system so that "payoffs" can be obtained without pain and coercion. Four general steps are followed:

Pinpointing the problem sequence involves deciding upon the degree of molarity or molecularity that punctuates family interaction in a treatment-valid manner. In other words, the therapist needs to determine whether to intervene at the level of moment-to-moment interactions (e.g., mother puts the adolescent down and the adolescent gets defensive) or at a broader level of analysis (e.g., mother-adolescent arguments result in the father's paying more attention to his family). A sequence has been pinpointed when the therapist can start with one member's actions and outline successive behaviors of the others until the original response recurs at a later point in time.

Identifying the functions involves specifying the payoffs for the family as a whole and each member individually within the sequence. The therapist can adopt either Alexander's (Alexander & Parsons, 1982) two-dimensional model of contact/closeness and distancing or Robin and Foster's (1989) interlocking contingency model to help specify payoffs.

Deciding upon a goal for change involves either planning to change the "payoffs" or functions within the sequence, or planning to leave the functions intact but change the topography of the responses emitted to achieve these functions. Changing the payoffs that maintain behavior is often more difficult than changing the way in which family members obtain their current payoffs.

Planning and implementing a strategy for change involves using molecular interventions, such as problem-solving training, communication training, cognitive restructuring, behavioral contracting (Stuart, 1971), or strategic/structural family therapy techniques (Haley, 1976; Minuchin, 1974), to achieve systemic change. The skillful therapist will combine in-session activities with homework assignments to accomplish strategic change.

The application of the four steps of structural/functional intervention will be illustrated with two common problem sequences.

1. WEAK PARENTAL COALITION/
HIERARCHY REVERSAL

When two parents disagree concerning rules and consequences for their adolescent, the adolescent is able to engage freely in proscribed, often risky, behaviors. Parental authority is diluted, and over time the adolescent assumes a controlling, coercive position. The normal hierarchy of parent-in-charge-of-child is reversed, and the parents do not support each other (e.g., they have a weak coalition with each other).

The pinpointed problem sequence may include seven steps: (a) the adolescent misbehaves or acts out; (b) the mother (could be the father, but we will use the mother for simplicity) issues a rule/consequence; (c) the adolescent ignores the mother's discipline; (d) the father issues a different rule/consequence; (e) the adolescent ignores the father's discipline; (f) the mother and father argue about appropriate discipline; and (g) the adolescent continues to act out, behavior unchecked.

What are the possible "payoffs" for each family member? The adolescent may obtain *positive reinforcement* from extrafamilial peer sources for engaging in risky, antisocial behavior or the adolescent may *avoid* unpleasant consequences such as effortful school/homework and parental punishment by ignoring parental discipline. The parents may *avoid* an unpleasant confrontation with their teenager or the parents may engage in a *reciprocally punishing* spousal interchange (e.g., "score a point" against each other).

The therapist's goal is to correct the reversed hierarchy by restoring a reasonable degree of parental control over the adolescent's behavior. Strategies that persuade the parents to reach clear-cut agreements concerning rules, regulations, and consequences are appropriate. The therapist can ask the parents to problem-solve an issue in the session while the adolescent is asked to listen quietly. It is often necessary to be very directive and persistent to get such a couple to reach agreement. Because the adolescent has little to gain and much freedom to lose from consistent parental consequences, he or she is likely to sabotage the discussion through attempts to change the topic, anger a parent, or create an argument; the therapist must block these distractions.

The therapist then assigns as homework the task of implementing the agreement, anticipating possible adolescent sabotage. Repeated use of this strategy usually helps build a strong parental coalition.

2. OVERINVOLVED MOTHER AND DISENGAGED FATHER

The overinvolved mother-son dyad argues frequently and intensely about a variety of independence-related issues. In these families the fathers are often workaholics, physically and emotionally absent from the family for extended periods of time. The mothers naturally turn to their children for emotional gratification, becoming overinvested "supermoms." Prior to the adolescence of the children, this arrangement may be adaptive, but when the young teenager begins to individuate, the arrangement flounders. The adolescent feels smothered and must rebel to distance from the mother. With her major source of emotional support threatened, the mother may become increasingly invasive, controlling, and depressed. Sensitive adolescents often experience a lot of guilt and anxiety about letting their mothers down, but nonetheless rebel to individuate. This pattern may be exaggerated when the adolescent has a chronic illness or psychosomatic ailment, a learning disability, or any other handicap that is likely to evoke maternal protective behavior.

The pinpointed sequence may be as follows: (a) the mother specifies a rule; (b) the adolescent fails to comply; (c) the mother issues a consequence; (d) the adolescent and mother argue unproductively; (e) the mother coerces her disengaged husband to discipline the adolescent; (f) the father issues a rule and consequence; (g) the adolescent briefly complies; (h) the father withdraws from the family again; and (i) the cycle restarts. In this interaction the adolescent *avoids* unpleasant limitations on his freedom by disobeying his mother; in addition, rebellion against the mother eventually results in increased contact with the father, a source of *positive reinforcement*. The mother maintains close contact with her son, even though the contact is somewhat unpleasant; coercing her husband to discipline her son is *negatively reinforced* by cessation of the son's rebellious behavior and *positively reinforced* by increased contact with her husband. For the father, maintaining a distance from the family permits him to *avoid* unpleasant conflict and obtain *positive reinforcement* by entering the family as a peacemaker. Disciplining his son also is *negatively reinforced* by cessation of his wife's coercive behavior. Thus the circular sequence may serve functions for each member, maintaining homeostatic functioning for the family as a whole.

The therapist who wishes to address the mother-son conflict must change the sequence by reducing mother-son involvement and increasing father-son and father-mother involvement. The family might be asked to pick an issue for problem solving. The mother might then be put on "vacation" while the father and son engage in a problem-solving discussion. The father-son dyad would be coached to negotiate and implement a solution, with the mother remaining on "vacation" throughout the week. The mother might be given a task to monitor her spouse and son, and the father might be prepared to help his wife avoid the temptation to involve herself in the problem solution. It might also be arranged for the spouses to earn reinforcers contingent upon successful father-son problem resolution. Instructions, modeling, and behavior rehearsal could be used to teach the father to interact directly with his son while his wife is restrained from taking over the interchange. In addition, cognitive restructuring may be helpful in alleviating the mother's ruinous fears about her husband's inability to deal effectively with their son. There are a variety of similar strategic-structural interventions available for changing patterns such as cross-generational coalitions, triangulation, and adolescent involvement in marital affairs. Readers interested in these interventions might consult Robin and Foster (1989).

V. TREATMENT OUTCOMES

A dozen outcome studies have been completed evaluating three blends of behavioral family therapy with parent-adolescent conflict: (a) problem-solving communication training (PSCT); (b) functional family therapy (FFT); and (c) relationship enhancement (RE). These investigations have indicated that the interventions produce significant improvement in parent-adolescent communication, significant reduction in specific disputes, and significant reductions in recidivism for delinquent samples (Robin & Foster, 1989). Treatments have been superior to wait-list controls and nonbehavioral alternative interventions, but component analyses delineating the active ingredients and mechanisms of change in the treatments are only in the rudimentary stages. While treatment gains have been maintained over three- to four-month follow-up intervals, there have not been many long-term follow-ups. The outcome studies also suffer from a variety of methodological confounds, including unanticipated improvement by wait-list controls, measures with questionable psychometric properties, small sample sizes, attrition of subjects at follow-up, and skewed middle-class samples of subjects.

A. Problem-Solving Communication Training (PSCT)

In an initial study, Robin, Kent, O'Leary, Foster, and Prinz, (1977) compared 11 mother-adolescent dyads treated with five sessions of PSCT to 11 dyads randomly assigned to a wait-list control. Dependent measures included audiotaped samples of dyadic interactions coded for problem solving and self-reports of conflict and communication. PSCT dyads showed large, significant gains compared with the wait-list dyads on the problem-solving code, but there were minimal changes on the self-report measures and there was no follow-up. Four additional studies using PSCT have been completed (Foster, Prinz, & O'Leary, 1983; Nayar, 1985; Robin, 1981; Stern, 1984). Treatments varied slightly in each study, yet the skill training component was identical across all of these studies. Nayar (1985) and Robin (1981) integrated cognitive restructuring with PSCT. Nayar (1985) and Stern (1984) also treated families in small groups while the others treated one family at a time. Self-report measures of communication/conflict and specific disputes common to three of these studies (Foster, Prinz, & O'Leary, 1983; Nayar, 1985; Robin, 1981) have been pooled (Koepke, Robin, Foster, & Nayar, 1989). Treated families improved significantly more than wait-list controls, with stronger effects when parents were reporters compared with adolescents.

The clinical significance of changes was examined by analyzing the percentage of families who improved at least one standard deviation: 68% of the PSCT patients reported clinically significant gains on measures of communication/conflict, compared with 34% of the wait-list parents; 54% of the PSCT parents reported clinically significant gains on measures of specific disputes, compared with 24% of the wait-list parents. These differences were highly significant. For adolescents, 39% and 27% of the PSCT adolescents reported clinically significant gains on measures of communication/conflict and specific disputes, respectively, compared with 24% and 31% of the wait-list groups; these differences were not significant. When follow-up data were analyzed for a reduced sample of 34 PSCT families (wait-list families had been treated), the treatment effects were maintained.

Subanalyses within the individual studies also suggested that PSCT is superior to eclectic, nonbehavioral family therapy on observational measures of problem solving and communication, but comparable on self-report measures of conflict and specific disputes (Robin, 1981). Subanalyses also indicated that PSCT with cognitive restructuring is marginally superior to PSCT without cognitive restructuring (Nayar, 1985), but that the generalization programming component of PSCT may not contribute to its effectiveness (Foster, Prinz, & O'Leary, 1983). Stern (1984) assessed the additive effects of a component designed to enhance anger control compared with skill training alone, finding improvement in both conditions on self-report and observational measures but no consistent superiority for the enhanced anger control group.

The social acceptability of PSCT has also been assessed in a series of studies asking potential consumers of the intervention to compare it with alternative treatments. Finfrock-Mittl and Robin (1987) asked college students to compare PSCT, behavioral contracting, medication, and paradoxical family therapy as interventions for parent-adolescent conflict. PSCT received the highest acceptability ratings, with behavioral contracting, medication, and paradoxical family therapy following, in that order. Two additional investigations replicated the high acceptability ratings for PSCT using psychiatric inpatient adolescents, parents, and mental health professionals as raters (Liu, 1988; Tzelepis, 1986).

Thus, the cumulative evidence points to the effectiveness and social acceptability of PSCT to produce amelioration of parent-adolescent conflict but leaves unanswered many critical questions about the active ingredients and long-term maintenance of change. In particular, the absence of a clear-cut comparison of PSCT with an attention placebo control precludes definitive conclusions about the role of nonspecific factors in the treatment outcomes.

B. Functional Family Therapy (FFT)

As outlined earlier, the functional family therapy model views parent and adolescent behavior as serving two primary interpersonal functions: achieving distance (separateness, autonomy) or closeness (intimacy, merging) (Alexander & Parsons, 1982; Morris, Alexander, & Waldron, 1988). Individuals have preferred levels of distance or closeness in interpersonal relations that may conflict (e.g., when an adolescent wishes to distance from his parents while the parents desire increased closeness). Functions are not valenced as "good" or "bad," although the behaviors, thoughts, and feelings that express them may be good or bad in the sense of promoting interpersonal pain and suffering. Conflicts occur when parents and adolescents desire incompatible functions, and the behaviors that express their functions result in negative consequences for one or more family members.

Treatment strategically combines skill training and cognitive restructuring to change the manner in which family members achieve their desired functions. In contrast to PSCT, where the therapist begins with problem-solving communication skill training and later incorporates cognitive restructuring, the functional family therapist begins with a cognitive restructuring phase called "therapy" and later moves to a skill training component called "education" (Barton & Alexander, 1981; Morris, Alexander, & Waldron, 1988). Family members often enter treatment with a mutually accusatory, individualistic interpretation of their problems (e.g., "He is a rotten kid"; "she is an unfair, misunderstanding parent"). The "therapy" phase is designed to modify family members' dysfunctional cognitions, attitudes, assumptions, expectations, and attributions through the use of relabeling and reframing techniques, so that family members have a nonblaming, relationship perspective on their problems. During the "education" phase, the functional family therapist teaches the family to produce behavior change through communication skill training, negotiation training, behavioral contracting, charting, and a variety of other social-learning-based skill training techniques. Specific techniques are selected to meet the needs of each family and to fit with the analysis of interpersonal functions for that family.

In an initial study, 40 families with delinquent teenagers on probation for status offenses were randomly assigned to an early version of FFT, individual therapy, FFT plus individual therapy, or a wait-list control condition. The FFT and individual therapy families received four weekly sessions, while the combined group received four sessions of each modality, representing a methodological confound. Three of the family therapists also conducted individual therapy, while three other therapists only conducted individual therapy. The dependent measure consisted of audiotaped conflict resolution tasks coded for the ratio of supportive to defensive communication (Alexander, 1973). Only the two groups receiving FFT improved on this ratio. Even though the data are limited by the differing amount of therapist contact across groups and the use of a measure relevant only to family therapy, the results did provide preliminary support for the effectiveness of FFT.

In a now-classic random assignment outcome study, Alexander and his colleagues (Alexander & Parsons, 1982; Parsons & Alexander, 1973) compared the effectiveness of FFT, client-centered family treatment, a church-sponsored psychodynamically oriented family counseling program, or no-treatment control group with 47 court-referred delinquent youth. The FFT and client-centered groups received 8 sessions of treatment, while the psychodynamic group received 12-15 sessions. Different therapists conducted each condition. Outcome was assessed with communication measures and recidivism. FFT improved more on the communication measures (talk time, silences, interruptions) than either the client-centered or control groups (these measures were not collected for the church counseling group), and recidivism averaged 26% for the FFT group compared with 46%-50% for the other groups. In an unusual three-year follow-up assessment, Klein, Alexander, and Parsons (1977) found lower recidivism for the siblings of the FFT adolescents (20%) compared with the no-treatment (40%) or the client-centered (59%) and church family counseling (63%) groups. Barton, Alexander, Waldron, Turner, and Warburton (1985) replicated the earlier studies in a series of minimally controlled one-group and/or successive case-study investigations, finding comparable recidivism rates of 20%-30% following FFT.

Critics have questioned the generalizability of Alexander's results because of the skewed middle-class, Mormon ethic composition of the samples, possible selection biases, possible therapist motivation biases due to the extensive supervision given the relatively inexperienced FFT therapists, unequal therapy time and duration across conditions, and relative dearth of meaningful interaction measures. Recently, Gordon, Arbuthnot, Gustafson, and McGreen (1988) conducted a replication of Alexander's work with a more severely delinquent, lower-socioeconomic class, rural population who had committed misdemeanors and felonies. This constituted the first replication by a group independent of Alexander. Gordon et al. also conducted treatment in the home, used an open-ended treatment duration, and conducted 28-month follow-ups, with careful controls on therapist training and contact time. A total of 54 court-referred families received FFT while an additional 27 served as a no-treatment comparison group. It was not possible to have random assignment; the FFT group was referred by the court, while the control group was a random sample of the remaining youngsters on probation through the court. However, referral patterns were such that the more severely delinquent adolescents were placed in the FFT group, providing an even more challenging test of the treatment. FFT was clearly superior to the control condition of recidivism (11% versus 67%) at postassessment and follow-up (20% versus 63%); unfortunately, no interactional or standardized psychopathological measures were reported, making it difficult to establish the link between family change and recidivism. The results were impressive, given the tougher treatment population than had participated in Alexander's earlier studies, but the lengthier treatment duration (mean = 22 weeks) and in-home setting for treatment may have contributed to the positive outcomes.

Taken together, the evaluations of FFT provide powerful evidence for the effectiveness of this blend of behavioral family systems therapy in producing lasting reductions in delinquent behavior and the superiority of FFT to more traditional, nonbehavioral family and individual counseling approaches. However, the very limited family interaction and psychopathological data make it difficult to determine the extent to which the reductions in recidivism are a result of the hypothesized change process in the functional family therapy model.

C. Relationship Enhancement (RE)

Guerney's relationship enhancement intervention (described earlier as a form of communication training) has been evaluated in three studies. Ginsberg (1981) compared RE to a wait-list control in a random assignment study with father-son dyads reporting mild adjustment problems. The treated group improved relative to the controls on a battery of self-report and observational measures of communication and conflict. Guerney, Coufal, and Vogelsong (1981) conducted a well-designed comparison of RE, an attention placebo control, and a wait-list control with mother-daughter dyads. The RE group improved more on self-report and observational measures of communication than the other two groups, indicating that the skill training components of RE were the active ingredients of the intervention. In a 54-month follow-up of dyads who participated in Guerney's 1981 investigation, Vogelsong (1975) randomly assigned half of the participants to a booster-session maintenance condition and half to a no-booster-session follow-up condition. Booster sessions involved weekly phone calls and biannual therapy sessions. Only the RE group benefited from the booster sessions, with the most pronounced effects on self-reported communication. These investigations have paid a great deal of attention to methodological details and, in return, have provided clear-cut evidence for the effectiveness of RE and the importance of its skill training components in producing positive outcomes. Unfortunately, the families treated have been limited to dyads with mild adjustment problems desiring to enrich communication, leaving unknown the effectiveness of RE with more severely distressed families and adolescents.

D. Summary of Outcome Research

While the evaluations of PSCT, FFT, and RE have provided promising indications that short-term behavioral family therapy can reduce conflict, improve communication and problem solving, and reduce recidivism, they have only begun to address issues of maintenance, the process of change, and the relative contribution of treatment components to outcome. They have, however, provided three excellent models of programmatic efforts that are likely to yield additional information in the coming years. Comparing the three approaches and the populations on which they were tested, it would appear that Alexander worked with the most severely disturbed families, while Robin and Foster worked with a more moderately distressed group, and Guerney's dyads were the least distressed. It is perhaps not surprising that Alexander found he needed to begin therapy with a cognitive component designed to shape a shared family perspective on the problems and overcome resistance, while Guerney moved directly into skill training with little difficulty. Robin and Foster (1989) typically began with skill training but have outlined conditions of more severe distress under which cognitive or structural components had been implemented first. The more severely distressed the family, the more important techniques for engagement and overcoming resistance become, with skill training used at a later time.

VI. FUTURE DIRECTIONS

The approaches to the assessment and treatment of parent-adolescent conflict reviewed in this chapter have been developed and refined within the context of behavioral family therapy. The tripartite emphasis on skill training, cognitions, and family systems variables viewed within a developmental context is a reflection of the general directions in which the field of behavioral family therapy has been moving (Epstein, Schlesinger, & Dryden, 1988; Falloon, 1988; Robinson & Jacobson, 1987). The initial fervor and enthusiasm of the family behavior modifiers of the 1980s and the 1970s have given way to a more sober, yet realistic, perspective (Falloon, 1988; Patterson, 1988). Four issues that have been identified as central to the future development of behavioral family therapy in general are particularly germane to the subspecialty of parent-adolescent conflict: (a) resistance; (b) extensions to more severely psychopathological populations; (c) further developments in assessment; and (d) the integration of family systems with behavioral approaches.

Behavioral family therapists have only recently begun to discuss resistance (Birchler, 1988; Robin & Foster, 1989; Weiss, 1979), conceptualizing it in terms of those behaviors of the client or therapist, or of the client-therapist interaction, that interfere with the progress of therapy. Robin and Foster (1989) have delineated specific sources of resistance to treatment for parent-adolescent conflict, including difficulty engaging family members in therapy, session control problems, difficulties maintaining rapport with clients, and noncompliance with therapist directives and homework assignments. They have outlined suggestions for coping with each of these sources of resistance. Alexander (Barton & Alexander, 1981) has designed his FFT based upon the premise that families with delinquent adolescents will by definition resist change, and the entire first phase of intervention must be devoted to cognitive relabeling designed to circumvent such resistance.

If resistance is operationalized in terms of interactive behavior between the therapist and family, then it is potentially subject to the same type of functional analysis conducted to pinpoint family interaction problems. Patterson and his colleagues have begun such a functional analysis. They developed an observational code for client noncompliance and therapist behaviors in parent training sessions and demonstrated in both correlational and single-subject experimental studies the relationship between selected therapist behaviors (e.g., teach and confront) and increases in maternal noncompliant responses (Chamberlain, Patterson, Reid, Kavanagh, & Forgatch, 1984; Patterson & Forgatch, 1985). Future research needs to extend Patterson's innovative start to parent-adolescent conflict and also evaluate the effectiveness of the various mechanisms for coping with resistance that were outlined by Robin and Foster (1989).

The degree of resistance varies directly with the severity of the psychopathology in various family members. Much of the work described in this chapter was done on populations without severe individual adolescent or adult psychopathology. The effectiveness of behavioral family approaches in families with mood disturbances, personality disorders, anxiety disorders, and other forms of severe pathology is unknown. Barkley (1987) is currently evaluating PSCT with attention-deficit-disordered adolescents, while Robin (1988a) is evaluating a variation on behavioral family therapy with anorectic adolescents and their families. Hopefully, additional extensions to similar psychopathologically disturbed families will shed light on the limits of these approaches.

In the assessment area, the need for further psychometric studies of the family interview and self-report measures has already been stated. The development of innovative measures of family systems variables as well as approaches to conceptualizing and assessing molar interaction sequences that depict the functions of behavior within the family are also important subjects of future investigations.

Finally, much of the work reviewed in this chapter is based upon a hybrid theoretical mix of cognitive-behavioral and family systems approaches. There is considerable disagreement about the appropriateness and feasibility of such integrative efforts without semantic reductionism of one approach to the terms of the other. It has been pointed out that there may be a basic theoretical incompatibility between the systems notion that the family as a whole is more than the sum of its parts and the cognitive-behavioral emphasis on reducing family interactions to elements of skills and cognitions (Leslie, 1988). More pragmatic comparisons of the two approaches have pointed out that they are similar with regard to the analysis of observable interactions and the increasing emphasis on resistance to change, but that they differ in regard to the unit of analysis, the reliance on digital versus analogic communication, the attention paid to skill deficits, and the degree of perceived objectivity of the therapist (Foster & Hoier, 1982; Todd, 1988). Of the three approaches to treating parent-adolescent conflict reviewed in this chapter, Guerney has not integrated any family systems constructs; Robin and Foster have integrated the concept of the family as a circular homeostatic system and specific constructs of hierarchy into their PSCT; and Alexander has gone furthest with integration, emphasizing the universality of resistance, analogic meanings of communication, meaning-change "relabeling" techniques, and the homeostatic nature of the family. Future researchers will need to examine the utility and effectiveness of varying degrees of integration between family systems and behavioral treatments.

With these integrative efforts and careful attention to empirical evaluation of assessment and treatment approaches, behavioral family therapy for parent-adolescent conflict has come a long way in a short time. The clinician now has a variety of options for treating the family in conflict with adolescent offspring, and a number of investigators are actively working to increase these options in the near future.

REFERENCES

Adams, K. M. (1987). *Revision and validation of the parent-adolescent interaction coding system: An observational coding system for parent-adolescent conflict.* Unpublished doctoral dissertation, Wayne State University, Detroit.

Alexander, B. B., Johnson, S. B., & Carter, R. I. (1984). A psychometric study of the family adaptability and cohesion evaluation scales. *Journal of Abnormal Child Psychology, 12,* 199-208.

Alexander, J. F. (1973). Defensive and supportive communications in normal and deviant families. *Journal of Consulting and Clinical Psychology, 40,* 223-231.

Alexander, J., & Parsons, B. V. (1982). *Functional family therapy.* Monterey, CA: Brooks/Cole.

Alexander, J. F., Waldron, H. B., Barton, C., & Mas, C. H. (in press). Minimizing blaming attributions and behaviors in conflicted delinquent families. *Journal of Consulting and Clinical Psychology.*

Anderson, S. (1984). Family measurement techniques. *American Journal of Family Therapy, 12,* 59-62.

Aponte, H. J., & Van Deusen, J. M. (1981). Structural family therapy. In A. S. Gurman & D. P. Kniskern (Eds.), *Handbook of family therapy* (pp. 310-360). New York: Brunner/Mazel.

Arrington, A., Sullaway, M., & Christensen, A. (1988). Behavioral family assessment. In I. R. H. Falloon (Ed.), *Handbook of behavioral family therapy* (pp. 78-106). New York: Guilford.

Barkley, R. (1987). *ADDH adolescents: Family conflicts, follow-up, and therapy.* Grant proposal funded by the National Institute of Mental Health.

Barton, C., & Alexander, J. F. (1981). Functional family therapy. In A. S. Gurman & D. P. Kniskern (Eds.), *Handbook of family therapy* (pp. 403-443). New York: Brunner/Mazel.

Barton, C., Alexander, J. F., Waldron, H., Turner, C. W., & Warburton, J. (1985). Generalizing treatment effects of functional family therapy: Three replications. *American Journal of Family Therapy, 13,* 16-26.

Beavers, R., & Voeller, M. (1973). Family models: Comparing and contrasting the Olson circumplex model with the Beavers systems model. *Family Process, 22,* 85-98.

Birchler, G. R. (1988). Handling resistance to change. In I. R. H. Falloon (Ed.), *Handbook of behavioral family therapy* (pp. 128-154). New York: Guilford.

Chamberlain, P., Patterson, G. R., Reid, J., Kavanagh, D., & Forgatch, M. (1984). Observation of client resistance. *Behavior Therapy, 2,* 144-155.

Conger, J. J. (1977). *Adolescence and youth: Psychological development in a changing world.* New York: Harper.

Cooper, C. R., Grotevant, H. D., & Condon, S. M. (1983). Individuality and connectedness; Both foster adolescent identity formation and role-taking skill. In H. D. Grotevant & C. R. Cooper (Eds.), *Adolescent development in the family* (pp. 43-59). San Francisco: Jossey-Bass.

DeRubeis, R. J., & Beck, A. T. (1988). Cognitive therapy. In K. S. Dobson (Ed.), *Handbook of cognitive-behavioral therapies* (pp. 273-306). New York: Guilford.

Dickerson, V. C., & Coyne, J. C. (1987). Family cohesion and control: A multitrait-multimethod study. *Journal of Marital and Family Therapy, 13,* 275-285.

Dryden, W., & Ellis, A. (1988). Rational-emotive therapy. In K. S. Dobson (Ed.), *Handbook of cognitive-behavioral therapies* (pp. 214-272). New York: Guilford.

D'Zurilla, T. (1986). *Problem-solving therapy: A social competence approach to clinical intervention.* New York: Springer.

D'Zurilla, T. J. (1988). Problem-solving therapies. In K. S. Dobson (Ed.), *Handbook of cognitive behavioral therapies* (pp. 85-135). New York: Guilford.

Edelbrock, C., Costello, A. J., Dulcan, M. D., Kalas, R., & Conover, N. C. (1985). Age differences in the reliability of the psychiatric interview of the child. *Child Development, 56,* 265-275.

Epstein, N. B., Baldwin, L. M., & Bishop, D. S. (1983). The McMaster Family Assessment Device. *Journal of Marriage and the Family, 9,* 171-180.

Epstein, N., Schlesinger, S. E., & Dryden, W. (1988). *Cognitive behavior therapy with families.* New York: Brunner/Mazel.

Falloon, I. R. H. (Ed.). (1988). *Handbook of behavioral family therapy.* New York: Guilford.

Feindler, E., & R. B. Ecton. (1986). *Adolescent anger control.* New York: Pergamon.

Felton, J. L., & Nelson, R. O. (1984). Inter-assessor agreement on hypothesized controlling variables and treatment proposals. *Behavioral Assessment, 6,* 199-208.

Finfrock-Mittl, V., & Robin, A. L. (1987). Acceptability of alternative interventions for parent-adolescent conflict. *Behavioral Assessment, 9,* 417-428.

Forman, B. D., & Hagan, B. J. (1983). A comparative review of total family functioning measures. *American Journal of Family Therapy, 11,* 25-40.

Foster, S. L. (1987). Issues in behavioral assessment of parent-adolescent conflict. *Behavioral Assessment, 9,* 253-269.

Foster, S. L., & Hoier, T. S. (1982). Behavioral and systems family therapies: A comparison of theoretical assumptions. *American Journal of Family Therapy, 10,* 13-23.

Foster, S. L., Prinz, R. J., & O'Leary, K. D. (1983). Impact of problem-solving communication training and generalization procedures on family conflict. *Child and Family Behavior Therapy, 5,* 1-23.

Foster, S. L., & Robin, A. L. (1988). Family conflict and communication in adolescence. In E. J. Mash & L. G. Terdal (Eds.), *Behavioral assessment of childhood disorders* (2nd ed.). New York: Guilford.

Gilbert, R., Christensen, A., & Margolin, G. (1984). Patterns of alliances in nondistressed and multiproblem families. *Family Process, 23,* 75-87.

Ginsberg, B. G. (1981). *Parent-adolescent relationship development: A therapeutic and preventive mental health program.* Unpublished doctoral dissertation, Pennsylvania State University, State College.

Gordon, D. A., Arbuthnot, J., Gustafson, K. E., & McGreen, P. (1988). Home-based behavioral-systems family therapy with disadvantaged juvenile delinquents. *American Journal of Family Therapy, 16,* 243-254.

Grotevant, H. D., & Carlson, C. I. (1987). Family interaction coding systems: A descriptive review. *Family Process, 26,* 49-74.

Grotevant, H. D., & Cooper, C. R. (1983). *Adolescent development in the family.* San Francisco: Jossey-Bass.

Guerney, B. G., Jr. (1977). *Relationship enhancement.* San Francisco: Jossey-Bass.

Guerney, B., Jr., Coufal, J., & Vogelsong, E. (1981). Relationship enhancement versus a traditional approach to therapeutic/preventative/enrichment parent-adolescent programs. *Journal of Consulting and Clinical Psychology, 49,* 927-939.

Haley, J. (1976). *Problem solving therapy.* San Francisco: Jossey-Bass.

Hay, W. M., Hay, L. R., Angle, H. V., & Nelson, R. O. (1979). The reliability of problem identification in the behavioral interview. *Behavioral Assessment, 1,* 107-118.

Haynes, S. N., Jensen, B. J., Wise, E., & Sherman, D. (1981). The marital intake interview: A multimethod validity assessment. *Journal of Consulting and Clinical Psychology, 49,* 379-387.

Herjanic, B., & Reich, W. (1982). Development of a structured psychiatric interview for children: Agreement between child and parent on individual symptoms. *Journal of Abnormal Child Psychology, 10,* 307-324.

Humphrey, L. L., Apple, R. F., & Kirschenbaum, D. S. (1986). Differentiating bulimic-anorexic from normal families using interpersonal and behavioral observational systems. *Journal of Consulting and Clinical Psychology, 54,* 190-195.

Jacob, T., Tennenbaum, D. L., & Krahn, G. (1987). Factors influencing the reliability and validity of observation data. In T. Jacob (Ed.), *Family interaction and psychopathology: Theories, methods, and findings* (pp. 297-328). New York: Plenum.

Joanning, H., & Kuehl, B. P. (1986). Family measurement techniques. *American Journal of Family Therapy, 14,* 163-165.

Karoly, P., & Steffen, J. J. (Eds.). (1984). *Adolescent behavior disorders: Foundations and contemporary concerns.* Lexington, MA: D. C. Heath.

Kinsley, K. E., & Bry, B. H. (1988). *Contingency analyses of adolescent-parent verbal interactions.* Paper presented at the Association for Behavior Analysis Conference, Philadelphia.

Klein, N. C., Alexander, J. F., & Parsons, B. V. (1977). Impact of family systems intervention on recidivism and sibling delinquency: A model of primary prevention and program evaluation. *Journal of Consulting and Clinical Psychology, 45,* 469-474.

Koepke, T. (1986). *Construct validation of the parent-adolescent relationship inventory: A multidimensional measure of parent-adolescent interaction.* Unpublished doctoral dissertation, Wayne State University, Detroit.

Koepke, T., Hull, B., & Robin, A. L. (1989). *Comparison of the Family Beliefs Inventory and the Parent-Adolescent Relationship Questionnaire.* Manuscript submitted for publication.

Koepke, T., Robin, A. L., Foster, S. L., & Nayar, M. (1989). *Treatment of parent-adolescent conflict.* Manuscript submitted for publication.

Laursen, B., & Collins, W. A. (1988). Conceptual changes during adolescence and effects upon parent-child relationships. *Journal of Adolescent Research, 3,* 119-139.

Leslie, L. A. (1988). Cognitive-behavioral and systems models of family therapy: How compatible are they? In N. Epstein, S. E. Schlesinger, & W. Dryden (Eds.), *Cognitive-behavioral therapy with families* (pp. 49-83). New York: Brunner/Mazel.

Liu, C. K. (1988). *Acceptability of alternative treatment techniques for parent-adolescent conflict.* Unpublished master's thesis, Wayne State University, Detroit, MI.

Markman, H. J., & Notarius, C. I. (1987). Coding marital and family interactions: Current status. In T. Jacob (Ed.), *Family interaction and psychopathology: Theories, methods, and findings* (pp. 329-390). New York: Plenum.

Minuchin, S. (1974). *Families and family therapy.* Cambridge, MA: Harvard University Press.

Minuchin, S., & Fishman, H. C. (1981). *Family therapy techniques.* Cambridge, MA: Harvard University Press.

Montemayor, R. (1983). Parents and adolescents in conflict: All families some of the time and some families most of the time. *Journal of Early Adolescence, 5,* 23-30.

Montemayor, R. (1986). Family variation in parent-adolescent storm and stress. *Journal of Adolescent Research, 1,* 15-31.

Montemayor, R., & Adams, G. R. (1985). Contemporary approaches to the study of families with adolescents. *Journal of Early Adolescence, 5,* 1-7.

Moos, R. H., & Moos, B. S. (1981). *Family Environment Scale manual.* Palo Alto, CA: Consulting Psychologists Press.

Morris, S. B., Alexander, J. F., & Waldron, H. (1988). Functional family therapy. In I. R. H. Falloon (Ed.), *Handbook of behavioral family therapy* (pp. 107-127). New York: Guilford.

Nayar, M. (1985). *Cognitive factors in the treatment of parent-adolescent conflict.* Unpublished doctoral dissertation, Wayne State University, Detroit.

Oliver, M. E., & Reiss, D. (1984). Family concepts and their measurement: Things are seldom what they seem. *Family Process, 23,* 33-48.

Olson, D. (1986). Circumplex Model VII: Validation studies and FACES III. *Family Process, 25,* 337-351.

Olson, D. H., Bell, R., & Porter, J. (1982). *FACES II: Family Adaptability and Cohesion Scales.* St. Paul: University of Minnesota, Family Social Science.

Parsons, B. V., & Alexander, J. F. (1973). Short-term family intervention: A therapy outcome study. *Journal of Consulting and Clinical Psychology, 41,* 195-201.

Patterson, G. R. (1982). *Coercive family process.* Eugene, OR: Castalia.

Patterson, G. (1988). Foreword. In I. R. H. Falloon (Ed.), *Handbook of behavioral family therapy* (pp. VII-X). New York: Guilford.

Patterson, G. R., & Forgatch, M. S. (1985). Therapist behavior as a determinant for client noncompliance: A paradox for the behavior modifier. *Journal of Consulting and Clinical Psychology, 53,* 846-851.

Perosa, L., Hansen, J., & Perosa, S. (1981). Development of the structural Family Interaction Scale. *Family Therapy, 8,* 77-80.

Powers, S. I., Hauser, S. T., Schwartz, J. M., Noam, G. G., & Jacobson, A. M. (1983). Adolescent ego development and family interaction: A structural-developmental perspective. In H. D. Grotevant & C. R. Cooper (Eds.), *Adolescent development in the family* (pp. 5-26). San Francisco: Jossey-Bass.

Prinz, R. J., Foster, S. L., Kent, R. N., & O'Leary, K. D. (1979). Multivariate assessment of conflict in distressed and nondistressed mother-adolescent dyads. *Journal of Applied Behavior Analysis, 12,* 691-700.

Prinz, R. J., & Kent, R. N. (1978). Recording parent-adolescent interactions without the use of frequency or interval-by-interval coding. *Behavior Therapy, 9,* 602-604.

Reiss, D., Oliveri, M. E., & Curd, K. (1983). Family paradigm and adolescent social behavior. In H. D. Grotevant & C. R. Cooper (Eds.), *Adolescent development in the family* (pp. 77-92). San Francisco: Jossey-Bass.

Riskin, J., & Faunce, E. E. (1970a). Family Interaction Scales, I. Theoretical framework and method. *Archives of General Psychiatry, 22,* 504-512.

Riskin, J., & Faunce, E. E. (1970b). Family Interaction Scales, III. Data analysis and findings. *Archives of General Psychiatry, 22,* 513-526.

Robin, A. L. (1981). A controlled evaluation of problem solving communication training with parent-adolescent conflict. *Behavior Therapy, 12,* 593-609.

Robin, A. L. (1982). Impasses in negotiating solutions in behavioral family therapy. In A. S. Gurman (Ed.), *Questions and answers in the practice of family therapy* (pp. 181-185). New York: Brunner/Mazel.

Robin, A. L. (1988a). *A controlled evaluation of family therapy with anorectic adolescents.* Grant proposal funded by the National Institute of Mental Health.

Robin, A. L. (1988b). Parent-Adolescent Interaction Coding System. In M. Hersen & A. S. Bellack (Eds.), *Dictionary of behavioral assessment techniques* (pp. 334-336). New York: Pergamon.

Robin, A. L., & Canter, W. (1984). A comparison of the Marital Interaction Coding System and community ratings for assessing mother-adolescent problem-solving. *Behavioral Assessment, 6,* 303-314.

Robin, A. L., & Foster, S. L. (1984). Problem-solving communication training: A behavioral-family systems approach to parent-adolescent conflict. In P. Karoly & J. J. Steffen (Eds.), *Adolescent behavior disorders: Foundations and contemporary concerns* (pp. 195-240). Lexington, MA: Lexington.

Robin, A. L., & Foster, S. L. (1988a). Conflict behavior questionnaire. In M. Hersen & A. S. Bellack (Eds.), *Dictionary of behavioral assessment techniques* (pp. 148-150). New York: Pergamon.

Robin, A. L., & Foster, S. L. (1988b). Issues checklist. In M. Hersen & A. S. Bellack (Eds.), *Dictionary of behavioral assessment techniques* (pp. 278-279). New York: Pergamon.

Robin, A. L., & Foster, S. L. (1989). *Negotiating parent-adolescent conflict: A behavioral family systems approach.* New York: Guilford.

Robin, A. L., & Fox, M. (1979). *Parent-Adolescent Interaction System coding manual.* Unpublished manuscript, University of Maryland.

Robin, A. L., Kent, R., O'Leary, K. D., Foster, S. L., & Prinz, R. J. (1977). An approach to teaching parents and adolescents problem-solving communication skills: A preliminary report. *Behavior Therapy, 8,* 639-643.

Robin, A. L., & Koepke, T. (1985). *Molecular versus molar observational coding systems for assessing mother-adolescent problem-solving communication behavior.* Unpublished manuscript.

Robin, A. L., Koepke, T., & Moye, A. (1989). *Multidimensional assessment of parent-adolescent relations.* Manuscript submitted for publication.

Robin, A. L., Koepke, T., & Nayar, M. (1986). Conceptualizing, assessing, and treating parent-adolescent conflict. In B. B. Lahey & A. E. Kazdin (Eds.), *Advances in clinical child psychology* (Vol. 9), pp. 87-124). New York: Plenum.

Robin, A. L., & Weiss, J. G. (1980). Criterion-related validity of behavioral and self-report measures of problem-solving communication skills in distressed and non-distressed parent-adolescent dyads. *Behavioral Assessment, 2,* 339-352.

Robinson, E. A., & Jacobson, N. S. (1987). Social learning theory and family psychopathology: A Kantian model in behaviorism? In T. Jacob (Ed.), *Family interaction and psychopathology: Theories, methods, and findings* (pp. 117-162). New York: Plenum.

Rodnick, J., Henggeler, S., & Hanson, C. (1986). An evaluation of Family Adaptability and Cohesion Scales (FACES) and the circumplex model. *Journal of Abnormal Child Psychology, 14,* 77-87.

Russell, C. S. (1980). A methodological study of family cohesion and adaptability. *Journal of Marital and Family Therapy, 6,* 459-470.

Skinner, H. A. (1987). Self-report instruments for family assessment. In T. Jacob (Ed.), *Family interaction and psychopathology: Theories, methods, and findings* (pp. 427-452). New York: Plenum.

Stein, M. D., & Davis, J. K. (1982). *Therapies for adolescents.* San Francisco: Jossey-Bass.

Steinberg, L. D. (1981). Transformations in family relations at puberty. *Developmental Psychology, 17,* 833-840.

Steinberg, L. D., & Hill, J. (1978). Patterns of family interaction as a function of age, onset of puberty, and formal thinking. *Developmental Psychology, 14,* 683-684.

Stern, S. (1984). *A group cognitive-behavioral approach to the management and resolution of parent-adolescent conflict.* Unpublished doctoral dissertation, University of Chicago.

Stuart, R. B. (1971). Behavioral contracting within the families of delinquents. *Journal of Behavior Therapy and Experimental Psychiatry, 2,* 1-11.

Todd, T. C. (1988). Behavioral and systemic family therapy: A comparison. In I. R. H. Falloon (Ed.), *Handbook of behavioral family therapy* (pp. 449-460). New York: Guilford.

Tzelepis, A. (1986). *The influence of mode of presentation, therapeutic modality, and subject characteristics on treatment evaluation.* Unpublished doctoral dissertation, Wayne State University, Detroit.

Valins, S., & Nisbett, R. (1976). Attribution process in the development and treatment of emotional disorders. In J. Spence, R. Carson, & J. Thibaut (Eds.), *Behavioral approaches to therapy* (pp. 261-274). Morristown, NJ: General Learning Press.

Vincent-Roehling, P., & Robin, A. L. (1986). Development and validation of the Family Beliefs Inventory: A measure of unrealistic beliefs among parents and adolescents. *Journal of Consulting and Clinical Psychology, 54,* 693-697.

Vogelsong, E. L. (1975). *Preventive-therapeutic programs for mothers and adolescent daughters: A follow-up of relationship enhancement versus discussion and booster versus no-booster methods.* Unpublished doctoral dissertation, Pennsylvania State University.

Webb, D. (1977). *Discriminant and concurrent validity of the structural scales of the Parent-Adolescent Relationship Questionnaire: A multidimensional measure of parent-adolescent interactions.* Unpublished doctoral dissertation, University of South Carolina, Columbia.

Webb, D., Young, M., & Robin, A. L. (1988). *Construct validation of the structural scales of the Parent-Adolescent Relationship Questionnaire.* Paper presented at the Association for the Advancement of Behavior Therapy Conference, New York.

Weiss, R. L. (1979). Resistance in behavioral marriage therapy. *American Journal of Family Therapy, 1* 3-6.

Weiss, R. L., & Summers, K. J. (1973). Marital Interaction Coding System III. In E. E. Filsinger (Ed.), *Marriage and family assessment.* Beverly Hills, CA: Sage.

Youniss, J., & Smollar, J. (1985). *Adolescent relations with mothers, fathers and friends.* Chicago: University of Chicago Press.

INDEX